Gezebel

A Journey of Identity

BEVERLEY WORRELL

ISBN 978-1-967362-00-4 (paperback)
ISBN 978-1-967362-01-1 (hardcover)
ISBN 978-1-967362-02-8 (digital)

Printed in the United States of America

My daughter Eliana drew this picture of me on mother's day. Smooches!

Special thanks to Mr. Silva for supporting this effort.

Additional thanks to family & friends for sharing in my excitement about this book.

Gezebel

Chapter One

———❦———

In Barbados, the afternoon sun coaxed a sleeping Gezebel from restful slumber, as it shone brilliantly against sheer curtains that graced her bedroom windows. The hue of the sheer fabric reminded Gezebel of sea-foam, tickling the shores of a pink Bermuda beach. She exhaled, and lazily propped her elbows on the fluffy over-sized pillows on the bed. Gezebel gazed sleepily at the alarm clock on her nightstand and it was 12:42pm; much too early to wake up. She positioned the fluffed up pillows behind her back and propped them against the headboard. Gezebel sat up and rested against the pillows in the queen-sized bed that faced the windows, and wished the sun would wait another two hours or so before visiting her room. She rolled her long wavy locks into a perilous bun on top of her head, oblivious to the loose strands that hung past her shoulders. Gezebel's dark hair contrasted with the unique tint of her gray eyes, and ivory toned skin. Her black ancestry was perfectly veiled in her multiracial makeup, that being, the product of a Caucasian woman and an Octoroon man. Gezebel daydreamed about the night before. She twirled loose strands of hair round her index finger and mused over her most recent exploit. A lazy smile flitted across her lips as she relived those thrilling moments between herself and ...

"Cuck cuck coo!" Crowed her aunt's pet rooster!

"Cuck cuck coo!" The rooster crowed louder.

Gezebel put her hands to her ears to block the irritating noise out of her head, but the rooster continued its jovial "Cuck cuck coo! Cuck cuck coo! Cluck, cluck, cluck! Cluck, cluck, cluck!" Gezebel hopped out of bed in a fury and unlocked her bedroom window. Sure enough, the rooster was royally perched on a fence in plain view, close to the window. Gezebel had an ongoing feud with this rooster whom her aunt nicknamed Boss because of the militant way in which he guarded eggs laid by the hen. He also seemed to have terrorized other animals housed on the estate because they scurried away whenever Boss was around. Gezebel rechristened the rooster "Nuisance" and her Aunt Bella laughed every time she referred to him by that name. She stuck her head out the bedroom window and admonished the temperamental bird.

"Go roost somewhere else before I cook you!" She shouted at the bird. The rooster stood on one leg and fluffed up his feathers as if preparing to fight.

"Go I said!" Gezebel ordered the big bird.

The rooster continued to "Cuck cuck coo! Cuck cuck coo! Cluck, cluck, cluck!" On the fence and Gezebel became infuriated with the animal's refusal to roost elsewhere. She convinced herself the rooster purposely wanted to antagonize her and she was going to wheedle him into roosting somewhere else. Gezebel hastily donned shorts under her nightgown and shoved her feet into a pair of slippers. The peeved teenager tramped out of the bedroom, hurried down the winding staircase and stormed into the kitchen.

"Good Morning, Aunt Bella." Gezebel quipped and sucked her teeth.

Bella tried to stifle the laughter winding its way through her gut, but it eventually erupted like a geyser and spewed forth from her lips. She knew if anyone or anything could lure Gezebel out of bed on a Saturday morning, it would be Boss. Gezebel and the territorial rooster shared a strong antipathy for each other.

"Good morning, Gezzy. How was your night out?" Bella asked, referring to Gezebel by her pet name.

"Fine!" Gezzy snapped.

She refused to break her stride to answer any more frivolous questions and stormed past her aunt. Her focus was on show-ing Boss, who the real Boss was around here! Gezzy grabbed a slice of bread off the table and opened the kitchen door, and there was Boss standing in front of it! It was as though he came to meet her at the battleground! This unnerved Gezzy and she refrained from stepping outside. Bella sensed her apprehension and walked in front of her niece. She stepped easily onto the grounds. Boss obediently moved away when Bella approached and Gezzy walked cowardly behind her aunt. Gezzy hated to admit that she was afraid of the cranky rooster. Bella ignored Gezzy and walked to the modest farmhouse to check on other animals she kept on the estate. Gezzy made a detour and walked briskly to a palm tree rooted twenty feet or more from her bedroom window. Boss studied Gezebel and cocked his head to the side with curi-osity. Gezebel stood under the tree and tossed the bread on the ground, hoping to lure Boss away from the window. Boss "clucked clucked" softly, and inched closer to the bread. But,

3

before Boss could peck a morsel of bread, one of her aunt's ducks waddled past her at full speed and swiped the loaf! Boss angrily chased the duck and pecked it on its tail feather! The opportunistic duck quacked in an agitated manner and stole away with an unexpected treat!

Boss gave up chase and trotted back to the tree where Gezzy stood smirking! She couldn't believe Boss was outsmarted by a lame duck! The rooster stopped in front of her and "clucked clucked" angrily. Gezzy attempted to sneak away from under the tree when Boss stood tall and fluffed his feathers as if boasting of his stamina and strength. She had a bad feeling about this! She backed up against the tree and shifted her body in the direction of the kitchen door that was still ajar. Gezzy was going to make a run for it as soon as Boss got distracted. The rooster "clucked clucked" menacingly in front of Gezzy and panic set in. The "cluck cluck" resounded deep in the rooster's throat and Gezzy thought it sounded demonic! The animal kept Gezzy in full view and sized her up. She resisted the urge to scream for help because that would mean being the butt of her aunt's jokes for the rest of the week. Gezzy couldn't believe the ridiculous situation she was faced with! Here she was, frozen in fear of a rooster that seemed larger than life! Gezzy perspired profusely and her body felt as though it was glued to the tree. She started to reason with the edgy rooster and held her palms out to show him there was no more bread.

"See Boss, all the bread is gone!" Gezzy explained in a voice that trembled with anxiety.

Boss clucked and leapt at Gezzy! He pecked at her hands in search of food.

"Argh!" Gezzy yelled and kicked at the rooster whom she thought was attacking her! She assumed the rooster had gone insane and was on a murderous rampage!

"Auntie, help me!" Gezzy screamed!

Bella bolted out of the farm house to see what the commotion was about and spotted Gezzy under the tree with Boss lunging at her! She grabbed a broom from the kitchen and sprinted towards the drama. She whacked Boss with the sweeper side of the broom and he stopped pecking at Gezzy. The stunned rooster recovered quickly from the blow and clucked in protest of Bella's intervention as he trotted off. Bella grasped Gezzy by the hand and led her shaken niece into the house. Gezzy was out of breath, and her skin was clammy with perspiration. She had a few superficial peck marks on her hands but other than that she was unharmed.

"Gezzy, how many times do I have to tell you to leave boss alone? You know that bird is crazy!" Bella chastised her hard-headed niece.

"Aunt Bella, my plan was to use a loaf of bread to lure Boss away from the fence but the duck got the bread first. I want him to stop crowing near my bedroom window!" Gezzy complained.

"Well, no wonder! The rooster wanted food! You're lucky you didn't end up looking like spongebob Square Pants!" Bella joked and handed her a glass of water.

"He crows by my window to purposely wake me!" Gezzy responded in an agitated manner.

"Gezzy, if that rooster didn't crow, you would sleep all day!" Bella stated and laughed. Gezzy sighed and fixed herself a breakfast of scrambled eggs, toast and orange juice.

After breakfast, she ventured back to her room and showered in her private bath. She adjusted the shower nozzle to a hard jet spray and lathered with strawberry cream body wash. Gezzy relaxed as the tepid water splashed over her six-foot frame. She adjusted the nozzle to gentle massage and the water soothed her frazzled spirit. The faint scent of strawberries and cream pervaded her senses, and softened her skin. Gezzy closed her eyes and continued the daydream that was cut short by the rooster. She guided the wash cloth over her breasts, stomach and thighs and conjured thoughts of Kendrick. They skinny-dipped the night before and made love on a deserted beach in the wee hours of the morning. It was as if they were the only people alive in the entire world. Gezebel shuddered and fantasized about Kendrick. The wash cloth glided over her sudsy body and Gezebel experienced a self-induced climax that left her sexually satisfied. The pungent scent of strawberries and cream lingered in the air.

(Telephone rings)

Gezzy hurried out of the shower to answer the phone and wrapped a towel around her glistening body.

"i've got it, Aunt bella!" She hollered downstairs to her aunt.

"Hello?" Gezzy answered.

"It's about time you got out of that shower!" Quipped Gezzy's best friend, Joi.

"Girl, you would not believe what happened to me this mor..." Gezzy started to explain.

"Oh yes I do! Bella called mummy and told her what happened! We couldn't stop laughing! I don't know whose worse, you or that rooster that rules the yard!" Joi exclaimed and chuckled.

"Oh great! I was attacked by a chicken wannabe rooster and everyone thinks it's funny!" Gezzy stated and giggled.

"Gezzy, Let's hang out. Meet me outside in half hour." Joi tells her friend.

"Cool!" Gezzy agreed and hung up.

Gezzy dressed in denim Capri's, a white T-shirt, and a pair of casual sneakers minus socks. She toweled dried her hair and ran a comb impatiently through it. That was followed up with a few strokes of a hairbrush and then it was pulled into a ponytail. She donned a denim cap and fished out designer sunglasses out of a drawer. Gezebel tossed the necessities into her designer handbag.

Cell phone – got that!
Bank card – got that!
Cosmetics – got that!
Keys – got that!
Chewing gum – got that!
Cash – of course!

Quick once over in the mirror - Caliente! Gezzy smiled to herself and prepared to leave.

"Aunt Bella, I'm not home!" Gezzy yelled to her aunt from the foyer.

"Where are you going?" Bella asked dutifully as she joined Gezzy in the foyer.

"To hang out with Joi." Gezzy replied.

"Do you have enough money?" Bella asked.

"Yes, and, I also have my bankcard. See you later." Gezzy kissed her aunt's cheek and left the house.

Before Gezzy made it down the steps of her aunt's two-story Victorian home, she spied Joi entering through the gates. Gezzy and Joi grew up together and graduated from the same secondary school. They were practically sisters. Joi was a brown-skinned, dark-haired beauty in every sense of the word, standing 5' 8" in height with thick long hair, which she wore in a variety of styles. Her father owned a law firm and her mother worked with him on a part time basis. The girls were fitness fanatics and frequented the islands' most popular gym, "Body Sculpt" where Gezzy met Kendrick, the personal fitness trainer. They worked hard to tone their bodies and maintain flat abs. As best friends, they shopped together, and knew each others taste in wardrobe. Both girls traveled with their families to international destinations to vacation and shop. They considered themselves local fashionistas and trendsetters.

Gezzy and Joi lived in affluent communities and their lives were full of sunshine and fun. They partied, drank, and enjoyed all the entertainment a small island could offer. During the yearly crop over festival, they didn't hesitate to join music bands and wear the scantiest costumes for sale. Frolicking in the streets with other merry makers was an invigorating experience for both of them. Making a mad dash for the beach at the end of the festival route was the best way to cool off after hours of dancing wildly in the sun. The beach was always littered with festival goers languishing in the cool turquoise waters of the Barbados seas. The best friends devoured local cuisines such as coo coo and flying fish, fish cakes, rice and peas, breadfruit chips, pickled fruit, and preserves from vendors operating food stalls. Baked goods such as rum cakes, pone, sweet bread, and a slew of other flour laden goodies were gulped down. Fruit juices, beers and stouts were consumed liberally in keeping with the other revelers. After they were too exhausted to rotate their hips and swing their buttocks to the beat of calypso tunes, they made their way home with sore limbs and aching muscles.

Gezzy and Joi's friendship survived physical altercations, verbal spats, petty jealousies and challenges from their peers. Joi appreciated Gezzy's adventurous spirit and Gezzy admired Joi's direct nature. They were best friends for life.

Chapter Two

Estele Sealy was Deighton St. John's wife, and mother of Ernest, Bella, and Jeffrey. Estele was a mulatto whose black mother worked as a housekeeper/cook for a local white businessman, named Mr. Crichlowe, and Estele was the result of an intimate relationship between the two. Estele's mother had another daughter from a previous relationship that never materialized into marriage, and she struggled financially to support herself and the girls. Mr. Crichlowe, being generous and kind hearted, gave liberally to Estele's mother and financially supported the family. At age five, Estele's father, Mr. Crichlowe, suffered a fatal heart attack that left her mother emotionally devastated and financially destitute. Her mother found other housekeeping jobs but the pay was always inadequate and never enough to keep her and the girls from being in a constant state of want. After years of living hand to mouth, Estele's mother secured a well paying job as housekeeper/cook job for the St. John family and they compensated her well. Deighton, the eldest son of the St. Johns, loved Estele from the first day he laid eyes on her. He was a tall young man with steely gray eyes that spewed intelligence and ambition. In his eyes, Estele was pretty as a flower with her long hair parted down the middle and braided in plaits at either side of her head.

In the afternoon after class, Estele and her sister reported to the St. John household and waited for their mother to finish work. There, she would have a snack and something cool for the girls to drink. After eating, it was time for homework, and the girls obediently attended their studies. Deighton crafted excuses as to why he was constantly in the kitchen where Estele studied and waited for her mother. He entertained Estele with silly jokes designed to elicit her laughter. Deighton engaged her in topics of a political and social nature, and valued her opinions. Estele eventually became comfortable enough with Deighton to vent her frustration with the subject of mathematics in which she was on the verge of failing in class. Deighton reviewed Estele's math homework daily and tutored her in the subject. Under his tutelage, her grades improved and she graduated with scores in the eightieth percentile. This teacher-student relationship gradually turned into friendship as they learned more about each other.

The school year came to a close and Deighton decided it was time to invite Estele out on a date. Permission was obtained from Estele's mother and Deighton was thrilled. Estele's mother purchased floral material from a fabric store and sewed Estele a new dress for the occasion. Her mother insisted she wear knee-length white socks, and black shoes, but she would have preferred to wear stockings just like all the other young ladies. Estele was self conscious about her floral dress and socks, but when Deighton commented on how beautiful she looked, Estele quickly forgot about not having stockings. Their first date paved the way to future outings and the young couple fell madly in love.

Deighton asked Estele to marry him even though he was only 23 and she was 18. His family was skeptical about his mar-

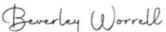

riage proposal to Estele because they would have preferred if he married a local white girl instead. But, Deighton's mind was made up, and the family acquiesced and gave the couple their blessing.

Wedded vows were exchanged in a traditional church ceremony followed by a formal reception. Estele was promptly moved out of the small one bedroom chattel home she shared with her mother and sister, and welcomed into the St. John family where her mother still labored as housekeeper/cook. Acclimation into this wealthy white family was a transition that took years in the making. Estele was a nervous wreck, especially at dinnertime and at social functions. At times, she felt out of place, even though Deighton's family went out of their way to make her feel at home. Estele sometimes longed for the simple life that was traded for this one, which was built on strict schedules, wheeling and dealing, and high stress. The desire to achieve, to accumulate, to own, and to control was paramount in this family. Estele was coached on the finer points of etiquette by Deighton's mother and three sisters. They suggested she practice proper diction, and frowned on frequent use of the local dialect. Estele learned to reserve her Bajan dialect for conversations held with her mother when assisting with chores around the house. She resided with the St. John family for three years while Deighton was busy having a new home built. When construction was completed, Estele and Deighton moved in right away, and she set about adding her personal touch. A year later, Estele bore Ernest. Bella followed two years later, and Jeffrey was not far behind. Their children passed for white, but tanned as golden as the sun. Estele's busy life as wife and mother of three young children was in full swing.

Deighton was well on his way to becoming a well-respected businessman, and he amassed a significant amount of wealth year after year. He invested his inheritance, and groomed the children into following the St. John entrepreneurial lineage. His daughter, Bella, was an obedient child who learned well and took her lessons seriously. Her brothers preferred to ride the waves at the beach, play cricket, chase girls, and goof off. They had it all; wealth, education, prestige and good looks. Ernest was the taller of the brood standing at 6'3" with hair the color of onyx and dark, flirtatious eyes. Jeffrey stood 6'0" feet tall with a boyishly handsome face and hair bleached by excessive exposure to sea and sun. Bella was shorter than both her brothers at 5'9" in height. She was a beautiful over achiever with an above average IQ. Deighton chose Bella as executor of his estate because she was practical, trustworthy, and demonstrated sound financial judgment. By the time Ernest turned nineteen, he was coined a ladies man out to score. He was the big brother, the confident one, the most handsome one, the one women loved to hate. He was cursed with good looks, a sturdy physique and a winning smile. Young ladies found him irresistible.

Ernest was sent to England to attend the University with grades that were barely good enough to get him enrolled. He attended Northampton Institute in London where he entertained the ladies, and partied more than he studied. Ernest graduated a year late at the bottom of his class with a degree in Sociology. Bella and Jeffrey attended Northampton, and Bella graduated with honors. She earned a degree in economics while Jeffrey impressed everyone with decent grades and a degree in Psychology. Deighton, known affectionately as "Daddy St. John" berated his sons for undertaking "sissy" courses instead of studying finance, business, or mathematics. How could they assist him with the running of his real estate company with degrees in Sociology and Psychology? Bella was the one who undertook a course with "substance," according to their father.

Deighton made up his mind to train Bella in all aspects of his real estate business. Bella became her father's pride and joy, and committed herself to the task at hand. Estele agreed with Deighton that "their Bella" was the most level headed of the brood. Bella and her brothers returned to Barbados after graduating, but it was Bella who accompanied their father to the office. She sat in on business meetings and was well on her way to becoming a valued member of his team. Her brothers viewed this as an act of favoritism by their father, and it incited their jealousy. Since Ernest was the eldest, he assumed that he should be going to the office every day with their father, but due to his lack of focus and immaturity, Deighton overlooked him. Ernest was furious, and ignited verbal spats with Bella every chance he got. He tried to ruin her credibility, and attempted to have their father view her as an emotionally weak, dumb girl, but Bella proved a formidable foe. She was sharp, tactful, and always managed to humiliate Ernest with in-depth knowledge, and logical reasoning about the debate at hand, much to the amusement of their father. Jeffrey on the other hand was more subdued in his invidiousness against Bella. He sided with Ernest but didn't think it was fair to constantly antagonize their sister, so he pretended she didn't exist.

Unable to cope emotionally with the rejection by his father, Ernest started to drink and his taste for loud, promiscuous women was cause for alarm. He spent money with disregard, and argued with everyone in the house. Estele threatened to eject him from the fold if he didn't cease causing strife! One night, while the family dined together at the house, Ernest passed out, face down into his bowl of soup! He had indulged in an all night drinking binge with his wild friends the night before, and was still intoxicated.

Estele pleaded with Deighton to send the boys back to England, in hopes that more job opportunities would be available to them. Ernest needed a change of pace in a different environment. Deighton agreed, and the family traveled to England so that they could settle Ernest and Jeffrey there. He secured a two bedroom flat in a London community called Notting Hill Gate, and furnished it with second hand furniture. He opened bank accounts, and deposited one thousand pounds into Ernest's account, and one thousand pounds into Jeffrey's account. Estele crammed the refrigerator and cupboards with food so that they would have plenty to eat. Deighton paid three months rent in advance for his sons, and hoped that one of them would find employment before rent was due. Estele and Deighton took their sons shopping for warm clothes, television sets, and basic necessities. They were satisfied that the boys were set up comfortably in their new flat with the basic comforts. Deighton, Estele, and Bella returned to Barbados, leaving Ernest and Jeffrey to eek out a living for themselves. Ernest was 25 years of age, and Jeffrey was 21. It was up to them to sink or swim because Deighton St. John was done.

Chapter Three

———

Ernest relished his easygoing lifestyle that was free of responsibility. Damn! It felt so good to finally have his father off his back! He frequented pubs and picked up women to have affairs with. His made a mockery of job hunting and his efforts were half-hearted. Ernest shopped for designer clothes, lounged at entertainment clubs and drank himself into oblivion. Jeffrey, on the other hand, found his new independence a challenge and embraced it. He visited museums, music clubs, and explored Britain. While Ernest succumbed to liquor, Jeffrey sought new experiences in food, culture and music. His choice of woman was starkly different from the brash types that Ernest entertained. Jeffrey was on the prowl for conservative, highly educated and ambitious young ladies. He rejected those that were overly sexed and dull. Nevertheless, Jeffrey envied his big brother's skill in winning many unsuspecting female hearts. Jeffrey was always a little shy and not as ruthless as Ernest when it came to dealing with matters of the heart. He was the kinder brother.

Within a month of his arrival in London, Jeffrey found a part-time job teaching psychology at a nearby business school. Weeks later, he applied for, and was hired to work nights as a doorman for a small hotel. Jeffrey's two paychecks allowed him to save half his earnings, along with the money his father deposited into his account. Ernest, on the other hand, had less than five hundred pounds in his account and cursed the world because he could not find work. Jeffrey ignored him, and was grateful that his day job and his night job kept him away from his disagreeable brother. Ernest had become a habitual drunk and a useless slob. Jeffrey always arrived home from work to a flat strewn with liquor bottles, cigarette butts, plates of half eaten food, soiled clothes scattered everywhere, and foul smelling garbage stinking up the place! He became the housekeeper and his brother's keeper. Jeffrey cleaned the flat with no help from Ernest, and usually discovered soiled panties, and dingy bras tucked between sofa cushions or left carelessly around the flat. Sometimes he came face to face with women that stumbled out of Ernest's room, appearing disheveled, and lost in a drunken stupor. Jeffrey prayed that his big brother would wake up and sabotage the downhill spiral he was headed in.

Ernest was devastated and severely depressed. Not only was he out done by his sister, but his little brother got himself two jobs! This couldn't be real, it just couldn't! He couldn't think straight! Ernest doused his emotional pain in liquor and women because he couldn't bring himself to cry. What he desired was a high paying job with an impressive title, not like the mediocre ones Jeffrey held. He couldn't fathom why Jeffrey would work as a lowly doorman. Ernest had to get a grip on life because he was losing himself in alcohol and sex.

Nine months after relocating to London, Ernest began to slowly pull himself together. His bank account reflected the minimum balance needed to keep it open, and he quickly sobered up! He borrowed money from Jeffrey just to get by, and was grateful to his little brother for taking charge of the bills while he was out having fun. Jeffrey had no choice but

to hunker down and do what was needed to keep them out of the cold. Ernest lamented to his female friends that he was in need of money and they picked up the slack.

On a day of sobriety, Ernest read the help wanted ads in a daily newspaper and came across an opening for a counselor at a reform school for boys. He decided to apply for the job, which paid thirty thousand pounds a year. Ernest arrived for the interview sober and immaculately dressed. He completed the application and was escorted to a private room where the interview was going to take place. A circular table and two sturdy chairs were in the room. Ernest seated himself, and waited for the interviewer to make his entrance. Minutes later, a dark haired beauty walked in and introduced her self as Corine Wilshire, the manager in charge of hiring. Corine was an attractive, twenty-three year old, 5'10", dark haired beauty, whose eyes swept over Ernest with interest. She was dressed tastefully in a snug fitting navy blue skirt and matching blazer. Her flirtatious smile didn't go unnoticed, and Ernest was smitten! The interview commenced, and Ernest provided concise answers to Corine's standard questions. He made a valiant effort to secure the job. Corine sat across from Ernest, and flirted with him by purposely keeping her long shapely legs in his view. Ernest fought the temptation to tell her how sensual her legs were, and how much she turned him on! Corine was so impressed with Ernest's vigor, and apparent passion for social work, she hired him on the spot! Later, Corine reflected on her impulsive hiring decision. She convinced herself that Ernest was the best candidate for the job, and she didn't hire him just because her interest in him was more personal than professional. So what if he wasn't qualified? She chided herself.

Corine worked in the administrative offices of the reform school, and genuinely cared about the students. Ernest was hired to counsel the boys, and engage them in creative activities. Corine invested a chunk of her time introducing Ernest to the school system, and bringing him up to speed. In doing so, she learned more about the handsome stranger that walked away with the job after a ten minute interview. Ernest made the rounds at the school, and familiarized himself with the students and staff. He found purpose in helping troubled kids make positive changes through teamwork and competitive sports. Over time, Corine became impressed with Ernest as he forged meaningful relationships with pupils. Their attendance soared and they paid more attention to their studies. Corine patted herself on the back and relaxed. Ernest was the right choice after all!

Ernest was seven months into the job, and he was certain that Corine was as attracted to him as he was to her. For the first time in his life, he was apprehensive about approaching a woman, especially since the object of his affection was his boss! Ernest had to figure out a clever way to make his move, so he came up with an idea for a summer program, and used that as an excuse to invite Corine to lunch. Corine readily accepted Ernest's invitation and was soon accepting invitations to dinner dates, walks in the park, and quiet time at the flat. Ernest courted Corine for five months before he agreed to date her exclusively.

After an evening out enjoying London's nightlife, Corine joined Ernest at the flat for a little quality time. Ernest unlocked the door to the flat and Corine walked in. He entered the foyer after her and locked the door. Ernest smiled shyly at Corine and reached for her. He drew her close. She touched her lips to his and kissed him softly. They stood in the cozy foyer, kissing and teasing each other with their lips. Ernest massaged her breasts and groped her curvy buttocks. His gaze lingered between Corine's thighs and she blushed. Ernest slipped off her jacket, and unbuttoned her blouse. He fought to control fleeting moments of nervousness which he never experienced before in the arms of a woman. He breathed rapidly and felt certain Corine could hear his heart pound in his chest. Ernest kneeled on the floor and lifted her skirt. He peeled her undies off and gently kissed her thighs before devouring her with his lips and tongue. Ernest rose, and lifted Corine by the buttocks against his hips. She slipped her shirt off and wrapped her legs around his firm hips. Corine's back arched when Ernest teased her nipples with his tongue and set her body on fire! He walked into the bedroom with Corine straddled to his hips and released her buttocks. Ernest unzipped his slacks and stood naked in front of her. She gasped at the sight of his sizable organ, and Ernest chuckled softly. Corine slowly unbuttoned her skirt, and it fell to the floor. Ernest hoisted her up by the buttocks again, and she wrapped her legs around his hips. He entered her with impatient desire and satisfied her pulsating body with rhythmic strokes perfected from years of sexual joyrides. He laid her on the bed and kissed every inch of her curvaceous body. Corine moaned with pleasure. Ernest straddled Corine, and rocked her body with powerful thrusts. Corine groped his buttocks and raised her hips to match his movements, determined to please him. Making love to Corine was unlike anything he had ever experienced. He was in love for the first time in his life. This was it! He maneuvered his manhood fervently inside Corine, and exploited her sensitive walls of delectation until she was satiated with pleasure. His manhood filled with love, and overflowed inside her. Multiple orgasms evoked squeals of delight from her lips.

Chapter Four

E rnest was in love and asked Corine to be his wife. He loved her intelligence, ambition, sense of humor, and vivacious personality. She took Ernest to meet her family in South Lancashire, which was located in Manchester, to a place known as "Old Town." Old Town was a poverty stricken area where Corine grew up. Her family resided in a two-storied terrace house built of brick, which some might refer to as a cozy cottage. In Ernest's opinion, it was nothing more than a run down tenement, which had seen better days. Potholes bedecked the roads, while garbage and animal feces fouled the air. Crooked paths leading to more dilapidated homes, and cracked cobblestone walkways, separated the closely-knit homes. Amidst all the squalor, the delicious aroma of baked meat pies, and mushy peas wafted through the air, reminding Corine of one good reason why it was always good to come home.

Corine's mother retired from her job in a fish market, and her father was a retired factory worker. The couple was content with their lot in life so long as they had a roof over their heads and food stocked in the cupboards. They preferred to spend their free time at local pubs, having a lark with old friends. They were fun loving, kind people, who would give their last dollar to help anyone in need, and most times, that's exactly

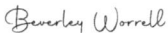

what they did. They weren't an ambitious lot, and spent their working years earning enough money to survive. Sunday was the perfect day for Ernest to meet them, because it was the one day of the week when Corine's mother prepared a sumptuous dinner.

The neighborhood in which they lived bordered middle class homes and Corine attended school with students of diverse economic backgrounds. She was an academically adept child who earned high grades, but, Corine's poverty stricken circumstances, always made her feel inadequate. She was sent to school in odd fitting clothes her mummy retrieved from places of charity, and the clothes never fit right. Her shoes were always tattered, and were either too big or too tight. Corine envied the middle class girls with new clothes and good shoes. She befriended a middle class student in her English Literature class named Emily. Emily liked Corine because she was smart and pretty. She knew Corine was in need of clothes and proper shoes so she asked her parents to help her friend out. Emily discreetly brought packages to school for Corine, and begged her not to open them until she got home. As soon as Corine arrived home, she tore the packages open, and was surprised by new shirts and skirts with the tags still on! She even had new shoes! These sporadic gifts made Corine less conscious about her appearance, and she was more comfortable interacting with her peers.

Education was Corine's ticket out of Old Town and away from boisterous neighbors. At age eighteen, she attended a London University and graduated a year early with a degree in social science. She held down a part time job as an office assistant to support herself and shared a one bedroom flat with another student. The roommates transformed the living room into a makeshift bedroom for Corine so she could have some semblance of privacy. After graduation, Corine was hired to manage the administrative offices at the reform school where she worked diligently to carve out a career for herself. Corine visited her parents every month, always on Sunday, and gave them two hundred pounds every time she visited. The small token to made their lives a little easier.

Corine stopped in front of one of the cottages in need of repair, and knocked gingerly on the weather beaten door. A stocky, middle aged woman with grayish hair opened the door and welcomed them with a toothy smile. It was Corine's mother. Corine entered the house and beckoned Ernest to come in. Ernest, being 6'3" in height had to bend his neck in order to step through the dwarfish doorway. Corine's mother gave him a warm hug as though she knew him all her life. Ernest returned her friendly gesture with a hug of his own and wrinkled his nose at the strong scent of disinfectant that pervaded the home and her clothes. A worn sofa and loveseat, along with a chipped center table, dominated the cramped, but tidy living room. A statuesque man stood in the room observing the jovial exchanges between Ernest and Corine's mother. He waited respectfully for his turn to greet Ernest. It was Mr. Wilshire, Corine's father. Corine's mother introduced the two gangly teenage boys seated in the room as Corine's younger brothers.

They sat down to a Sunday dinner of succulent roast with Yorkshire pudding, gravy, potatoes, steamed peas, and carrots. Mr. Wilshire topped their glasses with apple and blackcurrant juice while his wife heaped healthy portions of mouth-watering Banoffee pie on everyone's plates. The pie was made from bananas, cream and condensed milk and then baked on a biscuit and butter pastry. The meal was outstanding and Ernest cleaned his plate! The hearty dinner and conversation helped everyone to loosen up and Ernest began to feel comfortable and relaxed in the cozy home. Ernest talked with Mr. Wilshire about his family roots in Barbados and his intention to build a future with Corine. A few moments later, Ernest asked the entire family to gather around the intimate dining room. He took Corine by the hand and asked her to marry him. Corine was stunned by Ernest's unexpected proposal of marriage and didn't hesitate to say "yes." Her blue eyes were misty with love and admiration for her husband to be. The Wilshire's were pleased that a well-mannered, not to mention, dignified young man like Ernest wanted to marry their daughter. They gave the couple their blessing and Corine's mother fought back tears of joy. She couldn't wait to brag to her friends about the dapper young man her daughter was engaged to. Ernest removed a black velvet box from the inside pocket of his jacket, and placed a dainty diamond ring on Corine's finger. The happy couple kissed and Mrs. Wilshire, in her excitement, picked up the phone and invited friends over for Banoffee pie and drinks! They were going to celebrate Corine's engagement right away! She wanted to show off her son-in-law and Corine's pretty engagement ring. Mr. Wilshire emerged from the kitchen with a case of ale, and the atmosphere turned festive as they discussed wedding plans. The Wilshires' friends arrived in droves to congratulate Corine and meet Ernest. They even bought pies and delicacies of their own. The intimate dinner turned into a party with a house full of people, loud chatter, lots of drinking, and barrels of fun. Ernest and Corine departed Old Town well past midnight. They were legally drunk and hailed a taxi to take them home. The day was a roaring success!

Amidst wedding plans, work, and endless nights of making love, Corine was not feeling so good. She felt lightheaded, extremely fatigued, and dozed off at work, only to be nudged awake by snickering co-workers telling her to wake up. Corine couldn't figure out what was wrong, and Ernest rationalized that she was overwhelmed with wedding plans and work. The symptoms worsened when she woke up nauseated at her flat. Corine stumbled into the bathroom and vomited. The nausea subsided and Corine called Ernest to let him know that she was sick. Ernest met Corine at the flat and took her to the doctor's office right away. The nurse performed a series of tests, and informed the couple that Corine was six weeks pregnant! Ernest was shocked by the news. Corine lamented about being a pregnant bride and balked at the idea of having their baby out of wedlock. All plans for an elaboate wedding came to a screeching halt because they would have to get married sooner than they anticipated.

January 4, 1976, Ernest and Corine were married at a wedding chapel in Ilford. Jeffrey served as Ernest's best man and he was proud of his big brother for getting his life on track. It was an enchanting, intimate affair, witnessed by family and friends on a gorgeous Sunday afternoon. Corine was beautiful in a white, sleeveless silk, and lace gown with a full-length flowing skirt. The sleeveless top had an attached white pique of a shawl-collar combination. Long, silk gloves completed the picture of elegance and grace. Corine's hair was loosely curled and pinned softly at the top of her head with loose tendrils framing her face and shoulders. Ernest gazed lovingly at her and sported a gray tuxedo for the occasion. The St. John family flew from Barbados to be with Ernest on his wedding day. Estele and Deighton purchased south sea pearl silver drop earrings and a matching necklace as a special gift for Corine. They blessed the couple with a handsome monetary gift designed to give them a head start in life. They were pleased that Ernest had finally settled down and was a bit more serious about life.

Chapter Five

⸻※⸻

Corine moved into the flat shared by the brothers and Jeffrey was thankful for the extra help around the house. Corine cooked and kept the apartment spotless. Jeffrey no longer had to worry about Ernest not contributing to the household because Corine was there to help out. Corine gave birth to Gezebel, November 9, 1976. The seven pound, five ounce, bundle of joy kicked up a fuss when when the mid-wife tapped her behind. The baby hollered in protest every time nurses disturbed her rest for a diaper change! The infant owned a fiery personality and Corine determined that "Gezebel" was a fitting name. Ernest laughed, and the family grumbled about Corine giving the baby the name of a biblical vixen. Corine was undaunted, and explained that in her opinion, the biblical Jezebel was really an independent and assertive woman that was way ahead of her time, and vilified by men. Corine's views raised eyebrows among the St. John clan, and they took comfort in the fact the name was spelled with a G instead of a J.

Jeffrey was out of the house a lot due to his day job and his night job. This afforded Ernest and Corine time to adjust to their roles as parents. While Ernest was busy with his family, Jeffrey courted a lady that captivated his interest. Jeffrey met Sisi at the Natural History Museum located on Cromwell

Road in London. Sisi visited the museum with her mother, and observed artifacts that described the earth's ecology. Jeffrey was drawn to Sisi's aristocratic features and the intelligent manner in which she communicated her thoughts about the exhibit. He fantasized about whether her charcoal skin tasted like his favorite bittersweet chocolate! Sisi's black hair was thick and kinky. She wore it away from her face, to emphasize high cheekbones. dimpled cheeks and full lips. Jeffrey cleared his throat loud enough to break Sisi's concentration. She looked in his direction and batted dark lashes that complemented beautiful crescent shaped eyes. Sisi smiled shyly at Jeffrey. With that sign of encouragement, he hastily introduced himself to the women. The trio discussed the exhibit and exchanged critiques about the displays. Sisi's mother realized that Jeffrey was interested in Sisi, so she excused herself and left them alone to talk. By the time she returned, Jeffrey had Sisi's telephone number and she had his.

Jeffrey and Sisi dated regularly and discovered they shared similar tastes in cuisine, movies, literature, and music. Sisi's dream was to become a fashion designer. She worked for a top designer in London making patterns and working as a design assistant. It was a demanding position but she needed experience to succeed in the competitive fashion industry. Sisi learned merchandising, event planning, marketing and retail. She acted as liaison between sales and production teams and modeled pieces as needed. The hours were long, and the designers were impossible, but Sisi wouldn't have it any other way.

Sisi's father served as diplomatic representative to England from Ghana, and he spent the majority of his time traveling between the two countries on official business. The family previously resided in France and Germany when Sisi's father was required to do so by the government of Ghana. Sisi's appreciation of couture was influenced by the cultured ladies that wore stylish clothes at political events her father was required to attend. She was accomplished in French and was able to communicate effectively with Parisian designers. Her father's diplomatic affiliations rendered the family to upper class living in London, and their neighborhood teemed with political superstars. Sisi's accent amused Jeffrey because it was a confusing mix of all the places she lived. She often substituted French words for Ghanaian words, and English words for Ghanaian words. Sisi became Jeffrey's constant companion and their friendship blossomed into love, admiration and mutual respect.

Sisi introduced Jeffrey to her father and he was aghast that Sisi was in love with a white boy! He immediately suspected that Jeffrey wanted to bed his daughter to satisfy exotic fantasies. The politician was paranoid, and was sure that Jeffrey was sent by a political enemy to cause him scandal and embarrassment! Sisi apologized to Jeffrey for her father's unreasonable assumptions and explained that he was over protective. Sisi's father had Jeffrey's background investigated and was surprised to learn that Jeffrey came from a wealthy, multiracial family in Barbados. He had a sudden change of heart and acknowledged Jeffrey as Sisi's love interest. Once Sisi's father let his guard down, Jeffrey advised Sisi's parents that he wanted to marry their daughter. He was given their blessing and wasted no time shopping for the perfect ring.

The couple wed August 4th 1979, at Saint James Church in Piccadilly, London. Sisi was exquisite in a white silk gown embroidered with lace and pearls. The high necklace gown boasted a lace train and cape. Her mother hand picked six bridesmaids from a pool of their political friends and family members. Sisi's mother dressed them in shapeless but expensive frocks, ensuring that her daughter would be the only princess on her wedding day. Jeffrey's bridegrooms were friends from work, and his brother, Ernest, served as best man. Sisi's parents financed the entire affair and spared no expense. The reception soiree was held in London at the exclusive Gibson Hall where Sisi had the opportunity to blind guests with the 2.01-carat diamond solitaire Jeffrey placed on her finger. Guests were treated to cocktails in the courtyard while the wedding party was engrossed in photo sessions with family, politicians and other government officials. A sumptuous three-course dinner was served while attendees took the opportunity to personally congratulate the couple. Jeffrey and Sisi couldn't wait to escape to the Greek Isles and Barbados for their honeymoon because Sisi's parents had turned the wedding into a major society event.

They arrived in the Greek Isle of Agios Nikolaos in the early afternoon and strolled hand in hand through the picturesque streets. They ate heartily at a café and participated in a tour of the Venetian Fortresses before returning to their hotel. Sisi soaked her tired body in a tub filled with scented oil and emerged from the bath with a thirsty towel wrapped about her. She entered the bedroom of their honeymoon suite with droplets of water still clinging to her moist skin. Jeffrey admired her toned legs as she sauntered over to the plush bed where he lay naked in anticipation of being sexually intimate with her for the first time. Sisi nervously lay on the bed and faced Jeffrey. He cupped her face in his hands and slid his tongue into her mouth. Sisi was unsure of what to do because none of their kisses in the past were this sexy, so she closed her eyes and forced her self to relax. She felt stupid and sexually incompetent. Sisi stuck her tongue between his lips and wiggled it around in his mouth. Jeffrey understood that this was new to his wife and he whispered in her ear to take it easy. Sisi shivered when Jeffrey removed the towel and threw it on the floor. He gasped at the beauty of his African princess. Her breast nipples were the color of blackberries and Jeffrey took them into his mouth. He caressed her buttocks, and marveled at her tiny waist, flat stomach and perfectly contoured hips. Jeffrey couldn't resist the urge to slap Sisi's ample buttocks, and this aroused her even more. She wasn't sure how to respond. Sisi shifted her position and lay with her back against the bed. She closed her eyes. Jeffrey pierced her sunken belly button with his tongue and desire awakened in Sisi like cream slowly churned into butter. Jeffrey's tongue scorched a hot trail down her stomach until it reached her parted thighs. Throaty moans escaped her lips. He positioned himself and penetrated Sisi's virtue for the first time.

They flew to Barbados for the final leg of their honeymoon and stayed with Jeffrey's parents. The radiant couple arrived at the home of Deighton, and Estele, the picture of happily married couple. Estele gave Sisi a tour of their four bedroom three and a half bath home that rested majestically on 4, 000 square feet of paradise. The bedrooms had adjoining terraces that provided spectacular views of the ocean and gardens. Bella's old room overlooked the pool while the bedrooms once occupied by Ernest and Jeffrey had garden views. Sisi loved sitting in the oversized bamboo chairs on the terrace outside Jeffrey's room to gaze at the natural beauty of her surroundings. Her mother-in-law had a reputation for giving life to plants that others gave up on. Estele's gardens flourished with yellow and white hibiscus, desert roses, ixoras, and an interesting plant known locally as The Pride of Barbados. She pointed out banana, coconut, and mango trees that grew on the property, and singled out a green plant with white trumpet shaped petals, called Lady of the Night. Estele informed

Sisi that this unusual plant released a fragrance at dusk, and Sisi made a mental note to walk in the gardens this evening to experience it for her self.

Sisi sat on the terrace outside Jeffrey's room and watched the sun disappear behind the horizon. A soft flowery scent wafted through the air, and she couldn't figure out where it was coming from. Sisi sought Estele, who was in the kitchen preparing dinner. She reminded Sisi, the scent was coming from the plant, Lady of the Night. Sisi was astonished! She ventured out of the house where the scent was more intense, and roamed the gardens in search of the mystical flower that showered the night with beautiful fragrance. Sisi located the plant and her imagination scoured the possibilities. She stated out loud, "A perfume!" And broke off a few stems before returning to the house. Sisi placed the stems in a vase that rested on the bureau in the bedroom she shared with her husband. She couldn't wait to tell him about her idea! That evening, Estele baked chicken, cooked macaroni, rice with peas, and steamed vegetables for dinner. She got the opportunity to know Sisi on a more intimate level and concluded that Jeffrey made an excellent choice. Estele sensed Sisi's loyalty and love for Jeffrey was much like her loyalty and love for Deighton. She was pleased to have another woman of color in the family. It was nice to have someone to relate to.

Estele took Sisi to visit her mother and sister a few days after her arrival in the island. Estele's mother lived in a small three-bedroom bungalow with Estele's sister who had a daughter about the same age as baby Gezebel. The green and white bungalow reminded Sisi of the concrete bungalows in Ghana. Estele explained that she purchased the bungalow for her mom so she could have a worry free retirement. She visited her family every week and gave her mother a weekly allowance to spend as she pleased. Sisi was surprised that Estele's mother and sister were dark skinned, whereas Estele was so fair. Estele read Sisi's reaction, and disclosed that she was the only mulatto in the family. Sisi respected her mother-in-law because wealth and social standing never got in the way of her loyalty and generosity to her family.

Sisi's meeting with Deighton's white family was an entirely different affair. They were visibly impressed with her background but she was not what they expected from Deighton's son. They expected the boy to marry a white girl or someone of mixed race. They couldn't fathom the idea of having an African marry into their family because the continent of Africa seemed so remote, so strange. They greeted her warmly, careful not to upset Deighton or his son with expressions of surprise. But, behind closed doors, when Deighton and his immediate family left, the St. John Clan lamented about the darkening of their bloodline. Their tongues "tskd tskd" with disapproval, and they shook their heads with disappointment.

Sisi was pensive about her meeting with Deighton's family and was glad when it was finally over. She cringed when their hard eyes failed to match their smiles. Sisi got it! This was a lily-white family and she would never be able to immerse her self completely into it. Deighton married Estele who was part black and part white, obviously because he loved her. His family seemed to genuinely love Estele and the children, which was probably easier for them to do since their kids passed for white. Sisi understood that her situation was different from Estele's because she was a black African, and nothing was ever going to change that. Yes, they treated her with kindness, and made sure she was physically comfortable in their opulent home, but that was as far as her comfort zone went. Their icy stares and frozen smiles sliced through her Ivory Coast soul like a machete! Sisi clasped Jeffrey's hand in the back seat of the car. She came away from the visit with his father's family with renewed respect and admiration for her husband. Jeffrey was emotionally strong so she had to be emotionally strong when it came to race and prejudice. She thought about these things as the Mercedes winded through the narrow streets and rolled to a stop outside his parent's home. Sisi was exhausted, and made her way upstairs to Jeffrey's room. She couldn't wait to slip beneath the crisp sheets covering the queen-sized bed where she and Jeffrey made love almost every night since their arrival.

Deighton fancied him self a chef and roasted breadfruits, sweet potatos, chicken and fish on his grill. He served Sisi in grand style. Estele refused to be outdone by her husband and introduced Sisi to local cuisine such as coo-coo with flying fish and roti, which she found quite tasty. Deighton, in jest, declared war against Estele and whipped up fish cakes and bakes! The two of them enjoyed challenging each other with these light-hearted cooking competitions and cajoled Sisi into declaring who was the best cook. Sisi's only proclamation was that she enjoyed everything they prepared and gobbled it all up! Her sister in law, Bella, visited in the evenings and took Sisi shopping in bustling Bridgetown on Saturday. Bella purchased syrupy sno cones drizzled with condensed milk for Sisi, and Sisi was hooked! Jeffrey took her for drives in the country for a glimpse of rural life in the island. These drives were often abandoned to frolic on a sun drenched beach. They attended entertainment shows at hotels where Sisi cheered fire-eaters and danced to calypso. Sisi cried regrettably when it was time to leave the sland because it reminded her of Ghana in many ways. But, she and Jeff had

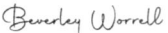

a new life waiting for them in England. One filled with work, prosperity, and children.

Sisi and Jeffrrey chose to reside in Hammersmith where they rented a two-bedroom luxury apartment close to theaters, restaurants and shops. Sisi decorated the apartment with modern furnishings and unusual artwork. Jeffrey resigned from his teaching job after he was offered a management opportunity with the hotel where he had been working nights. Hotel Executives were impressed with his leadership abilities and ideas to improve service, and Jeffrey was promoted. Jeffrey's agenda included managing a staff of fifty two, spearheading marketing campaigns, working with quality teams, and overseeing a limited budget. He was ready for the challenge and his days were booked solid with meetings, conferences, power lunches, and dinners. He earned advanced degrees in International Hotel Management, and Finance, in order to further his career. Sisi busied her self researching the idea of creating a fragrance from the plant, and Jeffrey gave her his full support. She sketched showpieces for designers, and in the evenings, worked on developing a business plan for her own design label. Within two years, she and Jeffrey were ready to start a family.

Chapter Six

L ife for Ernest and Corine was a financial struggle as they tried to make ends meet with a young child to care for. Ernest was no longer content with his job at the reform school and cursed his paycheck every payday. He enjoyed mentoring the boys and acting as a substitute parent but he wanted more. Ernest complained about his inadequate income and was determined to make more money. His ego was bruised by the fact that Corine was still his superior at work and earned more. Gone, were the splurges on expensive dinners, clothes, pubs, and frivolous things. He had a family to provide for. Out of frustration, Ernest would throw caution to the wind, and spend his entire paycheck on clothes, and whatever else struck his fancy, leaving Corine to foot the bill for rent and food. Corine solved this problem by opting to pay the rent, leaving him to pay utilities. Ernest accused Corine of treating him like a child because she suggested he take care of their share of monthly utilities which amounted to less than rent. As far as Corine was concerned, it was a practical solution to a recurring problem. Corine theorized that Ernest could find part time work in the evenings because they needed the additional income to save for a home of their own. She thought the idea of home ownership would motivate her husband into getting a second job.

"Ernest, It would be nice if we could start saving for a home." Corine voiced cheerfully.

"Yeah, our little potato could use a backyard to run around in, eh little potato?" He replied, and swung two year old Gezzy in the air.

"Well, we need to start saving our money." Corine emphasized.

"Corine, we don't have any money to save. I'm going to start looking for a job that pays more." Ernest replied.

"Ernest, that's fantasitic! Why don't you work an evening job until that happens?" Corine asked.

"What do you think I am? A mule? I don't have the energy to work a part-time job after running around with those kids all day! A man needs time to relax and unwind!" Ernest retorted in an annoyed manner.

"You make time for the pubs, and come home later than you should! I think you could use that time to bring me more money!" Corine berated him in an irritated voice.

"i've got a better idea! Why don't I quit this stupid job and focus on finding something better? I'll take care of Gezzy during the day when I don't have interviews. That would save on childcare expense!" Ernest retorted.

"What? Have you lost your bloody mind? You want to quit? There's no telling how long it will take you to find work, mate! I won't stand for it!" Corine shouted decisively.

"You have no say in the matter love! I'm sick and tired of those wayward brats treating me like I'm their father! I've got one child, Corine! One! I'm going to hand in my resignation first thing tomorrow morning!" Ernest hollered in frustration.

"Bye bye darling!" He cooed to baby Gezzy and slammed the door on his way out.

Corine cried and held Gezzy in her arms. She nuzzled her daughter's soft hair and thought hard about what her next move should be. Corine sat on the dingy sofa she found in the apartment when she moved in three years ago. She ran her hand along the rough fabric, and hoped to own fine furniture one day. Corine fondly remembered when Deighton and Estele furnished Gezzy's room with a brand new bed, wardrobe, dresser and matching nightstand. She remembered commenting about wishing there was a rocking chair in Gezzy's room so she could rock her to sleep and Daddy St. John added it to the bill of sale! They filled Gezzy's room with toys and her closet overflowed with new clothes. Corine felt fortunate to have such generous in-laws that wanted nothing but the best for Gezzy. What was she going to do now that Ernest was going to quit his post at the reform school? He was an irresponsible bastard, to say the least. But, he was her husband and she loved him. She dressed Gezzy and headed toward the community bank not far from their flat. Their joint account reflected a balance of fifteen hundred pounds. Corine withdrew one thousand pounds and redeposited it into an account she opened in her name. She left the rest of the money in the joint account so that Ernest could have access to it. From now on she would deposit her paycheck into her personal account. Corine was relieved knowing that Ernest couldn't spend what he didn't have access to. She

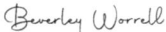

would not allow him to financially devastate their lives and took matters into her own hands.

Ernest walked to one of his favorite pubs near Lace Market, not far from their flat in Nottingham Gate, and ordered a dry London gin. He sat at the bar and downed the gin in one swallow. The spirit burned his throat and warmed his belly. "Ah" Ernest sighed as his body surrendered to the warming effects of the gin. He ordered another one and downed that too. This time he squeezed his eyes shut, and gritted his teeth as the liquor worked its magic. He ordered another one and held it in his hand while his eyes scanned the pub for a secluded area to nurse his drink. Ernest found a quiet nook in the rear of the pub where he could sit and not be bothered by women looking for Mr. Right in all the wrong places. It was time Corine knew how he felt about working at that blasted reform school! Ernest loathed the countless rounds of dull meetings he had to endure with the school establishment in order to update them on the progress made by the students. He detested having to listen to their nonsensical recommendations about how to improve his program. Ernest wanted the students to have fun and excel at athletics without having to adhere to more rules and regulations. The needs of the students drained him emotionally and he forced himself not to care too much. He didn't want to become emotionally attached to any of them. After all, this was just a job and all he got was a paltry paycheck for his trouble! Ernest accepted the low paying job because he wanted Corine and now that his mission was accomplished it was time to move on to bigger and better things.

His thoughts lingered on his little brother Jeffrey who had transformed himself into a smart-assed, nerdy, businessman indeed! What a showoff! Ernest thought bitterly. Jeffrey was trying to out-do him and prove to everyone that his big brother Ernest was a loser! Ernest was bewildered and outdone by his siblings. Here he was, struggling to make ends meet and his little brother was living the life he dreamed of! His brother had the respect of his peers and the respect of the family. Ernest felt that success should have happened to him first. He had to find a way out of the daily grind because he couldn't settle for less. He had to make money, lots and lots of money. He was accustomed to living a life of leisure with access to cash. Corine just didn't understand. She deserved to stay at home and raise children while he made the money. Jeffrey could waste his life slaving away behind a desk but he was going to be the one to discover the easy path to riches!

Ernest pondered Jeffrey's wife Sisi and smirked at the blue-black color of her skin. Sisi was a posh, dishy-looking woman, but as far as he was concerned she was too damned black! He would never marry someone so dark, no matter how impressive her background was! What was Jeffrey thinking? At least Corine was white and that had to be a feather in his cap, Ernest thought. Jeffrey might have done better in the eyes of their father's family if he'd declared himself a "Nancy Boy" instead! A silly image of Jeffrey walking and sashaying his hips like a girl played in Ernest's mind and he burst out laughing! Patrons stared at him curiously. He would have given anything to be there when Jeffrey had the gall to introduce his jigarooni teapot to the St. John Clan! He would have forfeited his inheritance to witness the expression of disbelief on their faces when Ms. Jungle Bunny walked in the door! Ernest laughed hysterically at his insensitive thoughts and patrons realized that he was officially on the piss so they chuckled and looked away. The beastly laughter subsided and Ernest considered his own ethnicity. Even though he and his siblings had a touch of the tar brush, it was no excuse for Jeffrey to find himself a tar baby from the motherland! He gulped the gin in

one swallow and some of it spewed out of his mouth when he started to guffaw again! His little brother sure did think in an anti-clockwise manner when it came to women! Ernest was in hysterics! He held his gut, doubled over and laughed loud! Why couldn't his little brother give Ms. Thick Lips a good bang and move on? Ernest snickered with insanity when he realized that 'thick lips' was derogatory of Sisi's ethnicity and possibly her woman hood! He stood up on rickety legs and hollered belligerently at the top of his lungs. "No pun intended ladies and gentlemen!" Patrons shook their heads and laughed at the drunken man! Ernest plopped down in his chair and placed his head on his arms in an effort to hide his face from patrons who leered at him for behaving lawlessly!

The manager of the pub walked briskly over to Ernest.

"Sir, may I help you get a taxi?" The pub manager offered. He was anxious to get this drunkard out of the pub before he caused another scene.

"Not bleeding likely!" Ernest yelled.

Ernest eased his leg up to "blow off" and laughed hysterically at his shameless act! The pub manager turned up his nose at the offending stench and requested Ernest control his outbursts or leave. Ernest thought the pub manager's speedy recoil from the skunk like odor was well worth the effort! He tossed money for his drinks on the table and left the pub. If he was able to coordinate his movements properly he would have knuckled sandwiched the pub manager. His tall frame swayed like a skyscraper caught in powerful winds as he shuffled down High Pavement Street. He laughed like an insane man and passersbys quickly got out of his way. Ernest cussed and laughed pugnaciously all the way home.

Chapter Seven

True to his word, Ernest handed in his registration for his post as student counselor and turned down a raise offered to him as an incentive to stay. Corine confided in Jeffrey about his brother's irresponsible decision, and Jeffrey promised to help financially until Ernest found employment. Ernest resorted to lounging with associates at upscale pubs. These associates held lofty titles in London's financial sector, wore designer suits, and drove flashy cars. They were lawyers, accountants, financial analysts and investors that discussed market trends and bounced ideas about investment banking off each other. Ernest tuned in to their conversations when they boasted about the wealth they accumulated from investing in the markets. His ears perked up as they rambled on about how easy it was to gamble with other people's money. It was during one of these happy hour meetings at the pub that Ernest learned his drinking buddies freelanced for an investment firm called "The Network" and touted themselves as officers of the company. In fact, these associates were exorbitantly paid salesmen whose main goal was to lure corporations, investors and philantropists into investing with the firm. They were charismatic experts in their field whose portfolios boasted fiscal management, financial planning, corporate accounting, and competence in operating and working capital. They worked under the direction of Lerwick, the creator of The Network.

Mr. Lerwick was an arrogant, flashy, young man, barely thirty years old, who stood 5'9" with a medium build, scanty hair and beady eyes. He had a boyish smile that camouflaged his cunning personality and above average intellect. Lerwick was a wheeler, a dealer, a salesman, a hustler. When he was five years old his mother died in a boating accident and his father never remarried. Instead, he raised the boy to be a replica of himself. As a child, Lerwick's hair was cut indentical to his fathers' and the boy dressed in business suits just like his father. His father walked or rather marched like a British soldier with his head up and back straight. Lerwick idolized his father so much that he mimicked his walk and the nickname "Young Lerwick" was bestowed upon him. Mr. Lerwick owned a profitable investment business and he taught his son how to be a savvy investor just like he was. At age twelve, Young Lerwick worked alongside his father in the business, and by the time his eighteenth birthday rolled around, he was a cut throat businessman.

The elder Mr. Lerwick's female companions fluttered like butterflies in and out of Young Lerwick's life. His father dated beautiful women who weren't necessarily smart and Young Lerwick's opinions about women stemmed from his father's romantic interludes. Women, according to the elder Lerwick, were to be spoiled, cherished, loved, and admired for their beauty. Once the infatuation with beauty was over, it was time to move on to the next. The birdlike pecks on his cheeks, and perfumed hugs showered on him by his fathers' ladies never came close to the nurturing a true mother could give.

Young Lerwick graduated from Oxford Brookes at the top of his class with degrees in business and international finance. He insisted on being called "Lerwick" by his family and friends and denounced his childhood nickname. After graduation, he accepted an enviable position in a finance company where he outsmarted the competition with his talent as an adept investor. Two years passed and Lerwick desired a company of his own. He promptly handed in his resignation and set his sights on building a financial empire for himself. Lerwick rented office space in the business district of Liverpool, and the investment firm called "The Network" was born. He hired a small administrative staff and opened the doors for business.

Within three years The Network turned a profit and Lerwick seeked out other money-making strategies. He was tired of watching other people's money and wanted a change. Lerwick was burned out because he had been in the investment business before he reached his thirteenth birthday. The Network needed a new direction and he needed to move on to something fresh and exciting. Lerwick net worth was 5.2 million and as far as he was concerned, he was dirt poor. He devised a plan to create a foundation within The Network, and this idea was the breeding ground for his interest in offshore banking and investing. Lerwick realized that if he turned The Network into a foundation, he could walk away with millions.

He reorganized "The Network" into "The Network Foundation" or TNF, and it was hyped as a fund dedicated to charitable giving. Its mission was to identify charitable causes and assist them financially. Lerwick became proficient in the laws and conditions pertaining to offshore investment banking and traveled to offshore destinations. He used his money

to buy those in positions of power in the banking, investing and real estate sector. Bank accounts were opened in
these countries to facilitate international transactions, which
Lerwick intended to initiate after his return to England. The
scheme went like this. Funds trusted to TNF would be fun-
nelled to TNF's off shore account, and then redirected into
one of Lerwicks' account in undisclosed offshore destinations.

Now that TNF was incorporated as an offshore enterprise,
the settlors, (Lerwick and the officers) were named benefi-
ciaries of all trusts bought into TNF. Lerwick appointed his
crooked attorneys as trustees who were directed by him as to
how to manage the trusts. When a trust expired, Lerwick and
his associates received payments milked from the interest of
the trust. To avoid suspicion, the TNF machine donated a
small percentage of their funds to community organizations.
Lewick duped heads of corporations and philantrophists
into donating and investing with the firm. The corporations
shared in the glory of charitable giving, and Lerwick's secret
was safe. Lerwick was constantly flying from one offshore
destination to the next and needed a break. He was ready
to pass the baton of travel to someone else. That individual
had to be ready at a moment's notice to travel. He needed a
quick learner, someone who was trustworthy and someone
who didn't ask too many questions.

Ernest answered the call, and was interviewed by Lerwick
and his officers before being asked to join the team. After a
background check proved he had no criminal record, Ernest
was on Lerwick's unofficial payroll, and agreed to be compensated in cash. TNF's administrative staff doled out crash
courses in offshore investment banking so that he could
understand what was expected of him and what to expect
from Lerwick's counterparts. After six weeks of study, Ernest

passed a series of written tests and proved that he was competent for the job.

The first assignment was in Austria where Ernest was instructed to open fictitious bank accounts with the assistance of Lerwick's contacts at the banks. He traveled to Lunchen, Salzburg, and Bratislava and did the same thing. Since Bratislava was his last stop, he spent the night there and departed for London the next morning. Ernest arrived in London and reported to TNF headquarters so that Lerwick could review reports of all transactions. Lerwick was pleased that Ernest executed his first mission expeditiously and presented him with an itinerary of international locales that he was required to visit. If the territory was sizeable, Ernest was required to travel from one city to the next in order to open fictitious accounts. Lerwick added an extra task to Ernest's job description. He instructed Ernest to liquidate physical assets donated to TNF and direct the proceeds to offshore accounts. Those funds would be further dissected and redistributed to Lerwicks' personal accounts in offshore countries. It was that easy! Ernest had reached his twenty-ninth year and reclaimed the good life.

While Ernest traveled continuously on behalf of TNF, Lerwick shopped for a chic three-bedroom penthouse in London and moved his favorite girlfriend in on a trial basis. But, there were conditions the girlfriend had to meet before moving in. She was required to sign a contract which stated that should their living arrangement go awry, she was expected to vacate his home within 30 days. The agreement had all the verbiage of a prenuptial agreement minus a marriage. The girlfriend was dismayed at having to sign such an agreement but moved into his lavish home anyway, certain that their relationship would conclude in marriage. Lerwick

spoiled his girlfriend and lavished her with money, exotic vacations, cars, furs and jewelry. Fifteen months into commingling, Lerick became bored and lost interest. He claimed his favorite girl was devoid of basic ambition, not too smart, and overly materialistic. Lerwick blamed her laxity in finding ways to invigorate their union as the main reason why their relationship was doomed. According to the terms of the contract, the girlfriend had thirty days to make alternative living arrangements, but she refused to heed his warning. He filed a motion in court, and she was ejected from his premises after missing the 30 day mark! His attorney sent her a paltry parting gift in the form of a five thousand pound check, while Lerwick turned a deaf ear to her cries for reconciliation. Two months later, a new girlfriend moved in under the same rules and conditions. Lerwick played the game. He was in search of a dynamic woman that would stand strong, even if the rug was pulled out from under her feet!

Chapter Eight

L erwick paid Ernest a weekly sum of two thousand pounds, in addition to all travel related expenses. Ernest traveled to Dubai, France, Germany, France, Liechtenstein and Portugal to conduct business with the banks on behalf of TNF. He iniatiated computerized bank transfers between offshore countries, and created a web of bank transactions that would take decades to unravel. TNF business was money laundering and Ernest was a key player in its success.

Corine was concerned about Ernest's activities and the huge sums of cash he brought home. She had a premonition that his involvement with the foundation would eventually lead to disaster. Corine played detective and visited TNF's headquarters in Liverpool. A buxom, red haired secretary, busy sorting mail, greeted her. The secretary insisted on handing Corine brochures about joining the TNF family of investors and shoved an application in her face. Corine attempted to cozy up to the secretary in hopes that she would divulge gossip about the internal affairs of the company, but the telephone kept ringing, and the secretary asked her to leave the completed application on the desk. A frustrated Corine completed the application with false information, and placed it on the desk. But, before Corine could get another word in, the secretary advised her an officer of the company would call in 24 hours. Corine left the office in a hurry and counted her blessings that Ernest didn't find her there. She would have to talk to him about his involvement with this instituiton because it stunk like a dead rat!

Ernest arrived home in the evening after playing cricket with buddies at a local park, and Corine fired off a barrage of questions at him before he could take his shoes off.

"Ernest, we need to talk! I want to know where all this money is coming from!" Corine stated in a concerned voice. She leapt up from the couch where she sat watching t.v., when she heard the key turn in the door.

"Damn, Corine! I just walked in! "Ernest replied in an exasperated voice. He leaned over to untie his athletic shoes.

"Every week you're flying off to different countries and you've become so secretive! I have a right to know what my husband is involved in!" Corine retorted with defiance and placed her hands on her hips.

"Do you want for anything Corine?" Ernest asked between clenched teeth.

"No, I don't! At least not now, but what does that have to do..." Corine stammered. She was unable to finish the sentence.

"Are the bills paid on time Corine?" Ernest growled.

"Yes, but that still..." Corine faltered and started to lose ground. Ernest refused to let her continue.

"Does our child have everything she could ever want?" Ernest asked menacingly and gritted his teeth.

"Yes she does! Ernest I'm trying to warn…" Corine blurted out and lost her focus when Ernest cut her off.

"We are now able to save for a home. Isn't that right?" Ernest asked with impatience.

"Yes!" Corine admitted in a crushed voice.

"Well, then, by the grace of god almighty, leave it alone!" Ernest yelled, and stormed into the bedroom, slamming the door. Corine leaned against the wall and closed her eyes. She was getting nowhere with Ernest and would have to find out about TNF on her own. It was the only way.

Ernest was busy flying to exciting destinations and Corine was left in charge of the household. He handed Corine fifteen hundred pounds every week, and kept five hundred for himself. Corine deposited half of the fifteen hundred into their joint account and the other half into her personal account. She cleared their debts and hoarded the money as the months sailed by. They were able to save more money in nine months than they were able to save in a year when they both worked at the reform school. Corine never had anything in abundance since her family was poor and now that she had money at her disposal, she wasn't about to spend foolishly. She wanted to save as much as possible just in case the money stopped rolling in. Corine deposited her biweekly pay into her personal account and never spent a dime of it. She accumulated more than ten thousand pounds in her nest egg and chose to keep it secret from Ernest.

Ernest passed time during his overnight stays in foreign countries by shopping for handmade shoes, leather belts and designer clothes. He was prepared to spend top dollar for any quality item worthy of his possession. Sometimes he walked around the cities and towns visiting places of interest. Other times he caught a movie or nursed a drink in a nearby lounge. Ernest was in Geneva, Switzerland, visiting the Conservatoire et Jardin Botaniques, to relax and take his mind off work before his early a.m. Flight the next morning. He was jet lagged and needed to walk off the feeling of fatigue. He roamed the park zoo and observed the caged animals. Ernest peered at the animals and pitied them because they weren't free. Shouldn't every living thing be free? He wondered. Well, at least they were well cared for and... something bumped his calves and interrupted his thoughts. He spun around to see a ball on the ground next to his feet. A boy, about four years of age ran toward him. Ernest assumed the child was playing with the ball when it rolled away and bumped his calves. He picked up the ball and threw it in the air, much to the delight of the tot. Ernest's roving eyes captured a 5'10" blond haired beauty charging after the toddler. He paused tossing the ball in the air to admire the athletic beauty racing in his direction. The toddler finally reached Ernest and he placed the ball in his chubby hands. The child hugged the ball possessively, happy to have it again.

"Allo, je m'appelle Paola." (Hello, my name is Paola) The blond beauty introduced herself and extended her hand for a handshake.

"Ernest here! Um... muy francais es mauvais?" (My French isn't good) Ernest blundered in French mixed with Spanish and shook her hand.

"Je suis enchanté de vous connaitre." (Nice to meet you) Paola replied.

"I'm enchanted too!" Ernest responded. He struggled to converse in French because he knew very little.

"Je suis un garder des entant pour Olaf. Merci pour le balle a propos!" (I'm a baby-sitter for Olaf. Thank you for the ball by the way!) Paola stated with enthusiasm.

"Look, it would be a gaspiller (waste) of your temps (time) for me to parler (talk) to you like this. Nice to meet, uh, enchante Paola!" Ernest spoke in English and French. He was embarrassed and turned to leave when Paola laughed.

Ernest swung around and stared at her. He wanted to know why she was so amused; and ran his fingers through his hair to make sure a bird hadn't pooped on his head! He checked the bottom of his shoes and his trench coat just in case he was dragging a sheet of toilet paper on his person after his last visit to the restroom! Paola and Olaf giggled at his erratic movements.

"Ernest, please forgive me! I didn't mean to make a mockery of you but I just couldn't help myself! In addition to speaking French, I also speak German, Italian, Romanic and English!" Paola laughed and winked.

Ernest let his guard down and grinned. Paola was happy he wasn't insulted by her teasing. Her words were coated with strong European inflection, and he had to listen intently to understand what she was saying. Paola viewed Ernest with interest. She had to take Olaf home, and desired Ernest's contact information before leaving the park.

"Do you live in Geneva?" Paola asked.

"No, I reside in London." Ernest replied and gazed intently into Paola's vibrant blue eyes. Paola blushed and the blood rushed to her face.

"Oh! London! I've been there once or twice. It's a lively city. How often do you come to Geneva?" Paola inquired. Her flushed face betrayed her emotions.

"This is my second visit." Ernest replied subtlety.

He faced Paola with hands shoved into the front pockets of his slacks. His unbuttoned trench coat revealed a black cashmere sweater that hid toned abs beneath.

"I can show you around if you like. Maybe we could meet somewhere in forty-five minutes to dine." Paola suggested with confidence. She was already five minutes late getting Olaf to his parents.

"I'm staying at the Quality Hotel in Geneva City Centre. Meet me there at 7:00pm." Ernest stated. His dark eyes searched hers and triggered every muscle in her racing heart.

"Sounds good!" Paola exclaimed. "A (très) bientôt, Ernest." (See you soon, Ernest.) Paola replied in French just for the fun of it, and picked Olaf up.

"Adios!" (Goodbye) Ernest hollered in Spanish! He smiled lasciviously, and leered at Paola's curvy buttocks in black leggings as she hurried out of the park.

"Adieu!" Paola hollered in French and chuckled when Ernest said good-bye in Spanish instead of French.

Paola walked briskly to Olaf's home. His parents expected employees to adhere to prompt schedules, and a few minutes of tardiness would give his mother a migraine! Her thoughts reverted to Ernest, the handsome stranger that captivated her as he strolled through the park. She thought he was incredibly sexy with jet-black hair, piercing dark eyes and arched eyebrows that appeared to be etched by an artist. He was meticulously groomed, and sooo good looking. Paola imagined him to be a great lover and couldn't pass up the opportunity to meet him. That's why she purposely kicked Olaf's ball towards him! Life was about making things happen! Her victory was short lived however, when she observed the wedded band on his finger.

Paola threw caution to the wind and arrived at the hotel on time! Ernest stood outside waiting for her. He dressed casually in black jeans, a knit sweater and black leather jacket. His hair was slick from the shower and it had a tousled look. Paola smiled sweetly as she approached him. She wore a knee length knit dress to show off toned legs, and strappy coal colored pumps completed her "leggy" look. Paola's hair fell lushly past her shoulders in loose bouncy curls down the small of her back. Ernest caught the faint scent of shampoo in her hair when she kissed his cheek. He was tempted to sweep her off her feet and take her to his room for "rumpy pumpy" but was too lethargic for that! He wanted to relax and enjoy getting to know all about her over a good meal. Paola chose a trendy bar-restaurant in Vielle-Ville, which catered to young professionals. They choose a quiet table, away from the crowd and chatted while a jazz band performed. Ernest learned that Paola was twenty-five and lived with her mother on the outskirts of Geneva. Her father died five years ago after an arduous battle with lung cancer, leaving Paola and her mom to carry on. His life insurance policy and investments kept them comfortable after he passed away. She studied business administration at a nearby University and worked part-time as a nanny, caring for Olaf. Her future looked promising.

"What about you? What do you do?" Paola asked.

"I'm a traveling businessman for a company called The Network Foundation." Ernest stated.

"What type of business is it?" Paola queried.

"It's a foundation dedicated to assisting communities in need. We also specialize in offshore investment banking." Ernest elaborated and his eyes feasted her substantial bustline.

"Sounds like a worthy organization." Paola responded breathlessly. She fidgeted in her chair while his gaze concentrated on her bosom. A blush elevated her body temperature, and Paola exhaled, hoping to thwart the heat that started to spread through her body.

"Ernest, when will I see you again?" Paola questioned him.

"That's hard to determine because I travel where the business requires me to go. My intinerary changes every week." Ernest answered.

He reclined in the chair and admired Paola's legs. His eyes trailed imaginary kisses from her toes, to her knees, to her stomach and lingered below her belly button. Paola perspired as the blush surged through her body like an electric current, and ended up looking like a red bell pepper! She grabbed a glass of ice water from the table and gulped it down. Paola prayed it would cool her off. Ernest smiled and Paola squirmed. She opted to ask about his wedded ring.

"You're married?" Paola probed and held her breath.Ernest shifted his gaze and his piercing eyes stabbed Paola's baby blues. He responded tactfully to her question.

"Yes. I also have a child. My wife doesn't appreciate my job because it requires an extensive amount of travel. She finds that difficult to deal with. Now I know why! You know…i've never felt the inclination to look at another woman until…" Ernest stated meekly, and stopped talking. He had given up his frivolous affairs and one night stands when his relationship with Corine turned serious.

"Until now?" Paola finished the sentence.

"Yes, until now." Ernest confirmed. He remained quiet. Content to admire Paola's beauty if that was all he was allowed to do. Paola cleared her throat.

"I was attracted to you from the moment I saw you." Paola remarked, and sipped a glass of wine.

He reached for her hand and gave it a gentle squeeze. Ernest was tempted to kiss the wine off of her pouty lips but refrained from doing so. They dined and danced the night away. The two of them strolled back to the hotel holding hands; laughing and chatting like lovers. Ernest hadn't laughed like that in such a long time. They arrived at the hotel and he instructed the concierge to summon car service to take Paola home. Paola was miffed! She wanted more time with him.

"Ernest, it's not that late. Maybe we could go to your room and have a drink?" Paola suggested.

"I'm really tired Love. Not tonight!" Ernest replied tactfully.

"Is it your wife?" Paola asked boldly. She linked her arms around his neck and embraced him.

"Actually, it isn't! Look, it's getting late and i've got an early flight!" Ernest uttered impatiently. He removed her arms from around his neck. Paola was perplexed by his rejection to her affections. She walked over to the front desk and snatched a pen and pad off of it. She scribbled her phone number and address on the paper and shoved it in his hand.

"Call me!" Paola stated in a hurt voice.

Car service arrived and Paola threw her arms around Ernest's neck and hugged him again. Ernest sternly removed her arms from around his neck, and escorted her by the elbow, from the lobby to the car. He opened the passenger door.

"Ernest, you led me on! You'll never return to Geneva and i'll never see you again! Paola protested and seated herself into the vehicle.

Paola couldn't fathom why she was so captivated by a man she met hours ago. How could he refuse her? Most men would die for an opportunity to spend the night in her arms but he turned her down! She was mortified! Ernest remained aloof and paid the driver. He closed the vehicle door and signaled the driver to push off. Ernest turned on his heel and disappeared into the lobby. Paola craned her neck and looked out the rear window, expecting to see Ernest staring at the car until it was no longer in view. By the time she turned around to wave goodbye, he was gone! Her ego was crushed! Paola dissolved into tears. She had never felt so foolish and rejected in all her life!

Ernest retired to his suite and was grateful for a full night's sleep. He tucked Paola's telephone number in his briefcase because Corine was forbidden to look in it. He lay back on the bed and images of sexy Paola seeped into his consciousness. What a lovely girl! The smell of her perfume lingered in his senses and he marveled about what their next encounter would be like. He wanted to give her time to think about getting involved with him. Ernest had no intention of calling Paola until he was back in Geneva. There was something about her that made him smile. He had a feeling she was going to be around for a while.

Chapter Nine

The 6:00am Air France flight arrived in Great Britain at approximately 7:50am, and Ernest stopped at an airport florist to purchase a bouquet of roses for Corine. He entered the flat, happy to be home, and was confronted by an irate Corine who stood in the living room and stared at him with her arms crossed against her bosom.

"I was up all night waiting for you to call!" Corine yelled. She was still in her bathrobe.

"Corine, not now! Here, these are for you!" Ernest replied. He was annoyed because she didn't express joy to see him, after a few days absence. Ernest pecked Corine on the cheek and handed her the roses.

"I don't need bloody flowers!" Corine ranted and tossed the bouquet to the floor.

He walked away from his fuming wife and went into Gezzy's room. She was fast asleep so he kissed her cheek and closed the bedroom door on his way out so as not to wake the sleeping child. Ernest ventured into the living room where Corine stood and glared at him angrily. He picked up his travel bag, and proceeded to the bedroom with Corine gnashing her teeth behind him! She stormed in after him and slammed the door shut!

"Where the bloody hell were you last night? I called the hotel several times and you never answered the phone!" Corine chided Ernest. He ignored her and unpacked. The slight enraged her!

"Answer me, Ernest!" Corine shouted. Ernest continued to give Corine the cold shoulder and was on his way out of the room when she jumped on his back and coiled her legs around his waist! She flung one arm around his neck and pummeled his shoulders with the other!

"How could you treat me this way?" Corine shouted and pummeled his back and shoulders with stinging blows. Ernest swung his body from side to side and Corine could not maintain a steady hold on him. She landed on the floor with a thud and her bathrobe became untied in the midst of the ruckus. Corine got to her feet and shrugged the bathrobe off her body. She was ready to wage war, clad in nothing but panties! She lunged at Ernest, hell bent on scratching his eyes out!

"You bastard! How dare you spend the night in the arms of another woman! I won't tolerate it!" Corine hollered hoarsely. Ernest protected his face by putting his hands up to block her quick jabs.

Suddenly, he dived beneath her arms and swept Corine up over his shoulder. Ernest spanked her buttocks playfully and tossed her on the bed. He hastily unbuttoned his shirt and took off his trousers. Corine quickly recovered and stood up on the bed. She ran at Ernest, and he caught her by the waist, and held her tight. Her movements were restricted in this position, so she yanked his hair with her free hands and slapped his head! His scalp was on fire! He let go of Corine and she delivered a slap to his face!

"Blasted woman!" Ernest roared and massaged his cheek. He grabbed her wrists and Corine fell down on the bed. She kicked like a wild horse and aimed at his groin.

"i'll make sure you have nothing left to cheat with!" Corine hollered vengefully.

Ernest hoisted her arms above her head and held her wrists with one hand. He leered with amusement into her infuriated eyes. Her raw passion sexually stimulated him and he wanted her. Corine was out of breath and her chest heaved rapidly when she breathed. Ernest flicked his tongue over her luscious nipples and her anger turned to lust as he provoked her sexually. She closed her eyes and surrendered her soul to his superb lovemaking. Ernest used his knee to part her thighs and caressed her insides with his finger. He straddled Corine and entered her. Ernest loved the feel of her body united with his. He nibbled her earlobes, and murmured lewd words in her ear until their slick bodies plateaued with ecstasy.

Lerwick was pleased with the progress Ernest made establishing offshore accounts for TNF. His international contacts were comfortable working with Ernest on Lerwick's behalf. He proposed Ernest become more involved in the day to day affairs of TNF which meant that he would travel less frequently. Ernest had become so valuable to Lerwick that he was compensated to the tune of four thousand pounds per week! Lerwick invited Ernest to social functions to meet leaders in the financial sector and other powerful personalities. He attended rounds of cocktail parties, dinners, and private affairs where he was instructed to promote TNF. Corine attended some functions and finally got the opportunity to meet Lerwick. He poured on the charm and flashed his winning smile but Corine distrusted him even more after their meeting. Corine was impressed with Ernest's ability to converse comfortably with these financial gurus and heads of corporations when talks turned to politics and banking. She listened for investment tips and strategies that were lauded as sound. Corine was motivated to learn about investing, so that she could invest some of her own money. The couple was invited by Lerwick to a black tie event hosted by a millioinaire corporate financier. The affair was to be held at a mansion in Surrey, and Corine was eager to attend. She pored over fashion magazines for ideas on what to wear and shopped for the perfect gown. She sought wardrobe and makeup advice from professionals in high end department stores, for valuable tips on hair, makeup and the type of gown that would best suit her needs. This was Corine's night to be Cinderella at a grand ball.

A chauffeured limousine sent by Lerwick drove the couple to Surrey and Corine sank into the luxurious leather seats. She and Ernest sipped champagne and enjoyed the sixty-minute drive. The vehicle entered a community dotted with mansions and Corine had no idea people really lived like this. They viewed the extensive lawns and opulent estates with awe. These were a far cry from the two bed room flat they lived in. The chauffeur cruised into the drive of a resplendent mansion where the event was taking place. Corine couldn't take her eyes away from the perfect gardens, immaculate lawns, private lake and Trout River. The mansion was at least six thousand square feet with open areas for entertaining. The limousine cruised to a stop at the entrance and the chauffeur opened the doors. They were graciously greeted by a uniformed staff that ushered them into a marbled entryway that led to a spacious ballroom where musicians strummed classical music. Buffet tables were heavily ladened with sumptuos foods and mouth watering treats. Corine feasted her eyes on the assortment of meats, desserts and pastries. She had every intention on sampling each treat before the night was over. They circulated the ballroom and chatted with other guests.

Lerwick emerged from a huddled group of brick faced men, and greeted them cheerfully. Corine envied Lerwick's sense of conceited entitlement. He engrossed Ernest in talking shop, and Corine took the opportunity to observe her female counterparts that arrived in furs and minks to conceal their elegant gowns. A few ladies wore stylish knee length dresses accentuated with shawls and silk gloves. Jewelry fashioned from a wide array of precious stones was worn but diamonds ruled the night. She ogled the huge rocks worn by some of the ladies and wondered if the gems were genuine. Corine sparkled in a 2-carat diamond and pearl earring, and necklace ensemble that was given to her by Ernest. She wore an off the shoulder wine colored velvet gown with a heart shaped neckline. Corine selected black stilettos with velvety straps which were a must have, for only two hundred pounds. This was her night and she spared no expense. Her hair was arranged in an elegant up do, kept in place by crystal accessories. Black mascara defined her eyes and red wine lipstick was applied to her lips with precision. Ernest was handsome in a tuxedo and diamond encrusted Rolex watch. Corine feigned interest in the conversation with Lerwick's newest girlfriend, and scanned the room for a suitable distraction. She observed a black woman who appeared to be held captive by a hunched over, doddering, tottering man. Corine realized it was Sisi,

Jeffrey's wife. She promptly disengaged herself from the company of Lerwick's girlfriend and made a beeline for Sisi.

"Sisi!" Corine gushed and gave her a hug.

"Corine? I didn't recognize you! You look fabulous!" Sisi replied blissfully.

"Thanks! You look wonderful too! Where did you get that gown?" Corine asked.

"It's my own creation. I blended Ghanaian and European styles. I wanted to bring something exotic to the world of fashion!" Sisi declared.

"Sisi, you'll make a great fashion designer." Corine stated.

"Mr. Pembleton, This is Corine. She's the wife of my husband's brother." Sisi introduced them.

"Nice to meet you, Corine. Sisi designed an exquisite gown! I'm impressed with her creativity. She also has a captivating personality I hate to share her company!" Mr. Pembleton fretted and shook Corine's hand.

"Sisi, it must have taken months for someone like you to design this gown!" Corine quipped, and a naughty smile surfaced on her lips. Sisi rolled her eyes at Corine's condescending comment.

"Oh Corine, I put this gown together in two days! It was so simple. I cut the pattern out of yards of black velvet, and sewed the sequins in place. I sewed red, green and yellow sequins to the cinch around my waist. These colors represent kente which is unique to my native Ghana. And there you have it!" Sisi informed them with pride.

"Ace!" Replied Corine.

"Brill!" Chuckled Mr. Pembleton.

"And that's no codswallop!" Sisi exclaimed and everyone laughed.

"Well, well, well, look who's here! What in heavens name are you doing here?" Ernest asked sarcastically.

"Oh Ernest, I live here!" Sisi answered and the others chuckled.

"I'm going off on a gander! Sisi, we'll talk soon." Mr. Pembleton interjected and ambled off.

"I assume Jeffrey is with you?" Ernest quizzed Sisi and furrowed his brow.

"Your assumptions are correct." Sisi replied haughtily and smiled when Jeffrey approached.

"Big brother! I had no idea you were going to be at this party! What a fluke!" Jeffrey announced. He and Ernest hugged briefly.

"Hey, if I knew you were going to be here, you could've caught a ride with us in the limousine." Ernest stated. He wanted to impress his little brother.

"Thanks, but we rented a limousine of our own. So, how long have you known Mr. Howsham?" Jeffrey asked.

"Actually, I don't, but my boss does. I'm progressing rapidly at TNF, so my boss insisted I meet the chap!" Ernest proclaimed.

"That's excellent news, man! The family will be happy to know that you are doing so well! Pukka!" Jeffrey exclaimed and winked discreetly at Corine.

Ernest cast his eyes down and hunched his shoulders. He shoved his hands in his pockets and rocked back and forth on his heels. The silence was deafening. Corine's stomach flip-flopped because she hoped Ernest wouldn't read between the lines, and suspect her of confiding in Jeffrey about TNF. She cleared her throat and ripped Ernest away from his thoughts.

"Let's have more champagne! Sisi, I want to dance, and show off my dress, don't you? Corine tried to perk up the mood.

"Of course I do! We never get the opportunity to party so let's make the most of it!" Sisi agreed. She clutched Jeffrey's hand and marched into the ballroom followed by Ernest and Corine.

The musicians strummed upbeat tempos, and Sisi rocked her hips, and shook her shoulders to the rhythmic beat. Jeffrey executed a 360 degree spin that garnered everyones' attention, and amazed everyone with fancy footwork in black patent leather shoes. Jeffrey's dancing got the competitive juices of Ernest flowing so Ernest whisked Corine onto the dancefloor to compete with his little brother. He rocked his shoulders, and moved to the beat, but he was no match for the sure-footed moves of his younger brother. Jeffrey danced like no one was watching, and received a rousing applause from guests. The tempo slowed and Sisi suggested they take a break.

"Sisi, is that you? You look absolutely stunning my dear!" Voiced a dignified man in his mid to late fifties.

"Mr. Howsham, it's good to see you again! Thanks so much for inviting us." Sisi replied graciously and Corine jealously looked on.

"Nice to see you, Mr. Howsham." Jeffrey interjected and extended his hand for a handshake.

"Jeffrey, I hear you're doing a marvelous job at the hotel by setting forth high expectations. I commend you for transforming The Beasley Hotel into a five star masterpiece. Keep up the good work and soon you'll be in charge of a whole slew of hotels and resorts!" Mr. Howsham advised Jeffrey.

"That's my overall goal. To restore old maidens to their former glory!" Jeffrey joked.

"Jeffrey!" Sisi scolded her husband playfully and everyone laughed.

"Let me introduce you to my brother Ernest and his lovely wife Corine. I would like you both to meet the host of this spectacular event, Mr. Howsham." Jeffrey announced.

"It's a pleasure." Corine murmured and extended her hand to Mr. Howsham.

"The pleasure is mine, Corine." Mr. Howsham asserted and turned his attention to Ernest.

"Mr. Howsham, it's very nice to meet you. This is a wonderful party; Ernest smiled broadly and shook Mr. Howsham's hand.

"Mr. Howsham, I see you've met Ernest St. John." Lerwick announced and approached the group. He observed the introductions from a few feet away.

"Lerwick! I'm glad you made it. So, this is one of your employees?" Mr. Howsham asked.

"Yes, he is!" Lerwick replied.

"Lerwick, I understand you want my company to donate to tnf but I have some concerns." Mr. Howsham stated.

"Such as?" Lerwick asked.

"TNF has yet to be approved by a number of key agencies in England. The approval of these agencies is imperative to every financial instittition." Mr. Howsham remarked dryly.

"TNF offshore status allows it to bypass these regulatory agencies." Lerwick replied smugly.

"Let me make one thing absolutely clear. If I decide to parlay a considerable amount of money to TNF, I expect to know how the charities are being served. I'm not comfortable with the fact that TNF offshore status won't allow me to be privy to such information." Retorted a grim faced, Howsham.

"Mr. Howsham, you and my father go way back. Are you telling me you don't trust me?" Lerwick asked shamelessly.

"Your father did not get rich by throwing money into half-hearted schemes, and neither did I! There's a sucker born every minute and I'm not one of them! Some foundations have business practices that are somewhat murky! Why don't I send my auditors over there to see what you're up to?" Sneered Mr. Howsham.

"Mr. Howsham, TNF's financial base is second to none. All articles have been validated and the foundation has been filed with the registrar of companies for five years. I'm willing to provide the premium binder with all certificates if you would allow me to. TNF's status as an offshore enterprise means tax benefits and savings in accounting fees, auditing services and reporting. These savings enable TNF to do more for communities and charities. We're even expanding our outreach to communities on a global scale." Lerwick recounted stiffly.

"Hm... I want to review TNF's secret letters of wishes from donators." Mr. Howsham stated.

"Those letters are not public record. You know that!" Lerwick remarked.

"Ladies! Gentlemen!" The group was greeted by a tanned fellow with a foreign accent. The turban on his head was indicative of his Arab ethnicity.

"Everyone, this is Prince Jabbar of Arabia. His family is in the business of oil and the stock market is his playground." Mr. Howsham quipped.

Gezebel

"Prince Jabbar, I believe you own several off shore entities. Is that right?" Mr. Howsham probed.

"Indeed! I've been involved in all types of off shore deals." The prince boasted.

"Have you donated funds or assets to TNF?" Mr. Howsham pressed the prince for information.

"Of course I have! The publicity garnered from giving to that foundation helps our image. The general public loves it when corporations give back to communities. It's a win/win situation." The prince replied.

"Now, doesn't that make you feel all warm and cozy inside?" Lerwick interjected, and elicited good-natured laughter from the group, including Mr. Howsham. Mr. Howsham was a business competitor with the prince's family. He would donate to TNF just because they did. This is why he wanted to know who the donators were.

"Lerwick, have TNF's offshore registrations on my desk first thing Monday. Once the documents have been proved legal and binding, i'll write a check for five hundred thousand. The Howsham Gas & Oil Logo should be at the forefront of all corporate givers. Is that understood?" Mr. Howsham asked.

"Consider it done Mr. Howsham!" Lerwick replied and sealed the deal with a handshake.

Lerwick licked his lips and tasted the nectar of another sweet victory. He earned Five hundred thousand in less than fifteen minutes. Corine wanted to warn Mr. Howsham that TNF was

69

nothing but a scam, but she couldn't prove it. What would she say? "I'm suspicious about Lerwick because he pays my husband four thousand a week?" No, that would never do. The group resumed socializing and Mr. Howsham excused himself in order to interact with other guests. Lerwick spoke privately to Ernest about the significance of the victory he just scored for TNF. First thing Monday, Ernest was to have the secretary expedite the documents to Mr. Howsham's head-quarters and the check should be at TNF's office by the end of the week. Ernest would schedule the next flight to Geneva and deposit it into a TNF account. The bank would make the funds readily available and Ernest would electronically redeposit the funds into multiple accounts at different banks around the world. Lerwick smirked with satisfaction because Mr. Howsham was a tough sell. That's why he enlisted the help of the prince to reel him in. Mr. Howsham didn't even see it coming! He motioned to his live in love Giselle that it was time to leave.

The party ended at 3:00am in the morning, and partygo-ers waited in the grand hall for their chauffeured limousines to pull up outside the mansion. The Howshams personally bid goodbye to their guests and thanked them for coming. Ernest and Corine's limousine pulled up and the chauffeur stepped out. He opened the door for the couple, and waited for them to climb in. They drove away from the mansion, past extensive grounds, and into the paved street. Corine gazed at the looming mansions, illuminated by twilight, and was spooked by the shadows cast by these gigantic structures. She shuddered in the comfy seat, and freed her aching feet from the punishing confines of her high heels. Ernest sat across from her in the limousine and Corine propped her legs on his knees.

"I had a wonderful time. Did you?" Corine asked Ernest.

"Yes. You were the most beautiful woman at the party." Ernest replied. He wasn't in the mood to talk because his mind was on the trip to Geneva. Paola was there. He was impatient to see her again.

"Lerwick is such a beast! Couldn't he conduct business at a more appropriate time?" Corine asked irritably.

"Corine, some business deals are sealed at events like this." Ernest replied vaguely.

"If it wasn't for the prince, I don't think he would've had a bloody chance in hell to get a donation!" Corine responded indignantly.

"Corine... Please!" Ernest replied in an irked manner.

"He just had to talk shop!" Corine railed.

Ernest sighed and resigned himself to her tirade about Lerwick. He interjected occasional "uh huhs, hums and ok's" to make her think he was tuned in. She seemed satisfied with his responses and dominated the conversation. It was just as well, Ernest thought. He kept his eyes glued on his wife, but his mind summoned images of Paola.

Chapter Ten

Jeffrey gazed out the bedroom window of the spacious flat he shared with his wife, and worried about Ernest. The information Corine disclosed about Ernest's involvement with TNF disquieted his spirit. He hired a private investigator to examine TNF and the report caused him great concern. Jeffrey learned that TNF started out as a small investment firm before doing business as an offshore foundation. Even though strict privacy laws protected TNF, the P.I. disclosed that donators' funds were deposited into numerous offshore banks and investment firms. Ernest was Lerwick's stealthy compatriot, and traveled to off shore countries for the sole purpose of misapproprating funds. The bottom line? TNF was a money laundering operation, Lerwick was a thief, and Ernest was up to his neck in horseshit!

"Blimey!" Jeffrey muttered and punched the wall with his fist.

"Jeffrey what's wrong?" Sisi mumbled; she was awakened by his angry outburst. Sisi was alarmed at the contorted expression on her husband's face and sat up in bed. She thought he was upset over something at work and rushed to his side. She put her arms around him.

"Jeffrey, what is it?" Sisi asked anxiously.

He freed himself from Sisi's embrace and turned toward the window. Jeffrey confided in Sisi about the unscrupulous line of work Ernest was involved in. She ambled back to the bed and sat down. Sisi thought about their friendship with the Howshams and didn't want Jeffrey to get caught in the middle.

"Jeffrey, I think we should tell Mr. Howsham!" Sisi stated.

"Mr. Howsham's business is not *our* business! If anything should happen to my brother because you tipped off Howsham, I wouldn't be able to handle the guilt! I won't be responsible for his demise!" Jeffrey uttered with finality.

"Alright, so what then?" An exasperated Sisi asked.

"We do nothing! If Ernest gets caught, chances are i'll be the first to know." Jeffrey reasoned.

"If you think this is the best way to handle the situation, then i'll respect your wishes." Sisi assured him and massaged his neck. He was tense and needed to loosen up.

"Jeffrey, come back to bed." Sisi murmured.

Jeffrey returned to bed and lay on his stomach. Sisi sat gingerly on his backside with her legs straddling his hips and kneaded his back with her hands. Jeffrey turned over and lifted her nightgown over her head. He caressed her breasts and licked her blackberry nipples. Sisi removed his brief and slid her body over his rigid manhood. Jeffrey held her thighs and moved inside her until all his worries about Ernest faded to black.

As promised, Mr. Howsham's check arrived at TNF's headquarters the week after the party and Ernest eagerly prepared for his trip. He fished Paola's number from its hiding place, and made reservations at the Warwick Geneva Hotel, which was a step up from the no-frills hotels he usually stayed in. Ernest booked an early flight to Switzerland, and dialed Paola in Geneva. He left a message inviting her to meet him at the hotel the next day, anytime after 7:00 pm. The day before the trip, Ernest remained at home to spend quality time with Gezzy. Ernest played hide and seek with his daughter, and she screamed in delight when he discovered her hiding places. Hide and seek was Gezzy's favorite game. Corine was in the kitchen preparing a hearty steak and potato dinner, leaving them alone to play.

After dinner, Corine put Gezzy to bed a little early, because she was looking forward to a night of lovemaking with Ernest. She bathed with exotic body scents to put him in the mood, and removed a new lace negligee from her dresser drawer. Corine put the negligee on and sauntered sexily into the living room. She dimmed the lights and joined Ernest on the couch where he sat engrossed in a television program. Corine ran her tongue along his ear lobe to ignite his passion and caressed his manhood through his sweat pants. Ernest had no intention of being intimate with Corine because he was saving his energy for Paola. Corine tilted his face towards hers, and kissed him sensuously. Ernest placed his hands on her shoulders to prevent her from going any further.

"What's the matter?" Corine asked. She was put off by his behavior.

"Can't you see I'm trying to watch the show?" Ernest replied and feigned annoyance with Corine. He raised his arms in the air and an exaggerated yawn escaped his jaws.

"Oh Ernest… why don't you be hanky and i'll be panky tonight!" Corine whispered sexily, and giggled. She slipped her hands under his shirt and massaged his taut abs. Ernest was resolute in his decision not be seduced by Corine and promptly removed her hands in an agitated manner.

"Corine, let's relax and watch the tele. I'm tired!" Ernest lied.

Corine sat rigidly on the couch and stared at him in disbelief! His rejection to her sexual advances was baffling because he was always ready for sex, and she was the one who begged for reprieve!

"It's not like you to turn me down! What's going on?" Corine questioned him with a smirk on her face.

"Can't a man say no to his wife?" Ernest asked innocently and tried to keep a straight face.

"No he can't! Especially if his name is Ernest St. John! I'm no fool!" Corine stated in an accusatory tone. She got up from the couch, and flipped on the bright lights. He was not going to choose a television program over her!

"Are you mad, woman?" Ernest asked as Corine worked herself into frenzy.

"I see what's going on here! You already shagged with someone else while I was at work, eh?" Corine spewed accusations at him.

Ernest ignored her and resumed watching television. He knew that silence would provoke her confrontational spirit. Much like gasoline to a fire.

"Answer me!" Corine shouted.

"I'm going to bed! I'm zonked!" Ernest's replied and switched off the television.

He walked into the bedroom and left Corine by herself. She was confused and suspicious. Could it be that he was really zonked? Maybe Lerwick was putting too much pressure on him at work. He did seem a bit subdued this past week. Corine felt ashamed for not being more understanding. So what if her hopes were dashed tonight? Knowing Ernest, he would more than make up for it during their next encounter. Corine laughed at herself. There was nothing to worry about. She switched off the light and walked into the bedroom.

"Ernest, I'm sorry. I should've been more understanding." Corine apologized.

"Um hum." Ernest replied and drifted to sleep.

The alarm sounded at 5:30am and Ernest jumped out of bed and headed for the shower. Corine awoke to the sound of running water in the bathroom and realized Ernest was no longer in bed. She was baffled because Ernest didn't wake this early unless he was leaving the country. Corine sought answers when he returned to the bedroom.

"You're up early!" Corine remarked. She sat up in bed and stared at him with a quizzical expression on her face.

"Yes, I am!" He replied and removed the packed suitcase from the closet. Corine realized he was taking a trip and her anger brewed like percolating coffee.

"You didn't tell me you were taking a trip!" Corine uttered in a shrill voice.

"I forgot to tell you about this one. It's not like my flight itinerary is committed to memory!" He replied with an apathetic air and dressed with alacrity.

"Don't you have any consideration for me? Don't I deserve to know that you'll be out of the country?" Corine demanded; hurt by his disregard for her feelings. She threw the blanket aside and jumped out of bed to confront him! Corine was on the verge of tears.

"Give me one good reason why I should tell you ahead of time? Everytime I have to leave on bloody business, you quarrel about it! I refuse to subject myself to that any longer!" Ernest replied arrogantly and adjusted his tie.

"Ernest, it's only because I'm worried about you working for TNF!" Corine stated in protest.

"My flight to Geneva leaves at 7:45. It's time for me to go!" He attempted to kiss Corine goodbye but she recoiled from him in anger.

"Suit yourself love! See if I care!" Ernest stated in a flippant manner. He grabbed his suitcase in one hand and his briefcase in the other. Ernest walked out the bedroom, and Corine in a fit of rage, unplugged the lamp that rested on the nightstand, and held it in her hand.

"Ernest!" Corine yelled, and gripped the lamp by its neck.

"What now?" He bellowed and returned to the bedroom.

"Watch your blimey back!" She hollered and hurled the lamp at him.

Ernest ducked and the lamp crashed into the wall! He glared at Corine as if she had finally gone barmy! He loved her devilment and couldn't resist the opportunity to mock her.

"Sorry love! You missed!" Ernest quipped. He dissapeared into Gezzy's room, and kissed her goodbye. Then, he was gone in a flash.

Corine was devastated. What was happening to her marriage? She sat on the bed and cried. Corine dressed for work but all she could think about was her stormy marriage. She made a mental note to search the contents of a briefcase Ernest kept locked under the bed. Picking locks was a valuable trick she picked up when living in Old Town. Breaking into that briefcase should be no problem. Her marriage was facing so many dilemnas. Perhaps whatever was in the briefcase held the key to an uneventful life?

Ernest finished conducting business in Switzerland Friday afternoon, and the city of Geneva was his until Tuesday. He feasted on shrimp salad ordered from room service, and showered. Ernest dressed comfortably in gray slacks and a forest green sweater. He poured himself a glass of wine and turned on the radio to soft music. Ernest reclined on the sofa and kept the blinds drawn. He dozed off, and was awakened by the incessant buzz of the telephone. It was 6:42pm. Ernest quickly answered the call.

"Mr. St. John, there's a young lady here to see you. She said you were expecting her." The representative at the front desk informed him.

"What's her name?" Ernest asked. He wanted to be certain it really was her.

"Paola." The representative replied.

"Send her up right away!" Ernest instructed the representative.

Ernest dropped the phone into its cradle and waited anxiously. Minutes later, there was a soft "rap rap rap" on the door and he rushed to open it. Paola stood there looking more beautiful than he remembered. Her blond hair was pulled away from her face, and tied in a ponytail with a black barrette. She wore a knee-length black dress, and a red wool coat. They stared at each other for a long time and Paola was unable to mask the pained expression on her pretty face. Ernest stepped aside so that she could enter the room. Paola wasn't sure if she should rush into his arms or slap his face for not calling for the past four weeks. She was elated when she retrieved his message and couldn't wait to join him. Her eyes kissed his slick black hair, long eyelashes, perfect lips and broad shoulders.

"Paola, I'm glad you came. I apologize for not contacting you sooner but I wanted to give you time to think about getting involved with me." Ernest offered persuasively.

He cupped Paola's face in his hands and gazed into her eyes. Ernest slipped his tongue between her glossy lips and Paola felt his manhood surge when he held her close. She reciprocated his kiss and yearned for his touch. He lifted her in his strong arms, and carried her to the bedroom. Ernest laid Paola on the bed, and explored her body with his hands and lips. Paola panted with anticipation as Ernest ripped off her dress and tossed the torn material on the floor! She kneeled on the bed and removed his sweater. Paola gasped at his muscled abs! Ernest stepped out of his brief, and Paola marveled at his impressive organ! She lavished it with tantalizing kisses and drove Ernest wild. He positioned Paola on her back and licked every crevice of her throbbing body. Forces of pleasure, too strong for her to contain, burst forth from Paola's thighs like fireworks on the fourth of July! Ernest lay back on the bed and Paola lowered her body on his manhood. His manhood engorged her core and her body pulsed with a sexual craving that only he could satisfy. Paola relished the thought of having Ernest all to herself and that put a smile on her face. Ernest was all she had ever dreamed of and he was a superb lover. She ran her fingers through the sparse hairs on his chest and fell asleep listening to the steady rhythm of his heartbeat. Ernest closed his eyes while Paola lay sleeping in his arms. Man! He thought to himself. She was well worth the wait! His thoughts turned to Corine.

"Blimey!" He muttered to himself. It was past 8:30pm, and he wanted to call Corine before it got too late. He reached for the phone.

"Hello?" Corine answered.

"It's me, checking in. How's Gezzy?" He asked before she could question him about anything else.

"She's right here. Say hello to Daddy." Corine cooed to the toddler.

"Da Da." Gezzy managed to coo over the phone."

"Daddy loves you, English muffin." Ernest cooed back.

"Da Da, ruv ru." Gezzy babbled. Corine took control of the handset again.

"So, when are you coming home?" Corine asked.

"Sometime Tuesday! I have a lot of paper work to complete and I need to tie up loose ends." Ernest informed Corine.

"So you'll be gone the entire weekend?" Corine asked incredulously. She was annoyed at finding this out while he was already in Geneva.

"Yes." Ernest confirmed.

"Don't you think I should have the number..." Corine started and Ernest cut her off.

"Look, I'll call tomorrow!" He sensed a storm was brewing in his wife and ended the call.

He sighed and caressed Paola's back as she lay on top of him. The feel of her soft skin aroused him. She opened her eyes and sensed his need. Her thigh brushed his erect organ and it stoked her longing. Ernest rolled on top of Paola, and his tongue flicked her raspberry nipples. He tasted her creamy center once more. Ernest penetrated Paola and electrifying sensations spiraled through her body. She cried out in ecstasy!

Ernest had paperwork to complete Saturday morning, so he sent Paola shopping. She returned with clothes, jewelry,

handbags, shoes, and gifts for her mom. Paola purchased vintages to savor with Ernest in the evenings when they made love. They dined at fine restaurants, took long walks and learned more about each other. Paola luxuriated in Ernest's company. This was the most exhilarating time of her life.

Their last night together was especially hard for Paola because she had no idea when Ernest would visit again. Her jovial spirit waned and her mood turned sulky. Ernest reassured Paola that he would be back and promised to call. That night, he whipped her body into an orgasmic blizzard, and Paola lay quivering in his arms. Paola was sexually tapped but oddly energized. She was in awe of Ernest's stamina, and was unable to muster the energy for another love making session. Paola dozed off. Ernest checked the clock on the nightstand and it was 5:17am. His flight was scheduled to depart Geneva at 8:00am so he got out of bed, careful not to disturb Paola. He thought about waking her to say goodbye but changed his mind. Instead, he decided to write her a brief note.

"Beautiful Paola,

Our time together was incredible and you will always be in my private thoughts. I arranged for car service to drive you home around noon, tomorrow.

Ernest."

He placed the note on the pillow and departed for the airport. Ernest arrived in England at 10:45am. Corine and Gezzy were already out of the house, and wouldn't be back until 5:00pm. He touched base with Lerwick and briefed him on the trip. Lethargy set in after his weekend of sex and he needed to rest. It was 11:28am and Ernest was fast asleep.

Paola stirred. Her eyelids were still laden with sleep. Paola's eyes darted at the clock on the nightstand, and it was 11:28am. She yawned and stretched her arms above her head. The air in the room was musky from the lovemaking she indulged in with Ernest. It aroused her sexually, and she was eager to have him fulfill her once again. Her eyes scoured the room for Ernest but he wasn't anywhere in sight. Paola knocked on the bathroom door.

"Ernest, are you in there?" Paola yelled.

She got no response and decided to open the door to see if he was in the shower. No Ernest! Perhaps he had to finish up some business, she thought. She ambled back to the bedroom and spotted a piece of paper on his pillow. Paola smiled at his thoughtfulness and sat cross-legged on the bed to read the note. She was crushed to learn that he was already gone! Just like that! Without so much as a goodbye kiss! Paola read the note twice and convinced her self that Ernest really did care. She breakfasted in bed, and called in sick to work, because she was too depressed to entertain little Olaf. Paola laid her head on Ernest's pillow where the scent of his cologne remained. Tears streamed down her face. She stayed in bed for the rest of the day with the blinds drawn, and refused to let sunlight in.

Chapter Eleven

Gezzy was seven years old and already a stunning beauty that towered over her peers. She was a spoiled child whose temper tantrums worked well in getting her whatever she wanted. Gezzy was energetic and craved adventure. She didn't mind resorting to naughty deeds just for a thrill. Gezzy earned good grades, but was often sent to the principal's office for refusing to obey her teachers, or, for getting into physical altercations with other students. She was the life of the class, a natural leader, a girl that relished being the center of attention. 1986 was a significant year for Ernest. He embarked on six years of work for TNF, and he acquired a surmountable amount of money. His family wanted for nothing and they settled into normal, everyday routines. But, the seeds of change started to take root.

Ernest relaxed on the leather recliner in the living room, and thought about the future. The recliner was his favorite piece out of the expensive furniture ensemble Corine purchased four years ago. He sipped a glass of rum & coke, and mulled over the events of the past three weeks. Corine, the buxom, long-legged, dark-haired beauty that secured a special place in his heart, was not as honest as he thought. In his down time from toil at TNF, Ernest performed an audit of his family's finances. He perused files where Corine maintained records of their financial documents, and deciphered that money entrusted to her over the years was not accounted for in their joint bank account. He never kept tabs on all that was spent within the household, but estimated that more money should be on the books. This was an "ah ha" moment in Ernest's life. It sparked the suspicion that she was siphoning off money from their joint account, but why? Ernest was suspicious and enlisted the services of an underpaid bank teller in need of cash. The teller was paid to find out whether Corine maintained a separate account. To his dismay, he learned that Corine sustained a personal account for six years at the bank. Ernest obtained copies of the statements and was flabbergasted to learn that Corine banked her paychecks for six years, had sound investments, and was basically running the household strictly on his pay! The impact of her actions weighed heavily on his mind because she hid this for so long. He shared all that he had with Corine so why did she have to hoard money? Ernest also invested with reputable brokerage firms, and Corine was included on all details. He was deeply troubled by her deceit.

Corine feigned ignorance when Ernest questioned her about the money missing from their account. She tried to explain it away as money he splurged on shopping sprees, money she spent on new furniture, family vacations, and extra curricular activities for Gezzy, but the numbers still didn't add up. Ernest, in retrospect of Corine's poverty stricken past, decided not to press the issue and micromanaged their finances instead. He demanded that Corine provide deposit slips proving that the thirty five hundred he gave to her out of the four thousand per week pay received from Lerwick, was deposited into their joint account. Ernest insisted she allocate one thousand out of her biweekly salary into Gezzy's trust fund. He reviewed monthly statements with tenacity and demanded Corine justify any discrepancies.

Ernest was ready to part-company with TNF but couldn't figure out what his next step would be. Maybe he could start a business and work for himself. He was mulling over the possibilities when Lerwick called an emergency meeting at TNF's headquarters. The 'out' he sought stared him right in the face! One of TNF's trustees owed hefty gambling debts and tried to blackmail Lerwick into giving him money. Lerwick refused to be blackballed, and the trustee resigned from his post, and demanded a payout from the board. The trustee leaked information to the press about the unsavory activities of TNF, and went into hiding.

The press shone the spotlight on TNF, and Lerwick set his pit bull attorneys after them. Snippets about the scandal was publicized in the media and made headlines. TNF's lawyers threw the press temporarily off TNF's trail by questioning the credibility of the former trustee. They exposed his gambling debts, and illicit affairs, much to the embarrassment of his snooty wife! They dredged up negative facts and innuendos that reflected on his character. His professional and personal reputation was ruined! Juicy testimonials from former play-mates, and details about his gambling debts were splashed across the front pages of newspapers that exposed the sordid life of the snitch.

While the media and public focused on the troubled life of the former trustee, Lerwick and his cronies lined their pock-ets with millions. They discreetly liquidated TNF's physical assets and divided the spoils. These crooks planned for some-thing like this years in advance, and were unified in their belief that if their plans to escape prison should go awry, suicide would be a better alternative. They intended to secure their freedom, along with their millions, no matter the cost. One by one, officers and trustees mysteriously vanished as authorities started their investigation of TNF.

Ernest had to save himself. He wasn't an officer or a trustee, and didn't have millions coming his way. Ernest hatched a plan to secure financial security at tnfs' expense. After months of watching the events unfold, he booked flights to Panama, Seychelles, The Caymans and Geneva. These were the offshore destinations where he had the most favorable contacts. Corine came home from work with Gezzy in tow, to find Ernest packing.

"Ernest, are you going somewhere? I was going to prepare bangers and mash for dinner." Corine remarked with a worried expression on her face. She followed TNF's troubles in the news and feared for her husband.

"I'm flying out tomorrow. I'll be gone for at least two weeks!" Ernest explained in a distracted manner.

"Two weeks? You've never been away for so long!" Corine stated with alarm.

"i've got a lot to take care of in a short a space of time!" Ernest replied impatiently.

"Mummy, I'm hungry. Make butty for me." Gezzy implored and pouted.

"Put one together for me too!" Ernest interjected. He wanted to derail Corine's questions.

Corine ventured into the kitchen and removed the condiments from the fridge. She prepared the butties and placed them on separate plates. She handed a plate to Gezzy who sat at the kitchen table. Corine walked out of the kitchen with another plate in her hand. She handed the plate to Ernest with the butty on it.

"Sweetheart, here's the butty." Corine stated.

"Thanks!" Ernest responded. He took a generous bite of the sandwich layered with butter, chips, a touch of vinegar, and tomato sauce. Um, Ernest uttered, and savored the tangy butty.

"Ernest, are you in trouble with the bobbies?" Corine asked nervously.

"No, I'm not. I've never held an official position with TNF, and, i've always been compensated in cash!" Ernest replied.

"Am I going to have cameras shoved in my face and Bobbies waiting at the door when I come home?" Corine asked with trepidation.

"Mummy, is anything the matter?" Gezzy asked as she hurried out of the kitchen. She overheard Corine's stress filled voice.

"No! Let us have some privacy!" Corine snapped and Gezzy retreated to her room.

"Ernest, I warned you to refrain from this unethical line of work!" Corine stated in an accusatory tone.

"Unethical? You didn't seem to mind spending the unethical money!" Ernest echoed with disdain.

"I accepted that money with forgiveness in my heart! There were other opportunities out there! You didn't have to settle!" Corine replied haughtily.

"That's a bloody lie!" Ernest seethed. He took hold of Corine's arm, maneuvered her into the bedroom, and slammed the door!

"Have you gone completely bonkers? Take your bloody hands off me and stop talking rubbish!" Corine yelled.

Ernest refused to let go, and snarled sinisterly in her ear. "You think I'm a fool?"

"You're bonkers!" Corine protested and tried to wriggle free.

"What kind of git do you take me for? You think the daughter of a fishmonger and factory worker could ever outsmart me?" Ernest shouted with fury.

"I'm gobsmacked! I don't know what you are talking about!" Corine cried.

"The money, Corine!" Ernest yelled. The anger in his eyes almost made her faint and tears welled in her eyes.

"What money? I can't suss this out!" Corine protested.

"Does account 59177 sound familiar?" Ernest huffed. She was aghast that he knew her personal bank account number and cried. Corine was weak in the knees, but Ernest maintained a hold on her arm, and kept her on her feet.

"Ernest, I was going to tell you about that! I saved my pay after you started working for Lerwick! I was putting money away for a rainy day! That's all! I swear!" Corine lamented.

"Saving for a rainy day eh? You hid this for six years! If I didn't review our statements, I never would have known!" Ernest yelled bitterly. Corine's deceit was more than he could stomach.

"It was never meant to be like this! I always considered it our money! An emergency fund in case things didn't work out with TNF, and look! Look, at what is happening! Can you blame me?" Corine beseeched him.

"Why don't you trust me?" Ernest hissed.

Corine hung her head and remained silent. Ernest released her arm and lifted her chin with his hand. Corine averted her gaze and avoided making eye contact.

"Look at me!" Ernest demanded. She stared at him and tears streamed down her face. Corine loved Ernest but she did not trust him.

"Corine, despite our disagreements, I love you. I would give my life for you and Gezzy. I continue to be at Lerwick's beck and call so that you could have the best!" Ernest reassured her.

"I dont' want this to come between us." A panic stricken Corine sobbed.

"It already has, hasn't it?" Ernest responded derisively.

Corine sniffed. She couldn't fathom losing her husband over money.

"What are you going to do?" She asked with caution.

"I'm taking this trip to safeguard our future and there are some sacrifices you have to make. You must give the reform school two weeks notice as of tomorrow. Book one way flights to St. Lucia, West Indies. We'll take a schooner from St. Lucia to Barbados under assumed names and Barbados will be our new home. Close all accounts and have the bank issue cash. We leave two weeks from today. Do I make myself clear?" Ernest asked dryly.

"Yes... but are you sure about this? I have a well compensated position as director of programs at the school... Gezzy has her friends... and I have my family. Isn't there some other way?" Corine sniffed. She reached out and touched him.

"Corine, it's the least you can do!" Ernest snapped, and moved away. Corine choked back tears.

Chapter Twelve

Ernest's two-week excursion from London was communicated to Lerwick as a much-needed vacation he needed to take with his family. Lerwick agreed that would be a good idea because he wanted everyone connected to TNF to keep a low profile. Ernest traveled to Panama, Seychelles, and the Caymans, to pilfer money from TNF's accounts. The funds were hidden in barrels, and shipped to Barbados. Deighton and Estele were informed of his impending move back to the island, and were excited to have their son and his family home. Ernest stressed to his father that valuable cargo was stowed in the barrels, and Deighton alerted his contacts at the port.

Geneva was Ernest's last stop before his return to London. He reserved a five-day stay at Hotel d'Angleterre's, by Lake Geneva, because he wanted this experience with Paola to be extra special. Ernest arrived in Geneva, and visited a jewelry store on State Street, where he purchased diamond and gold hoopla earrings for Paola.

Paola arrived at the suite and threw her arms around Ernest's as soon as he opened the door. Lusty kisses ensued and they peeled each others' clothes off, anxious to make love. The raunchy couple ordered meals through room-service, content to lie in bed, and satisfy their carnal desires. The next morning, Ernest rose early and showered. He had a fun-filled day planned for Paola and wanted to get an early start. Ernest opened the blinds and Paola awoke to a room drenched in sunlight. She put the pillow playfully over her face and peeked at Ernest, already dressed in jeans and a blue knit sweater. She tossed the pillow aside and spoke seductively in French, "Venir ici, mon amour." (Come here, my love.)

"Paola, as tempted as I am, I can't! I planned a fun-filled day, and I don't want to miss out. I intend to tie you to the bedpost every night, so it's best you take the opportunity to get some fresh air!" Ernest joked.

Paola snickered and got out of bed. Ernest attempted to take her in his arms but Paola playfully backed away and ran into the bathroom. She squealed with laughter when Ernest pinched her bottom before she had the opportunity to close the door.

The streets of Geneva were filled with the ambiance of the Fete del la musique. Music concerts were in full swing around the city, and they danced at most them. They cooled their heels on a boat tour to appreciate the serenity of the city. Ernest sat on deck, and admired Paola's pulchritude as the breeze blew wisps of hair across her face. Paola was loyal to her love, but the six-year affair had to end. Ernest was going to miss her energy, sincerity, and her willingness to give him her all sexually. The drastic changes in his life made further association with Paola impossible. Ernest thought he could be in love with her but never allowed himself to dwell on that possibility. They capped the night off at the Boutde-Monde stadium, and watched fireworks electrify the sky.

Afterwards, they returned to the Hotel d'Angleterre, exhilarated and famished. Ernest reserved seating for two at the hotels' restaurant, and they retreated to their rooms to wash up before dinner. Ernest donned slacks and a dinner jacket while Paola choose a red, off the shoulder number, and cream colored pumps. She blow dried her hair straight, and parted it down the middle, for a simple, yet elegant effect. Paola wanted no other man but Ernest, and reassured herself that he must love her after six years of flying back and forth to Geneva. She especially enjoyed those rendezvous where he arranged for her to meet him in another country. He always managed to put an exhillarating spin on their relationship. Ernest whistled his approval when Paola modeled en vogue around the suite for his amusement. She always made him laugh. Ernest held her by the waist and steered her out the room, toward the elevator. She shuddered when the door to their suite slammed shut.

They dined on succulent steak, and sipped expensive wine from crystal goblets. Paola was in awe of the resplendent restaurant. This was a night she would never forget because the amenities and grandeur of the hotel made her feel like Cinderella. They chatted intimately and exchanged kisses at the table when a familiar silhouette caught Ernest's attention. The body language of the man, the hair cut, the way he cocked his head, was all too familiar. The man sat with his back turned and Ernest could not see his face. He decided to keep his curiosity in check just in case it was someone he didn't want to be bothered with. The stranger turned in his seat to get the attention of a passing waiter but Ernest's view was obstructed when the waiter leaned toward the man to listen. The waiter finally went on his way, and the man locked eyes with Ernest. It was his brother, Jeffrey! Jeffrey waved and was about to come over when he realized that the woman whispering in his ear was not Corine! Jeffrey's emotions got the better of him and his face flushed with embarrassment! He remained glued to his seat because Sisi was seated next to him. He didn't want her to witness Ernest's indiscretion.

Jeffrey was in Geneva for two days conducting business with members of the hotel's management team and Sisi joined him. He watched with disdain as Paola placed her fingers on Ernest's chin and kissed his lips. Ernest found her flirtations irresistible and returned her sexy kiss. He obviously didn't care if Sisi caught him in the act! Jeffrey swiftly excused himself and Sisi from the company of their hosts, citing an upset stomach as the reason for his departure. Sisi grabbed her purse and managed to utter a few cursory "nice to meet you's" before Jeffrey rushed her out of the restaurant! He guided her to the opposite end of the room to avoid Ernest and his lover. Sisi was perplexed by Jeffrey's sudden ailment, and the speedy exit they were forced to make from the lovely dinner, and interesting company. She was peeved and still hungry! Jeffrey was certainly not ill and she intended to demand an explanation. Before they exited the restaurant, Jeffrey looked back and berated Ernest with his eyes. Ernest nodded and raised his glass toward Jeffrey in appreciation.

Ernest and Paola returned to their luxury suite, and resumed kissing as soon as the door was closed. This was the perfect time for him to present her with the gift. He halted lip-lock, and retrieved the velvet jewelry box from the pocket of his blazer. Ernest hid it behind his back.

"Guess what I have for you!" Ernest stated jovially.

"What are you hiding?" She asked.

"You get three guesses!" Ernest replied and grinned.

"Hum… a yacht?" Paola asked.

"No!" Ernest snickered.

"Hum… a mansion?" Paola joked.

"No!" Ernest replied and chuckled.

"Hum!" Paola mumbled and scratched her head in jest. "Oh, I know! It's the lost city of Atlantis!" She blurted out and both of them were in an uproar.

The laughter subsided and Ernest presented Paola with the jewelry box. Paola kissed his lips before opening it. Inside the box was an exquisite pair of diamond earrings. Paola lifted them out, and her eyes filled with tears. The expression of gratitude, and love on her face said it all. Ernest replaced the earrings she currently wore with the diamond set, and tears cascaded down her face. They undressed each other and Ernest held Paola's nakedness against his. He kissed her, and feelings of love he fought to suppress surfaced. Ernest was consumed by her love.

The next day, Ernest broke the news to Paola of his having to return to Barbados and she was crushed. Paola wept and he consoled her best he could. He tried not to make promises he couldn't keep but Paola remained steadfast in her refusal to accept the possibility that this might be their very last night together. Ernest reasoned with Paola that she deserved better. She deserved someone that would be devoted to her but Paola shunned the thought. Over the years, Paola rejected other suitors because of her love for Ernest so she wasn't about to let it go. Not now, not ever! Paola argued with Ernest, and begged him not to let go of all they shared for the past six years. She beat him down emotionally and Ernest relented. He promised to continue the relationship and Paola emerged victorious. She suggested he allow her to visit Barbados for their next encounter, and Ernest agreed. Paola came close to losing him and it scared her. She was playing for keeps and was determined to keep him in her life. As long as he still desired her, needed her, and loved her, she would be there, waiting for him with open arms.

Back in England, Ernest and Corine were invited to dinner at Jeffrey's and Sisi's new penthouse in the greater London area. The penthouse afforded spectacular views of the city and Ernest felt as though he were king of the world! Sisi announced that she was three months pregnant and Ernest and Corine were elated by the joyful news. Sisi prepared a Ghanaian dinner of Jollof, which is rice cooked in chicken stew. She served it with baked chicken and Lamujii. Lamujii is a non-alcoholic, homemade wine made from maize and salad. There was ice cream for dessert, much to the delight of Gezzy. Ernest and Corine enjoyed the exotic meal and Sisi was pleased. After dinner Corine helped Sisi load the dishwasher and they caught up on what was going on in each other's lives. Jeffrey garnered the opportunity to have a private discussion out on the terrace with his brother.

"Nice seeing you in Geneva!" Jeffrey remarked with sarcasm.

"I was surprised to see you there too!" Ernest stated and grinned.

"Ernest! Blimey, this is serious! Corine and Gezzy deserve better!" Jeffrey exclaimed with disgust.

"Look, I don't need a lecture from Prime Minister Jeffrey! I never intended to cheat on Corine. I met Paola on a business trip and things happened!" Ernest explained with a casual air.

"How long has it been going on?" Jeffrey inquired.

"Six years!" Ernest replied nonchalantly.

"Blimey! That's almost as long as your marriage! My God! It's a good thing you're returning to Barbados, otherwise this bloody thing could blow up in your face!"Jeffrey responded with disbelief.

"I haven't ended the relationship with Paola. She, too, deserves better!" Ernest retorted dryly.

"I'm sure she does, but Corine is your wife, not Pala!" Jeffrey insisted.

"Her bloody name is Paola, not Pala, and I'm not leaving her!" Ernest shouted.

Both brothers stood on the terrace and admired the view in stony silence. Jeffrey realized his argument on the issue of Paola was futile because a six year affair was serious. His brother was in love with two women! What a mess! Jeffrey thought. He decided to change the subject.

"I'm glad you've managed to stay clear of the TNF scandal. Exactly, what is it you did for that foundation?" Jeffrey asked coyly.

"I managed TNF's international affairs!" Ernest spat back, and sucked his teeth in an aggravated manner. Jeffrey chuckled at his brother's callousness, and resolved not to waste anymore time trying to have a heart to heart.

"Let's go inside and have a toast." Jeffrey suggested.

Everyone stood in the dining room and Jeffrey bought out the champagne. He popped the cork and Sisi filled the glasses. Gezzy lay on the couch and watched t.v. While the adults spent time together.

"To love and happiness!" Sisi toasted.

"Here's to the new addition of our family!" Corine gushed.

"Ernest, i'll miss having you here in England, and life will be lonelier without you. May life in Barbados be sweet like the sugarcane that grows in the land! Here's to a safe trip!" Jeffrey toasted in a voice choked with emotion.

"Well, where do I start? Corine, you are the love of my life and I promise to make this move as easy as possible. I love you and Gezzy with all my heart. Sisi, you make my brother happy, and that makes me happy. Jeff, you have my respect and admiration. Not only are you my little brother, but you are also my best friend!" Ernest finished and the teary-eyed brothers embraced. Corine dabbed her eyes with a tissue. The move to Barbados was a drastic change for their family, and she was bitter.

The clink of crystal glasses being touched together, and misty-eyed adults made Gezzy wonder what all the fuss was about! They made her sick with their sentiments and heart felt wishes. Her daddy and uncle were acting like girls as far as she was concerned! She agreed with her father that Uncle

Jeffrey never should have married an African but at least she was pretty and smelled nice! Sisi mistook Gezzy's expression of disgust for one of sadness and rushed to comfort her. Gezzy cringed but relaxed once she glimpsed the foreboding look on Corine's face. If she revealed the slightest bit of prejudice against Sisi, Uncle Jeffrey would be infuriated, so she smiled and allowed Sisi to comfort her.

Ernest and Corine were offered the option to purchase the flat by the realtor of the building in which they lived. Corine tripled the initial down payment of three thousand pounds and persuaded her parents to retire Old Town and relocate to the fully furnished apartment she onced shared with Ernest. The neighborhood was nicer, and her brothers would be closer to their places of employment. Her parents agreed to make the move, and Corine blessed them with ten thousand pounds so that they would have money. That, along with their pensions, and her brother's income should be more than enough to give the family a head start. Corine's heart swelled with pride because she was in a position to improve their standard of living. Her family promised to visit Barbados after she settled comfortably into her new life.

Chapter Thirteen

During the summer of 1988, Ernest and his family boarded a flight from London to the island of St. Lucia. He celebrated his thirty-sixth birthday by sharing a glass of wine with Corine on the uneventful flight. The family arrived in St. Lucia and promptly boarded a private schooner headed for Barbados. The schooner sailed rapidly on the bumpy seas and Corine was nauseated. She clutched her stomach as the schooner swayed and voyaged to their destination. Her head spun, and food regurgitated in her throat. Corine's skin was clammy with perspiration in the humid weather. Her flawless complexion was mottled and pale and she had reached a debilitative state. It seemed as if an unseen force was using a syringe to drain her energy. She laid her head on Ernest's shoulder and his face was awash with concern. Corine was suffering from motion sickness, and there was nothing he could do to make her feel better. He reassured her that they would soon arrive in Barbados and urged her to relax.

The schooner finally reached the shores of Barbados, and Ernest immediately assisted Corine off the bobbing vessel. As soon as her feet touched dry land, Corine clutched her stomach and vomited on the dock! Ernest attended his wife until she emptied the contents from her stomach. A worker provided a chair for her to sit and a glass of water. Corine was dehydrated and accepted the water with gratitude. Gezzy was embarrassed because her mother vomited in front of everyone. She thought Corine was disgusting!

"There you are!" Bellowed a scabrous male voice behind Gezzy.

Before Gezzy could see who it was, she was hoisted in the air and hugged. She was spun around and around by her grandfather until she was dizzy. Estele waited impatiently to shower her with kisses. Once they were done fussing over her, they observed Corine sitting in a chair, apparently sick. Estele requested Daddy St. John get the car while she helped Corine to her feet. Daddy St. John drove the Mercedes to the front of the port, and helped Ernest load their luggage into the trunk. The Mercedes sped to the parish of St. John where Ernest and Corine's new home was located. The air-conditioned vehicle eased Corine's discomfort and she started to feel a lot better.

Ernest supported Corine as she exited the Mercedes when they arrived at their new home. She smiled at the quaint villa. It was painted white and breathtakingly beautiful in the gorgeous sun! Corine couldn't wait to go inside. Gezzy skipped up the steps to the wrap-around porch, and there was her aunt, Bella, waiting for them. Gezzy ran into her arms and Bella hugged her. Bella was overjoyed at having her niece reside permanently in Barbados because that meant she had someone to spoil! Estele aided Corine as she walked up the steps with trebly legs into the villa. Estele remanded charge of Corine's care and ushered her up the stairs into the shower. Corine relished the cool water on her clammy skin and emerged invigorated. She towel dried her hair and retrieved a cotton dress from her suitcase before sprawling her exhausted body across the four poster bed. The breeze wafted gloriously into the open windows and soothed her to sleep like a baby's lullaby.

Estele enlisted a domestic to assist Corine with the upkeep of the villa and to prepare meals. Beulah was a thirty-five year old housekeeper with admirable cooking skills, and she was pleased to serve Ernest and his wife. The St. John family was known for being fair and just to their employees, and Beulah hypothesized that working for Ernest should be no different. Beulah's mother worked for Daddy St. John's sister before she retired, and when Beulah was a teenager, she accompanied her mother to work on the weekends. She vaguely remembered Ernest and his siblings when they stopped by to visit. Beulah recalled Ernest as the handsome, mischievous brother that broke hearts. He was still as handsome as she remembered, and still carried himself with an arrogant air. Beulah peeked at Corine when Estele assisted her up the stairs. She assumed that the frail wife should be no trouble at all. Beulah contemplated these things and remained in the kitchen chopping scallions, onions and fresh herbs. The family suggested she prepare a local dish called coo coo, with flying fish for dinner. She stirred cornmeal, okra, and water, in a pot on the stove with a wooden coo coo stick. Beulah seasoned the flying fish, and placed them into a steamy broth enhanced with curry and vinegar. Beulah mixed mauby, which is tree bark boiled in water and sweetened. She added a splash of vanilla essence to make it more flavorful. Beulah chopped cucumber and diced avocado. She tossed cucumber and avocado into a bowl, and added salt, pepper, and vinegar to taste. Beulah put the bowl in the refridgerator and resumed stirring the coo coo. She wanted to make a good first impression. Beulah eavesdropped on the animated conversation taking place in the living room as she set the table.

"Son, what brings you back to Barbados?" Daddy St. John asked. He sat cross-legged in a rattan chair across from his son.

"I think Gezzy and Corine need to experience life where I grew up. I saved a considerable amount of money, and the time was ripe for change." Ernest replied.

"We're glad to have you back. How much money are you talking about?" Daddy St. John inquired.

"Let's not get into that, right now!" Ernest responded. He was apprehensive about how his father would react to the figure.

"How much?" Daddy St. John demanded.

"Could be a million dollars!" Ernest exclaimed.

"You swindled that money didn't you? The world knows about the scandal!" Daddy St. John barked. Ernest felt like a wayward teenager about to be scolded by a parent. He held his breath in anticipation of the ridicule that was sure to follow, but to his amazement, his father chuckled.

"I always knew you would be the one! You were the rebel, the risk-taker, the pain in the ass! I've been worried sick about you! Thank goodness you jumped ship before it was too late! You were clever enough to beat that vagabond at his own game! You've proved yourself worthy of being called a "St. John!" Daddy St. John exclaimed and hugged his son for the first time in years. Ernest blinked back tears. Now that he had an inkling of his father's respect, he didn't want to lose it by crying like a sissy.

"Son, where's the money?" Daddy St. John asked.

"Hidden in barrels at the Bridgetown port." Ernest disclosed.

"My contact there has been keeping a watchful eye on your cargo. Let's take care of it right now!" Daddy St. John insisted and they headed to the port to claim the loot.

Ernest cleared customs at the port with his father's help, and the barrels were delivered to a bank where Daddy St. John was a member. The money was deposited and converted into local currency, totaling $2.6 million BDS. Ernest was a millionaire in his own right!

Corine stirred and sat up in the luxurious bed. The dizzy sensation was gone and the day cooled off considerably. She inhaled, and filled her lungs with fresh air. The reality of all she gave up in England began to sink in. Corine could hear cheerful voices talking and laughing outside, so she got out of bed, and peered out the window. Gezzy, Bella, and Estele were playing hide and seek in the courtyard. Gezzy screamed with glee when Bella flushed out her hiding place behind a tree. Gezzy was drunk with joy at being able to run barefoot in the pebbly courtyard. Corine stood by the window and laughed at her daughter having the time of her life. She leaned against the window and daydreamed about a bygone era, where genteel guests were greeted in this courtyard by the owners of the house. She wondered what those plantation days were really like.

Corine backed away from the window and her eyes searched the spacious room. The bedroom had a private terrace that afforded a view of the courtyard and the mahogany trees. There were three bedrooms upstairs. Gezzy's room was adjacent to the master bedroom but separated by the staircase leading downstairs. The guestroom was situated between the master bedroom and Gezzy's room. Gezzy's room was decorated with pastel colors and all the frills and lace a little girl could hope for. Corine ventured downstairs and familiarized herself with the rest of the house. She walked to the study, which housed a small library filled with encyclopedias and journals. Arched ceilings separated the rooms and gave the home a cathedral look and airy feel. Corine loved the modern kitchen with new ceramic tiles and cherry cabinets. The villa even had a cellar which was accessible from the kitchen by descending a few steps. The washer and dryer were located in the cellar along with relics from the houses' past. The glorious wrap-around porch was her favorite part of the house, because she could lounge on the cushioned chairs and appreciate the beauty of her surroundings. The house was built by Daddy St. John's great grand parents, and it was where he spent his early years as a boy. After his mother gave birth to a fifth child, the home was no longer adequate for the growing family, and it was abandoned for something more suitable. Villa Coral was left vacant and neglected until it was willed to Daddy St. John after his father passed away. Estele renovated the villa and made it available to family and tourists who wanted a private retreat. She and Deighton were pleased to return the villa to its original purpose, which was to house a family.

The Mercedes cruised into the courtyard and slowed to a stop. Daddy St. John stepped out of the vehicle, and talked loudly in his thick island accent. His accent reflected this European family's assimilation into island culture, but Corine thought it odd for a white person to employ anything other than a European accent. Ernest and his father walked briskly up the front steps, and Corine greeted them happily. Daddy

St. John marched into the house, and Gezzy clamored up the steps behind them, followed by Estele and Bella.

"How are you feeling?" Ernest asked Corine.

"Now that i've had time to rest, I feel much better. I'm starving, though." Corine replied.

"Beulah! De food ready yet? Yuh wuz cooking um fuh years!" ("Beulah! Is the food ready? You've been cooking for a long time!") Daddy St. John barked good-naturedly in Bajan dialect, and everyone laughed.

"De food did readie eva sense! You jus late, Mista St. John!" (The food was ready a long time ago! You're just late, Mr. St. John!") Beulah shot back and everyone laughed.

Beulah's coo coo and flying fish was delicious. Corine loved the cucumber and avocado delight, but the mauby brew was something she would have to acquire a taste for. After dinner, Ernest's parents, and his sister, Bella, retired to their respective homes. Beulah cleared the table and cleaned the kitchen. Ernest advised her she was free to go and Beulah drove off in her second hand Suzuki. Gezzy was sound asleep upstairs and Corine sat with Ernest on the porch. They listened as crickets chirped and toads called in the bush. They were prisoners to their private thoughts, and wondered about their future in Barbados. Corine felt right at home in the island and this was an unexpected surprise for her. Perhaps it was the epic English architecture that surrounded the island that made her feel connected to the place. In Barbados, she would live a life of leisure.

"Well, what do you think?" Ernest asked.

"This is a lovely house! Better than I imagined. Ernest, Estele asked me to figure out a schedule for the domestic. I think she should work Mondays, Thursdays and Saturdays. What do you think?" Corine asked.

"Whatever you decide, is fine with me. She's here to serve you. By the way, you look beautiful." Ernest complimented her. His eyes swept over her bosom.

Corine flipped her hair over her shoulders and smiled. Ernest reached for her and she clasped his hands. She stood up and faced him. Ernest gazed into her eyes and her eyes pleaded for his touch. He knew the love was still there. She yearned for him to make love to her, to make her scream in ecstasy. Ernest kissed Corine and ran his tongue over her lips and slid it into her mouth. His fingers slipped inside her panties and caressed her moist body while she unbuttoned his slacks. The feel of his hardened muscle against her stomach caused her to gasp with lust, and the excitement reached feverish pitch. Ernest peeled her panties off and hoisted one of her legs around his hip. Corine bit her lower lip to stifle the moans that emanated from her lips when he penetrated her. His organ penetrated her with precision, and infinite plea-sure consumed them. Corine cried out with pleasure! The Crickets and toads were silenced by the sounds of humans caught in the throes of sexual bliss.

Chapter Fourteen

E rnest rose early to meet his father at the familys' business headquarters in Bridgetown. Deighton, (Daddy St. John) was in the process of constructing a hotel in the parish of St. James, and he wanted Ernest to be actively involved in the project. The hotel was slated to be up and running in 1990, which left little time for unnecessary delays. Deighton was aging and he wanted to relax and enjoy all he labored to achieve for his family. He put Ernest in charge of overseeing the construction and engineering site. That morning, Deighton met with Bella, Ernest, and members of his team to brief them about the new chain of command at the site. After the meeting, Deighton drove Ernest to the parish of St. James to meet the crew.

Deighton was erecting a five-story luxury hotel, complete with spa, pool, dining, and work out facilities. Estele christened it "Wynter Haven Resort," and Ernest spent his first day on the job being introduced to key people involved in the operation. Deighton was confident that Ernest was capable of conducting affairs at the site while Bella continued as the company's' CEO. Deighton executed these arrangements, and spent a great deal of time mentoring his son; teaching him the business from the ground up. The demands of overseeing the construction site were great, and Ernest was thrust into the hectic role of managing conflicts between construction workers, foremen, inspectors and engineers. Despite the setbacks and complaints, he pressured the crew to have the hotel completed on time. Deighton slept soundly, knowing that two of his children were at the helm of his empire. He was finally able to slow down and enjoy his golden years with Estele. They wanted to travel, see the world, and enjoy spending quality time together.

Back at Villa Coral, Corine awoke to a bright and sunny day. It was 10:05am and Ernest was long gone. It was his first day on the job at the construction site and she was pleased that he was upbeat about working for his father. She daydreamed about their lovemaking session on the porch and hoped for many more nights like that. Corine was determined to steer her marriage in the right direction. The past was the past and they had a new beginning in Barbados. There was commotion coming from downstairs and the noise made her ears ache! Corine froze! No one else should be in the house but she and Gezzy! She slipped out of bed and grabbed a can of insect repellent to spray in the face of the intruder! Corine sneaked downstairs, and crept stealthily into the living room. She hid behind the couch. The racket was coming from the kitchen, so with her back against the wall, she inched closer and peeked to see where the vagabond was! Beulah! It was Beulah causing the racket with pots and pans! Corine became incensed!

"Beulah! Beulah! You're making too much noise! You woke me up, and soon you'll wake Gezzy!" An irate Corine yelled.

"Oh, Mistress St. John, uh sorry, uh din mean tuh wake yuh." ("Oh, Mrs. St. John, I'm sorry. I didn't mean to wake you.") Beulah apologized.

"How did you get in this house? I don't remember giving you a key!" Corine questioned Beulah suspiciously.

"Oh, yuh mudda in law gimme de key las night so uh cuh geh in if nuhbodie wuzzun hey wen uh come." ("Oh, your mother in law gave me a key last night so I could get in if no one was here when I arrived.") Beulah replied nervously. The last thing she wanted to do was upset the woman of the house.

"I see. Stop whatever you're doing and get my morning tea!" Corine ordered Beulah coldly.

"Yes, Mistress St. John. Sorrie bout de noise, hear?" ("Yes, Mrs. St. John. Sorry about the noise, ok?") Beulah replied. She turned her back to Corine and rolled her eyes. Beulah removed the kettle from the stove and filled it with water. She turned on the range and placed the kettle on the burner.

"Well, aren't you going to ask me what I would like for breakfast?" Corine asked Beulah in a terse fashion.

"Uh dine fuhgit yuh. Uh din waan mek de tea furst." (I didn't forget you. I wanted to make the tea first.") Beulah replied in a jittery fashion.

"I want eggs and toast!" Corine advised Beulah in a crude tone.

"Lemmuh mek um fuh yuh now, boah!" (I will make it for you right now!) Beulah replied in an abrupt manner and busied herself preparing Corines' breakfast. She decided to run the dinner menu by Corine just to be on the safe side.

111

"Mistress St. John, uh gine bake ah chicken, cook rice an peas, an mek salad fuh dinner. How dah soun?" (Mrs. St. John, I'm going to bake chicken, cook rice and peas, and make salad for dinner. How does that sound?") Beulah asked.

Corine considered the meal plan, and was on the verge of agreeing with Beulah, but then she changed her mind. Beulah didn't give her the opportunity to come up with a meal plan first, and Corine was livid. Beulah was not going to control the house!

"Beulah, I don't want baked chicken and rice and peas for dinner!" Corine responded testily. She opened, and slammed shut, the doors of the cupboards in search of pasta. Beulah moved out of her way! Corine looked in the freezer in search of shrimp, but all she found was chicken, fish, and beef! Her dark hair hung wildly around her shoulders and Beulah was convinced that Corine was medusa in the flesh! Corine turned her attention back to Beulah.

"Beulah, here is what I want you to do. As soon as Gezzy wakes, make her breakfast. Then, I want you to drive us to the nearest supermarket so that I could buy pasta, shrimp, and suitable groceries. Tonight, I want pasta with shrimp marinated in garlic sauce for dinner. Also, the floors are to be mopped before you leave today! Is that understood?" Corine quipped and delegated chores for Beulah.

Beulah listened to Corine order her around like a common servant, and she felt like a subservient slave. Beulah wanted to tell Corine to mop the blasted floors herself, but she bit her tongue and replied, "Yes."

"Yes, whom?" Corine barked. She wanted Beulah to understand that she was her servant, not family, not friend, but servant!

"Yes, Mistress St. John!" Beulah replied and resumed making breakfast. When Corine left the room, Beulah pushed her mouth in the air and sucked her teeth.

Corine felt more in control, now that she asserted herself as a woman in charge of her household. She stuck her nose in the air and returned upstairs to shower and dress. By the time she returned to check on Beulah, Gezzy was already dressed and eating breakfast at the island in the kitchen. Gezzy chatted happily with Beulah about England while Beulah stood over the kitchen sink and scrubbed bits of egg off the frying pan. Corine ate her breakfast in stony silence and watched as Beulah placed the frying pan into the dish rack. She got up and inspected the frying pan to make sure Beulah didn't miss a spot! Beulah wanted to give Corine a tongue-lashing but refrained from doing so because she needed the job. After breakfast, they departed for the supermarket.

The trio returned to find Estele sitting in a rocking chair on the porch, waiting patiently for them. Corine was happy to see Estele and greeted her mother-in-law with a warm hug. Estele announced that she wanted to take them to meet her family and Corine agreed to go. Corine excused herself to go upstairs and freshen up. Estele was left alone with Beulah and noticed the anguished expression on her face.

"Beulah, what's wrong? You don't think I should take them to meet my family?" Estele asked. She was confused by Beulah's reaction.

"Estele, uh jus doan tink dat wun ready!" ("Estele, I don't think that one is ready to meet your family!") Beulah stated with her mouth pushed up.

"Gezzy or Corine?" Estele asked for clarification.

"Not de lil girl!" ("Not the little girl!") Beulah replied and sucked her teeth when Corine sailed down the stairs.

"I'm ready." Corine breathed, and stepped onto the porch where Estele and Beulah stood.

"Very good, let's go." Estele replied.

"Beulah, don't forget the instructions i've given you for the day. These floors must shine by the time I return!" Corine reminded Beulah in a snippy fashion.

"Yes, Mistress St. John!" Beulah answered quickly and ducked into the house. She swished her ample hips and backside in defiance.

The dictatorial method Corine employed to communicate with Beulah caught Estele by surprise. She felt ashamed for Beulah because she remembered when her own mother worked as a maid. Estele didn't recall her mother being talked down to like that so she assumed that Corine was getting used to having domestic help. Corine and Gezzy stepped into Estele's white convertible and Estele drove in the direction of her mother's house. Estele's mother lived in a lively neighborhood alive with girls jumping rope on the paved street and boys chasing each other through gaps. Estele's mother lived in the parish of St. Michael, not too far from Deighton's office. She informed Corine that this area was known as Bayland.

Estele parked in front of a concrete, three-bedroom bungalow, with a front porch. A rose tree with white roses flourished in the garden outside the house, and it gave the home
a fresh appeal. Estele entered the house and was greeted by
her sister Pamela, and her daughter. She introduced them
to Corine and Gezzy. Estele's sister fussed over Gezzy, and
her daughter, Sophie, grabbed Gezzy's hand and took her on
the porch to play a game of jacks. Estele's mother was in
poor health, due to her age, and Pamela kept constant vigil
at her bedside. She was a slight, dark complexioned woman,
with fuzzy, snow-white hair. She sat up in bed with her back
supported by pillows and watched television with disinterest.
Fresh roses from the garden were placed in a vase filled with
water, and placed on top the dresser, along with pictures of
the family. The flowers added cheer to what would otherwise
be a dull room.

"Hi mummy." Estele announced loudly because her mother's
hearing wasn't too good. She walked into the room and gave
her mother a warm hug. Remember I told you that Ernest
was here with his wife and your great-granddaughter Gezzy?
Estele hollered at her ninety-three year old mother.

"Yeah, uh rememba. Ernest? Com hey!" ("Yes, I remember.
Ernest, come here!") The old lady spoke in a frail voice.

"Ernest will come later. His wife Corine is here from England
and so is little Gezzy." Estele explained.

"Gezzy, com, lem muh see yuh." ("Gezzy, come let me see
you.") The old lady stated and managed a weak smile.

"Gezzy!" Estele yelled for her grand daughter to come into
the room.

Gezzy rushed in and approached the wrinkled old lady hesitantly. She hugged the old woman, and the faint smell of medicine and liniment engulfed her. The old woman gave her a kiss, and Gezzy quickly disengaged herself from her embrace. She ran off again in search of her playmate. The old woman frightened her.

"Corine, com, com, Leh muh see yuh, nuh!" ("Corine, come and let me see you!") The old lady requested in a feeble voice."

Corine stepped closer to the bed, and the old woman held Corine by the arms. The elderly woman gasped for air when her eyes met Corine's disdainful stare. The old woman sensed contempt and scorn emanating from Corine's icy demeanor, and she shut her eyes to protect her soul from Corine's aversion! Corine was uncomfortable in her grasp and tried to disengage her arms from the old woman's iron grip but she wouldn't let go. The old woman's eyes shot open again, and she verbally attacked Corine!

"Yuh betta tek care uh muh Ernest an muh great-gran! Oddawise uh gine haunt yuh wen uh ded!" ("You better take care of Ernest and my great-grand child! Otherwise I will haunt you after I die!") The old woman warned Corine in a frightening manner! She released her arm, and turned her face to the wall. The old woman refused to look at Corine any longer! Corine backed out of the room in horror, and Estele stopped short of yelling at her frail mother!

"Mummy, that's not a nice thing to say!" Estele exclaimed. She and her sister were dumfounded by their mother's unkind words. Estele thought it was best to leave, because the old woman started to cuss! After they departed, the old woman called Estele's sister to her bedside.

"Dat woman doan like we cuz we too black!" ("That woman does not like us because we are black!") She complained, and Pamela tried to calm her down.

Corine was relieved to get away from Estele's family because their black skin made her uncomfortable. She didn't like being surrounded by dark people. Estele was different because she had a fair complexion and straight hair, like hers. It hadn't occurred to her that Estele's family would be so dark. She took one look at the prunish black woman sitting up in bed, and her stomach felt queasy. Corine desperately wanted to wash her hands because touching black skin made her feel dirty. It was toxic! The trio made a quick stop to Bridgetown, and visited the family's corporate headquarters. Corine headed straight to the restroom, and washed her hands. Bella gave Corine and Gezzy a tour of the operation, and briefed Corine on the family's various business endeavors. Corine was amazed at how much Bella controlled. Why, the St. Johns were filthy rich! It finally dawned on Corine that she married into wealth.

They returned to Villa Coral, and Corine entered the house in search of Beulah.

"Beulah! Beulah!" Corine yelled impatiently.

"Yes, Mistress St. John!" ("Yes, Mrs. St. John!") Beulah answered. She was breathless from running downstairs when Corine called for her.

"Didn't you hear me calling you?" Corine hollered.

"Uh wuz mopping de floors. Uh hey now, doah!" ("I was mopping the floors. I'm here now, though!") Beulah replied in an aggravated tone.

"Make us lunch if it's not too much trouble!" Corine requested flatly and marched upstairs to change. Estele was speechless at the mean spirited fashion in which Corine spoke to Beulah!

Corine returned and found Estele relaxing on the porch, watching Gezzy jump rope in the courtyard. She sat next to Estele, while Beulah served spicy corned-beef sandwiches and juice. Estele complimented Beulah on the wonderful job she did with the floors and thanked her for preparing the tasty sandwiches. Corine remained silent on both issues, and wolfed down the sandwiches. She chatted with Estele about life in England while Estele talked to her about life in Barbados. Estele escorted Corine around the island for the next couple of weeks, helping her get acclimated to Barbadian lifestyle, its people and culture. She taught her the finer points of gardening and Corine found it to be a relaxing and rewarding hobby. Corine and Gezzy weeded, planted and dug in the soil with tools to redefine the pretty gardens. Corine tended colorful roses and red hibiscus that hugged the perimeter of the villa. Gardening helped her pass time, and gave her life daily purpose.

Chapter Fifteen

E rnest purchased a new vehicle for Corine so she could explore the island on her own. He worked long hours at the construction site extinguishing spats between construction crews, and engineers. The stress and demands of the job left him physically and mentally drained when he returned to Villa Coral in the evenings. Gezzy was enrolled in private school and Corine was free to spend her days doing whatever she wanted. Corine added a few decorative touches to the villa to reflect her personal style and taste. She lunched at various restaurants and shopped for clothes, jewelry and anything else she fancied. Sometimes she visited idyllic beaches, and lounged on beach chairs with an interesting book.

Corine eventually grew bored with her leisurely lifestyle and volunteered her services at the public library where she met new people. The St. John's introduced her to their friends and soon Corine was immersed in her own society clique. She was more comfortable in the company of Deighton's family because they were of British descent just like she was. Corine bent over backwards to win their acceptance, and cozied up to his three sisters. The sisters loved Corine and treated like a little sister, but, she was jealous of the affection they lavished on Estele and competed with her for their attention. Even though Deighton's family adored Corine, she felt as though they loved Estele more, and that should not be. Corine resented being treated as though she was second best when Estele was around. She wanted to be the one they turned to for advice and support. The one they shared personal information and gossip with first. After all, she was one of them while Estele was a mulatto that lucked out in life! The situation finally came to a head while the family sat down to a Saturday night feast at the home of Emeline; one Deighton's three sisters. His two other sisters, Catherine, and Sherry were also present, along with Deighton, Estele, Bella, Ernest, Corine and Gezzy.

"Umm, that pudding and souse was good, Emeline!" Deighton complimented his sister's cooking skills.

"An hot wid pepper! Jus de way uh like um!" (And hot with pepper! Just the way I like it!) Sherry remarked. She was the youngest of Deighton's three sisters and preferred to speak Bajan dialect.

Everyone nodded in agreement.

"You have Estele to thank for that! After all, she's the one that taught me how to prepare souse!" Emeline stated with pride.

"Estele, you should open a restaurant with your cooking skills!" Catherine commented.

"Dah's tru, yuh kno! Ain like yuh doan hav de means! Yuh cuh call um, Estele House of Souse!" ("That's true you know! It's not like you don't have the money! You could call it, Estele House of Souse!") Sherry joked, and everyone laughed.

"I wouldn't mind owning a restaurant. As a matter fact, I could whip up English delights for all of you!" Corine interjected jealously. She was annoyed with everyone for giving Estele so much attention and praise.

"What would you name the restaurant, love?" Ernest asked with interest. The idea of Corine slaving away in a kitchen was very far-fetched.

"She'll name it Beulahs!" Estele joked, and the group snickered at the absurd idea of Corine opening a restaurant. Sherry almost fell out of her chair with laughter, and Emeline chuckled into a napkin. Catherine flushed red and coughed from laughing so hard, and Bella held her side and guffawed. Gezzy giggled at the amusing scene.

"Estele, you aren't the only one in this family who can put a meal together!" Corine retorted with a sharp edge to her voice. Her lips were pursed in a tight line and she was stone faced.

"Calm down love, mummy was just joking." Ernest stated.

"Well, I'm not!" The atmosphere turned tense and Estele thought it was best to apologize. She didn't mean to offend Corine.

"Corine, we have a bad habit of poking fun at each other. It was not my intention to hurt your feelings." Estele apologized and resumed eating. Corine glared at Estele with contempt! She refused to accept her terse apology!

"You, of all people, should be honored to sit at this table with the rest of us!" Corine responded with impudence.

The group was stunned into silence and Gezzy kept her eyes glued to her plate. She couldn't believe her bampot mother would insult Grandmother! Deighton lost his appetite and pushed his plate aside. He slammed his fist on the table and silverware toppled to the floor.

"Gezzy, please leave the room!" Emeline ordered and the other sisters nodded in agreement. Deighton had an explosive temper and Corine was going to get a taste of it.

"I think you're the one who should feel honored! Estele has always been a part of this family! She has done more than anyone else to help you settle into a comfortable life, here in Barbados! It was her idea to give Ernest that villa, so that you could move right into your own home, and this is the thanks she gets? You are no longer welcome in my house!" Deighton stated in a scathing manner and stormed out. Estele tried to pretend the implication of Corine's words didn't affect her, but the hurt was etched all over her face. She got up from the table and followed her husband out of the house.

"Corine, I want you to leave, and its best you don't come back until you get your feelings sorted out! Ernest and Gezzy are always welcome, but you, stay away! Emeline stated stoically.

"Yuh bey apolagize tuh Estele!" ("You better apologize to Estele!") Sherry stated in a brash manner.

"Apologize for what? I spoke the truth!" Corine blurted out.

"You miserable thing! Don't you have any shame?" Catherine asked with derision.

"Corine, enough is enough! Let's go!" Ernest yelled. He stood up from the table with such force that the wrought iron chair he sat on fell to the side. His body shook with anger! He had never been so humiliated in all his life!

"Ernest, Gezzy can stay with me tonight!" Bella suggested. She didn't want her niece to witness the ensuing turmoil.

"Fine!" Ernest yelled in response.

He grabbed Corine by the elbow and forced her out of the house and into the car. Ernest drove dangerously on the roads, and the tires screeched in protest around the perilous bends. Corine was terrified! She gripped the edge of her seat and cried for Ernest to slow down! She breathed a sigh of relief when the vehicle zoomed into the pebbly courtyard of Villa Coral, and he turned off the ignition. Corine hastily opened the car door and ran up the steps leading into the villa.

"Ernest, please let me explain!" Corine whined when Ernest ran up the steps after her, and slammed the front door shut!

"How could you insult my mother?" Ernest yelled in a tormented voice.

"Your mother put me down in front of everyone! I wanted to give her a taste of her own medicine and rightfully so! She needed to be reminded of what she is!" Corine implored without remorse.

"What am I hearing?" Ernest asked. He was stunned by the audacity of her words.

"Ernest, your mother's family is so dark!" Corine cried.

"Yes, they are! And, my father's family is white or have you forgotten that?" Ernest shouted and balled his fists.

"Yes, they're white like me, but they seem to care for her more than they care for me, and I'm one of them!" Corine ranted irrationally.

"My God! Who are you? I feel as though I don't know who you really are! You're as mad as a box of frogs!" Ernest stated and shook his head in amazement. Corine put her hands to her face and cried.

"What do you see when you look at me?" Ernest asked.

"I see you... Ernest! I see my husband!" Corine replied and sniffed back tears.

"Rubbish! What do you really see?" Ernest barked.

"You... I ..." Corine faltered, unsure of what he was getting at.

"Do you see a black man with a big penis?" Ernest asked sardonically. Corine was stupefied by his question, and realized the situation was out of control!

"I see a white man! You're white and our Gezzy is white!" Corine lashed out bitterly.

"Corine, I may look white because my father is white, but, I also have the blood of a black grandmother coursing through my veins! I've never lied to you about my family; you knew my mother was mulatto! Didn't you realize then, that my father's family made up half the picture?" Ernest asked dryly.

124

"I didn't! I didn't think about it!" Corine wailed and clutched her stomach. She dropped to her knees and cried in desperation.

"I knew you were prejudiced to some extent, and I admit to having prejudices of my own, but you are a disgrace! Your ignorance stops right here and right now! Your prejudice against my mother is something I can't handle!" Ernest stated with obdurance. He looked down at Corine with a vacant expression in his eyes and a chill ran down her spine.

"Ernest, please!" Corine whined. "I didn't mean those things I said to your mother!" Corine begged him to understand.

Ernest grimaced and turned away. The sight of her made him sick! Corine gripped his shoulders with her hands. She tried to make him face her, but he shrugged his broad shoulders aggressively, and she stumbled backwards and fell to the floor! He turned around and glared at her with fury!

"I need a bitch piss!" He snarled, and ran his fingers through his hair in an agitated manner. Corine scrambled to the bar where Ernest kept a well stocked supply of liquor. She hurriedly prepared the English brew of mixed fruit with alcohol, and gave it to Ernest with trembling hands. Her body quivered with anxiety and her muscles tensed. She needed a lifeline to make the situation better.

"Ernest, I love Estele! I really do! I'll apologize! I'll do anything! As a matter fact, i'll drive over there right now and beg her forgiveness! Let me get my car keys!" Corine announced neurotically. She fished the keys out of her handbag and headed for the door. Ernest ran after her and snatched the keys out of her hands! He threw the keys at the glass vase perched on the living room table and it crashed to the floor! Shards of glass were sent flying everywhere, and water from the vase dripped all over the floor! Ernest bolted the door and approached peevish Corine in a hostile manner! Corine wanted to scream but who would come to her rescue? She trembled when Ernest mashed the broken glass on the floor beneath the soles of his shoes when he walked. The "crunch" of glass heightened her anxiety, and she backed up against the wall in fear. Ernest grinned demonically and stood in front of Corine with his face an inch away from hers.

"Why, Corine? Why?" Ernest screamed in her face. Tears rolled down his cheeks.

Corine cried helplessly. She held his face in her hands and kissed him. Her lips lingered on his and she wanted to calm him any way she could. Ernest dropped to his knees and nuzzled his face on her stomach. Corine kneeled down and unbuttoned his shirt. She marveled at how physically fit Ernest had remained after all these years. His abs was still taut with a well defined six-pack. Corine stroked his abs and Ernest wasn't sure why he felt the urge to make love. She slipped out of her floral dress and lay back on the tiled floor. Ernest straddled Corine and made love to her with all the outrage he felt inside. Corine welcomed his inflexible organ and gasped at his vigorous energy. Ernest needed to physically release his tension. The fury within, had to find a way out, otherwise, he could physically hurt her! Corine gripped his shoulders as his rigid organ delved deep inside her. She was sexually dehydrated and Ernest replenished her garden of eden. Corine cried out with passion and reaped bountiful orgasms. This meant he still needed her, still desired her, and still wanted to remain a family! Ernest's passion reached its climax, and he released his outrage, his emotional pain, and his fury! They lay on the floor in a precarious lovemaking session. A physically spent Ernest retrieved his clothes off the floor and headed upstairs to shower. Corine was still wary of her husband, but followed him anyway. She washed his body thoroughly and lavished him with passionate kisses. They dried each other off and ventured into the bedroom. Corine slipped a sheer nightgown over her head, fluffed the pillows, and got under the sheets. Ernest threw on a pair of boxers, and left the room!

"Ernest, aren't you coming to bed?" Corine inquired. It was almost midnight and she wanted to lay in his arms.

"No! Not with you! Not tonight or any other night! The next time you degrade my black family with your racist filth; I will make you bleed like a stuck pig! Sleep tight and don't let the bed bugs bite!" Ernest stated vengefully. He ventured into the guestroom, and locked the door.

This couldn't be! What about the heart stopping love making they just shared? Corine leapt out of bed and spent the next two hours banging on the door of the guestroom begging Ernest to come out! She sought a hairpin and attempted to pick the lock, and when that didn't work, she resumed banging! Corine slouched against the door and cried profusely. She was sorry for her callous behavior. Corine finally gave up banging around three o'clock in the morning. She returned to bed, and fell into a disturbed sleep.

The next morning, a disheveled Corine hurried out of bed and headed for the guestroom. She was desperate to make amends with Ernest but he was already gone. Beulah was downstairs shifting furniture around in an effort to mop the water off the floor and sweep up the broken glass. Corine slammed the bedroom door and returned to bed. She would leave Beulah to her own devices today, because all she wanted to do was sleep.

Beulah arrived at the villa to find broken glass and water all over the floor. Corine still hadn't come down for breakfast but she heard her rummaging around upstairs. Something was definitely amiss because Corine stayed out of sight. It was just as well, Beulah thought. She scrawled a message on a notepad, letting Corine know she stepped out to purchase a new mop and a new broom. She drove away from Villa Coral and wondered what in the world was going on. Beulah intended to keep her eyes and ears open for juicy tidbits she might be privy to. She had a hunch that whatever happened was most likely Corine's fault and Ernest probably had enough! It was about time, Beulah theorized!

Chapter Sixteen

The St. John family distanced themselves from Corine, and she befriended other housewives, and mutual acquaintances that operated in the same social circles. An eventful year passed, and Corine was ready to re-enter the work force. She sought a new career in the financial sector and applied for a job at a bank. Corine was hired on the spot to work as a teller where she became adept at handling various bank transactions. While working at the bank, she established a close friendship with an accountant, named Clyde. Clyde was a white Barbadian, whose family resided on the island for generations. He was romantically interested in Corine but she refused to cheat on Ernest. Clyde didn't make her heart flutter like her handsome husband, but Corine knew he would cherish her in ways Ernest never would. Clyde knew Corine was sorely unhappy in her marriage to Ernest and disliked the brute.

Ernest remained in the guestroom of Villa Coral and refused to share a bedroom with Corine. When he was groped by the desire for intimacy, he surrendered himself to her affections, but, the emotional bond they once shared ebbed, and the relationship became increasingly strained. Corine was mindful of her manners and comments whenever she was in the presence of Estele, and penned letters of apology to Estele

and the family, but it was months before she was welcomed to their homes for family get togethers. Eventhough her heartfelt apologies were accepted, and her relationship with the family was re-established, Ernest refrained from taking up residence in their bedroom. Corine assumed she had not done enough to appease him and decided to reconcile with everyone in a big way.

The year was 1990 and Gezzy was approaching her tenth birthday in a couple of months. Corine came up with the brilliant idea to throw Gezzy a birthday bash and transformed Villa Coral into a childrens' paradise for the occasion. She had an inground oasis shaped pool constructed at the rear of the home, and it was outfitted with water slides and pool lights. Landscapers were hired to beautify the land surrounding it. Ernest agreed to the change because it increased the villa's property value. Gezzy invited her friends, Corine summoned a few acquaintances and their children, The St. John family, and Estele's family.

While Corine was occupied with work and the pool project, Ernest tended hotel operations. The Wynter Haven Hotel was off to a good start with a 90% occupancy rate off-season, and 100% occupancy rate during The Crop Over Festival. But, his extended hours away from home weren't always business related. Paola visited Barbados twice during the first year of Ernest's return to the island. She was his best-kept secret, and her visits were arranged at secluded hideaways. Paola was tired of their long distance affair, and was willing to relocate to the island to be closer to Ernest, but he wouldn't hear of it. She was currently in the island, and was scheduled to depart Barbados the same day as the party. That meant Ernest would have to leave the birthday bash to pick her up from the hotel where she was lodged, and drive her to the airport. Corine communicated to Ernest her desire for him to refrain from conducting business on Gezzy's birthday and commit himself to spending the entire day with the family. Ernest agonized over these conflicting interests.

The party was in full swing on the grounds of Villa Coral, and Gezzy was a birthday princess in a red and white polka dot dress. She greeted her friends with joyful shrieks and they chased each other through the courtyard. They played hide and seek, and crouched behind majestic trees with wide girths. The children trampled in the gardens with abandon, and splish splashed in the pool. Corine kept a watchful eye on Ernest as he assisted Beulah serving refreshments to the guests, while she welcomed new arrivals. Ernest's fidgety body language signaled to Corine that he was uneasy about something. He seemed distracted and constantly kept track of the time by glancing at his watch. She watched as Ernest abruptly handed the serving tray to Estele's sister, and excused himself from serving refreshments. He rushed into the villa to make a phone call, and Corine wondered if the situation with Lerwick was rearing its ugly head again. Was Ernest in some kind of trouble? She couldn't put her finger on it but something was wrong. Suddenly, Ernest bolted out of the house and hare footed down the front steps of the villa! He approached Corine in an exasperated fashion. She observed the car keys in his hands and scowled.

"Corine, we're almost out of ice cream. I have to run out and get some more." Ernest stated and dismissed the scowl on her face.

"Ernest, have you looked in the freezer? We should have more than enough ice cream." Corine replied curtly.

"i'll be back!" Ernest responded and hurried away. He got in his car and drove away before Corine could utter another word.

"Corine, Ernest is not conducting business today, is he?" Estele asked.

"No. He left to buy more ice cream. I need to use the restroom, would you mind playing hostess for me?" Corine asked.

"i'll be glad to." Estele replied.

Corine hurried into the villa and went upstairs to powder her nose. She observed a rumpled piece of paper on the floor, close to the bathroom door. Corine picked up the paper and unfolded it to see what it was. The note read: British Airways Flight # 302 Depart 4:50pm, today! She recognized Ernest's handwriting. What's going on? Corine asked herself. She glanced at the clock and it was 1:30pm. She studied the paper again and wondered whose flight information it contained. Corine tucked the paper into her brassiere, and went into the bathroom to empty her bladder. Suspicion and curiosity took possession of Corine's mind as she washed her hands and dried them. Corine bounded down the stairs and hurried into the kitchen. She opened the freezer door and there were unopened tubs of ice cream! More than enough for their party needs! Corine was infuriated by Ernest's deliberate lie and slammed the freezer door shut!

"Corine, wuh yuh lookin fuh?" ("Corine, what are you looking for?") Beulah asked and hoped she remembered to buy everything specified by her employer.

"Last time I checked, this was my house! I can look wherever I want!" Corine spat out.

"Uh did onlie wan kno ef dey wuz sumting uh cuh git fuh yuh! Dahs all boah!" ("I only wanted to know if there was something I could get for you! That's all!") Beulah stated. She sucked her teeth and stormed out of the kitchen.

Corine placed her hands on the marbled kitchen counter, and steadied herself. She took a deep breath and shook her head. Corine made a mental note to fire Beulah as soon as she found a suitable replacement! She turned her attention to the piece of paper and read it once more. Corine ruefully swiped the car keys off the hook on the kitchen wall, and walked onto the porch. She seeked Deighton and Estele to inform them that Ernest needed her help, and they were in charge until she and Ernest returned. Corine got into her car and sped toward the airport. Her heart beat ferociously in her chest, and she gripped the steering wheel so hard, her knuckles ached! Her throat was parched from anxiety, and it was difficult to swallow. A lump lodged in her throat and she was forced to breathe through her mouth.

Corine arrived at the airport at 2:00pm and headed for the British Airways terminal. She tried to be as inconspicuous as possible, and hid behind concrete pillars. She peeked around the pillars and stealthily scanned the faces of passengers waiting to check in. Her radar detected Ernest standing in line. Was he going somewhere without telling her? He chatted with a pretty blond that stood in front of him. Corine sized her up to be in her early thirties, about 5'9", with skin kissed by the Barbados sun. The blond wore a black tank top to amplify her enviable bosom and white hip hugging shorts to accentuate tanned legs. To Corine's horror, Ernest hugged the woman around the waist, and the mystery woman turned her head and kissed his lips! His eyes caressed her lovingly, and he reciprocated her smooches! They looked like they were so in love! Corine rested her head against the pillar and cried. When was the last time he held her like that? When was the last time he kissed her like that? She was forced to face the truth because it was staring her right in the face! Corine's heart was crushed into a million pieces! How could he leave Gezzy's party to succumb to the whims of another woman? The saliva in her mouth had an acrid taste, and her tears manifested into vengeance. How could he betray her like this? After all she sacrificed, for him?

Corine lurked behind the pillars and watched the interaction between her husband and the woman. The blond finally checked in, and whispered a few words to Ernest before leaving his side. Corine watched covetously as she disappeared into the restroom. Equipped with Old Town orneriness, a bruised heart, and a confrontational nature, Corine was well armored, and deserted her hiding place! She was prepared to battle! Jealousy and rage overcame her and emotion presided over reason. Corine was going to confront this blond, and inform her, that she was Ernest's wife! She was blinded by fury and stormed passed curious onlookers who got out of her way when they saw the hardened, contorted expression on her face. Perspiration trickled down Ernest's spine. He had a sense of doom that he couldn't shake. He nervously looked around the airport and witnessed a dark–haired lass hiking in his direction! The color drained from his face like sand in an hourglass! He couldn't believe his eyes! Blimey! It was Corine!

Ernest looked to the left and looked to the right! He was trapped! The situation was hopeless! How could he remedy this indiscretion? How could he explain it away? He stared at Corine with trepidation and braced himself for the verbal, and possible, physical onslaught of rage. But, Corine made a detour and was lost to him in the crowd of people! He grew increasingly apprehensive and hoped Paola would hurry up so that he could alert her. Ernest checked his watch and it was 2:20pm; still not time to board the plane. He skidded over to customs agents at the departure gate and waited for Paola as agreed. Corine entered the ladies restroom and found Paola brushing her blond tresses. Paola put the brush on the counter and reapplied her lipstick. Corine lingered in front of the mirror and pretended to fuss over her own hair until they were alone. Then, she pushed the steel trashcan in the restroom against the door so no one could enter. Paola was startled by the woman's actions and wondered why she blocked the door. She eyed her quizzically, and wondered if the woman was mad.

"Excuse me, but I need to get out of here!" Paola announced to the dark haired beauty.

"Don't you know who I am?" Corine stated with anger. Her chest heaved rapidly with every breath.

"No, I do ..." Paola's voice trailed off. She scooped the cosmetics off the counter and into the oversized bag. She knew who this woman was! Ernest described Corine numerous times and recanted vivid stories about her temperament. Paola was scared but refused to show it. Her heart boomed in her chest.

"You must be Corine!" Paola replied sarcastically, sounding more hawkish than she felt.

"That's right bird! So, you're the one! You're the one who's trying to wreck me household!" Corine's proper British diction had morphed into a cockney snarl.

Paola realized she was trapped and had to deal with this fiesty creature by herself. She mustered up her courage and assumed an aggressive disposition. Paola resigned herself to a fistfight and refused to be bullied.

"How long have you been getting starker for me husband eh?" Corine yelled vehemently.

"Longer than you would care to know!" Paola flung the words spitefully at Corine.

"You're nothing but a headcase!" Corine hollered belligerently. She cocked her head to the side, balled her fists and rested them akimbo on her hips.

"i've been in Ernest's life for seven years and I'm not going anywhere! He doesn't want you! He's with you because of his daughter so get out of my way!" Paola shouted viciously.

Paola flung the overstuffed handbag over her shoulder and stormed past Corine. She purposely allowed the heavy handbag to thump Corine's arm. Corine seized a fistful of Paola's hair in her hands! She yanked Paola's head backwards, causing her to fall back on the restroom floor! Corine dragged Paola by the hair along the restroom floor as if she were a mop! Paola hollered in distress, and tried to claw at Corine's hands, but she could not free herself. Corine stopped dragging Paola over the floor and released her hair. She bent over Paola, balled her fists, and pummeled Paola's face and head! Paola closed her eyes and flailed her arms wildly, trying to fight back! She tried to sit up but Corine shoved her in the face, and kneed her in the chest! Corine was furious! She started to yank fistfuls of hair out of Paola's head! Paola wailed as bunches of wispy blond hair littered the restroom floor! Paola delivered a well-aimed blow to Corine's shoulder and caused her to fall to the side! Corine quickly regained control and delivered jabs to both sides of Paola's head with her fists! An airport worker forced the door open and shrieked at the sight of the two ladies wrestling with each other on the floor! Corine scrambled to her feet and exited the restroom while the worker alerted security. She returned to her former hiding place and watched happily as the security officeres entered the restroom to see what the commotion was about.

Ernest witnessed the officers heading in the direction of the ladies room and followed their lead with a sense of dread. He waited anxiously for the women to come out. To his sorrow, Paola was the only one who emerged, looking grimy and beaten! Ernest rushed to her side and hugged her. Paola remained tightlipped about the incident, and security departed, leaving her and Ernest alone. The bald spots around her hairline and the middle of her head stunned Ernest. Her signature mane was reduced to a patchy, stringy, ugly mess! Ernest was speechless! He consoled Paola, but it was obvious his she-devil wife won the fight! Paola's flight was boarding and she didn't want to leave in this condition. She was mad as hell! Ernest reassured Paola that he would visit her in the next week or two and she agreed to board the plane. Paola walked on wobbly legs through the departure lounge and boarded the flight. Passengers and flight attendants pitied Paola's physical state. Her face was red and the bald spots in her head threatened to bleed. She claimed her first class seat, and flight attendants offered her icepacks for her swollen face. The confrontation she knew would eventually happen was now over.

Paola turned her face to the window and willed herself not to cry, as the plane prepared for takeoff.

Corine returned to Gezzy's birthday party full of smiles; seemingly delighted to be back in the swing of things. Gezzy and her friends played by the pool and the adults mingled freely and enjoyed themselves. Ernest soon arrived and Corine avoided him at all costs. He feigned pleasantries with guests and darted dirty looks in Corine's direction whenever their eyes met. Corine's fleeting nervousness and Ernest's stiff composure almost went unnoticed as they masqueraded like a happily married couple. Beulah observed their staged behavior and knew they were putting on an act. Corine seemed overjoyed about something and Ernest was unusually tense. She hoped Corine's joy would last a while because she needed to modify her work schedule. Working for Corine motivated Beulah to consider changes in her professional life. Beulah was fed up with Corine's nagging and condescending attitude. No matter what she did or how hard she tried, she could not please the woman.

The nursing profession appealed to Beulah and she enrolled in a nursing program, determined to get off her knees scrubbing floors. It wasn't too late for her to make a change. Beulah was only thirty-four years old, with an adolescent son, and there was nothing stopping her from reaching for higher goals. She wanted to prove that she had the ability to do more than clean someone else's house and wipe the rear ends of children. Beulah was a curvaceous size fourteen with a full bosom, small waist, and an ample backside. Her beauty was always concealed beneath the uniform dress Corine insisted she wear, but her down to earth personality and witty sense of humor could not be contained. Beulah rubbed her copper colored arm that itched due to an insect bite and pursed her lips. Her eyes roamed Ernest's tense shoulders and she wanted to massage the tightness out of them. She noticed the fire in his eyes and wondered what was going on. Beulah sashayed over to him with an empty serving tray in one hand and rested the other hand akimbo against her hip.

"Ernest, yuh luk like yuh cuh use ah drink." ("Ernest, you look like you could use a drink.") Beulah remarked.

"Beulah, you seem to know what I need and when I need it! Get me a bitch p…" Ernest started, but Beulah put her hand up to stop him from finishing the sentence!

"Uh kno wuh yuh wan but doan suh it, nuh man! Uh doan like de name uh dah drink becuz it soun real rude!" ("I know what you want so don't say it! I don't like the name of that drink because it sounds rude!") Beulah declared. She sucked her teeth and pouted sexily.

Ernest chuckled. Beulah's colorful dialect reminded him of his school days on the island. She always managed to put him at ease and he liked having her around. Beulah was sassy and her personality captivated him like a rough diamond in need of refinement.

"Beulah, I had no idea you felt this way! I'll rename the drink "bitch piss," "BP," just for you. How does that sound?" Ernest replied jovially. Beulah threw her head back and laughed good-naturedly, pleased that he considered her feelings.

"Uh huh! A BP coming right up!" ("Alright! A BP coming right up!") Beulah stated and walked briskly up the front steps. She disappeared inside the villa to fix his drink.

Beulah sauntered away with pep in her step and her hips swayed seductively. Ernest licked his lips and was mesmerized by Beulah's rear end that wiggled in front of him every time she swayed her hips. He wondered what treasures lay hidden beneath the polyester confines of her plain uniform. Ernest blinked, but could not look away. He cleared his throat in confusion. He must be going a bit barmey, he thought to himself. Lusting after Beulah? He needed a vacation!

Chapter Seventeen

A weary Paola arrived in Geneva after a grueling seventeen hour trip from Barbados. A fellow passenger pitied Paola and offered her his baseball cap to cover her patchy head. Icepacks offered by flight attendants helped to reduce the swelling on her face. Paola kept the baseball cap on her head when she arrived home so her mother wouldn't see the damage done to her hair. She arrived home exhausted, and her mom was ecstatic to have her safely back in Geneva. Paola's mother disapproved of Paola's involvement with Ernest, and encouraged her to date other men, but Paola was shunned the idea. She wanted no one else but Ernest.

Paola consulted a doctor about treatment for her injuries, and was prescribed antibacterial solutions. Paola's scalp was badly bruised, and the doctor suggested she cut the hair off to speed up the healing process. Paola wailed as remnants of her golden tresses was chopped off, leaving her with a bald head. She would have to wear a wig until the hair grew back! Paola visited a wig shop and was presented with a diverse selection of chic and sophisticated styles. She experimented with various looks and settled for a blond wig with straight hair that resembled her original mane. She hoped her mother wouldn't be able to tell the difference. Hiding the truth from her was going to be a challenge. Paola was satisfied with her selection and started to feel upbeat and lighthearted once again. The trauma she experienced left her mentally and physically exhausted, and she decided to return home. The bus traveling in the direction where she lived, trudged slowly uphill to the bus stop. Paola stood across the street and observed the bus driving at a snails' pace. She rummaged through her handbag for a hand held mirror because she was unaccustomed to the feel of the wig on her head and wanted to make sure it wasn't lopsided. Paola was preoccupied with searching through the handbag and didn't look to see if it was safe to cross the busy street. She was immersed in shuffling through the contents of the overstuffed bag, and walked across the road.

"Hey, you don't have the light!" Shouted a male pedestrian that was waiting for the light to change.

Paola looked up and realized she was sandwiched between fast moving vehicles on the road! Angry drivers swerved in their lanes and barely missed her! Paola clutched her hand-bag and held it to her chest in panic. She waded through oncoming traffic, desperate for a way out! The frantic pedestrian spied the bus driving up the hill, and bolted through traffic, risking life and limb to rescue her! He flailed his arms frantically to garner her attention, but Paola kept moving in the direction of the oncoming bus. She looked back at the pedestrian and tried to make sense of what the man was trying to communicate, but his animated gestures confused her. Finally, there was a lull in traffic. Paola made a run for it! The bus rumbled over the hill and barreled towards her. Paola screamed in terror!

"No!" Paola cried, but it was too late!

The bus driver mashed the brakes and the tires screeched in protest! Passengers braced themselves for impact! Paola was hit and hurled back into oncoming traffic, where she was run over by passing vehicles! She lay motionless on the pavement and was barely alive! The pedestrian rushed to her aid and cried because he was so close to saving her. He held her hand and offered words of encouragement until the ambulance arrived and whisked her off to the hospital. Paola whispered her telephone number to the paramedics and willed herself to live until her mother arrived.

Paola's distraught mother arrived at the hospital and erupted into tears at the sight of her daughter's broken body. She was hooked up to all kinds of machines and swathed in thick bandages. Doctors' solemnly informed her that there was nothing they could do to save Paola because her vital organs were ruptured and she bled internally. She also suffered from a broken back. Paola's mother maintained a devoted vigil at her daughter's bedside and prayed. Her daughter was all she had left! She pleaded with her not to die!

"Mother, promise me you'll tell Ernest i'll always love him." Paola murmured. Uttering those few words seemed to suck the life out of her.

"Oh, Paola, I promise! I love you! Please don't go!" Paola's mother sobbed with sorrow.

Her mother hollered out in agony because her only child was dying right before her eyes! Paola's raspy breath alarmed her and she frantically left her daughter's bedside! She opened the door of Paola's room and screamed in the hospital corridors for doctors to tend her child! Paola raised her eyes to the ceiling and could no longer hear her mother's anguished sobs.

Visions of Ernest and the times they shared flashed before her and she smiled. Her deceased father appeared before her, seemingly radiant and in excellent health. He smiled and waited for her patiently. She remembered him taking her for piggy back rides when she was a little girl! She heard her mother cry out with sadness and Paola was plucked back to reality!

She looked at her mother and murmured, "Don't be sad, mother. I love you!" Paola was at peace.

The light went out of her sparkling blue eyes and her spirit was free. The doctor closed her eyes with his hands and covered her lifeless body with a white sheet. Paola's mother was unable to utter a sound and pain knifed her broken heart! On the verge of heart failure, she clutched her chest and wheezed! She fainted in the emergency room from the reality of it all!

Chapter Eighteen

C orine rose earlier than usual the day after the party and arranged for Gezzy to spend the weekend with Bella. While Ernest was in the shower, Corine slipped into the guestroom and waited patiently for him. He emerged with a towel wrapped snugly around his waist and, after all these years, she couldn't help but marvel at his physically fit body. She wanted nothing more than to be intimate with him this very moment, but images of Ernest and his blond lover crowded her mind and she snapped back to reality. She had questions about the state of their union and needed answers.

"Ernest, we need to talk!" Corine stated when he sauntered into the bedroom. "Who was that woman?" She asked, in a shrill voice. Her nerves were frazzled and she stood before him with trembling hands on her hips. Ernest removed the towel from around his waist and tossed it on the bed. He glared at Corine in a peevish manner.

"Well?" Corine beseeched him. Her eyes devoured his nakedness and she hated being aroused by the sight of his beefy organ. Especially at a time like this!

"i've been having an affair for the past seven years with the woman you attacked!" Ernest replied flatly, without a hint of regret. Corine was humiliated by his casual admission to infidelity and slapped his face! Ernest laughed.

"You bastard! That's almost the duration of our marriage!" Corine cried in an edgy voice.

"I didn't plan for it to happen, Corine! I met her on a business trip and one thing led to another. I tried to end the affair several times, but she refused to let it go!" Ernest explained with an arrogant tone. Corine's eyes narrowed at the audacity of his words and she pursed her lips. She slapped his face again and Ernest gritted his teeth with impatience.

"She refused to let it go? You're the one that's bloody married! I've given you a beautiful child… i've sacrificed my career for you… and this is what I get? I've been a devoted wife, and you can't even share the same bed with me! The only thing keeping us together is sex!" Corine cried bitterly.

"It's better than nothing!" Ernest retorted cruelly. Corine sucked in her breath with astonishment and raised her hand to slap his face again, but this time, Ernest grabbed her hand.

"Let's not get carried away, love! I stayed in this marriage because I loved you but you've changed and i've changed! I'll remain married to you forever, if that's what you want, and that's the only promise i'll make!" He stated decisively, and flung her hand away from his face. Corine stumbled backwards but regained her balance.

"And, what about her? I hope you don't plan on seeing her again, because if she comes back to Barbados… I swear… i'll rip her pubic hairs out!" Corine yelled spitefully. Ernest was silenced by Corine's obscence words. He wasn't sure if he should laugh or have her head checked for loose screws.

"Corine, I can't promise you i'll never see her again! I've lied to you enough!" Ernest responded with brutal honesty. His words smashed Corine's pride to bits like the force of a sledgehammer. She faced Ernest with a blank expression, and her shoulders drooped. Corine put her hands to her face and cried.

"I can't believe you won't give her up to save our marriage! I gave up everything for you! I won't stand for it!" Corine sobbed.

"I know you won't!" Ernest reiterated dryly.

"So, this means our marriage is really over? It's all over?" Corine wailed. She was dazed at Ernest's willingness to let her go. The marriage was headed for divorce.

Ernest reached out to Corine and held her in his arms. He loved her so much but love was no longer enough. It was over and he was ready to move on. Ernest no longer desired to be married. Corine gazed into his eyes, which were now shrouded in emotion. They looked at each other and kissed. Ernest slid the straps of her black satin nightgown over her shoulders and picked her up in his arms. He laid her on the bed in bedroom they once shared, and kissed her curvaceous thighs, and shapely legs. His manhood throbbed with yearning. Ernest straddled Corine and pleased her with every stroke of his instrument. Corine's hands clasped his strong back and their hands caressed each other's bodies as if trying to embellish this moment forever in their souls. They remained in bed and made love until they were physically spent. Ernest

refused to leave her side, and Corine clung to him because she knew in her heart that this was their last dance.

The dawn of a new day was welcomed in the island of Barbados, and a green monkey scurried across the mossy courtyard which glistened with morning dew. The monkey climbed up a tree and disappeared into the thick foliage. Corine slept soundly. Ernest awoke and retreated to the gues-troom in a dispirited fashion. Yesterday would be the very last time he would know Corine intimately as his wife.

Chapter Nineteen

E rnest arrived in Geneva two days after receiving a phone
call from Paola's distraught mother, informing him of
Paola's tragic death. He advised the family he had urgent business in Geneva, and would be back in a couple of days. There
was no time for explanations of any sort. Ernest booked a
cheap room at a motel for the duration of his stay instead of
the customary luxury accommodations he reserved for his
trysts with Paola. Ernest opened the door to his room, tossed
his travel bag in, and left.

He wandered the streets of Geneva aimlessly in search of
Paola. Ernest visited the petting zoo where they met and
could hear her distinctive European accent as she amused
him with heartfelt sentiments. He heard her laugh and call
his name. Ernest roamed the park in search of her smiling
face, only to realize it was just a fantasy. He hunted the faces
of every longhaired blond he passed on the street, hoping to
detect glimpses of Paola in their smiles or mannerisms. He
watched jealousy as lovers chatted and exchanged kisses over
drinks at the same cafes they frequented. Ernest roamed the
streets till dusk with tears streaming down his face, and didn't
realize he was crying. He stopped at a liquor store and purchased a large bottle of vodka. Ernest had not craved alcohol
since he married Corine, but he was despondent, and needed

something to dull the emotional pain. He returned to his seedy motel room and made a beeline for the ice bucket on the counter. Ernest tossed ice cubes into a glass and filled it with vodka. He gulped the drink down in one swallow. His throat was on fire, and an alcohol-induced warmth pervaded his body. The wake for Paola was to be held at a nearby funeral parlor this evening but he couldn't bring himself to attend. Instead, he ordered long stemmed red roses to be delivered at the somber occasion. Ernest poured him self another drink, winced, and gulped it down. He lay on the bed and cried himself to sleep.

Ernest arrived promptly at the chapel on the day of Paola's funeral, wearing a black three-piece suit. He looked every bit the gentleman Paola fell madly in love with. He sat in a rear pew because he didn't want to be bothered with anyone. Ernest was in his own private hell and preferred to battle his demons alone. Touching eulogies were shared by those who loved Paola, and he wept silently through all of them. The casket remained opened, and it was time for friends and family to pay their final respects. Ernest stood to his feet and walked sluggishly to Paola's casket. He gazed sadly at Paola, sleeping eternally on a plush pink pillow. Ernest grasped the metal rail at the side of the casket, and wept uncontrollably. The sight of Paola lying there, frozen in time, unable to call his name or give him a kiss, dismembered his heart.

A middle-aged woman with short blond hair consoled Ernest and led him away from the casket. It was Paola's mother, who realized that this weeping stranger could only be Ernest. She felt he really did love and care for her daughter, after all. The grief stricken man whom she loathed from across the seas, simply because he was married, touched her. But, now, she loved him as if he were her son. They embraced each other and cried. The one thing they had in common was their love for Paola. Ernest handed her an envelope stuffed with enough money to cover funeral expenses, and she was speechless. Once the casket was interred into the earth, Ernest hastily departed the chapel grounds. Ernest returned to the motel and entered his room. He filled a glass with vodka and winced in pain as the liquor scorched his parched throat and ignited a fire in his chest. He tossed the glass on the floor, and gulped from the bottle as if it were juice. His vision blurred and he ambled over to the bed to lie down. Ernest miscalculated the distance from where he stood, to the bed, and collapsed on the floor in a drunken stupor where he remained for the night.

The incessant ringing of the telephone and the urgent, "rap, rap, rap" at the door, jolted Ernest awake. He stumbled over to the telephone in a disoriented fashion and answered it. The receptionist at the front desk advised him car service had been waiting outside for ten minutes to drive him to the airport. He dropped the telephone receiver and reached for the bottle of vodka. His cakey mouth covered the opened bottle and he drained the last remnants from it. He threw the bottle at the wall with miniscule energy and it bounced off and fell to the carpeted floor. Ernest tried to walk in a straight line but his coordination was off. He stumbled over his feet and fell to the ground with a loud "thud." He got to his feet and reached for his bags. Somehow, he made his way to the front desk and signed himself out of the seedy motel. The irate taxi driver honked impatiently. Ernest ambled out of the lobby and plopped into the rear seat of the car.

Ernest took his first class seat on the British Airways jet and remained aloof to the disapproving stares from flight attendants and passengers. His hair was matted and his clothes were smelly from having urinated on him self while he slept last night. He had no recollection of vomiting violently during the night, and his clothes were soiled from dried vomit. Overnight stubble crowded his smooth face and his pores reeked of alcohol. Ernest didn't bother brushing his teeth or washing his face before he left the motel and his stale breath was repulsive to everyone around him! He couldn't keep his bloodshot eyes open and drowsed off before take off. He snored obnoxiously for the duration of the flight and flight attendants decided it was in their best interest to let him sleep. The plane arrived in London one and half-hours later, and Ernest shuffled his way through the airport and waited for Jeffrey to pick him up. Two years passed since he had left England and he looked forward to seeing his little brother again. Ernest meandered clumsily to a newsstand to buy a cup of coffee when his eye caught a newspaper headline.

The caption read: "TNF founder, Mr. Lerwick, perished in an accidental fire at his home last night!" Ernest found the information he had just read mind-boggling. He tried to focus on the story and read on. Authorities speculated that Lerwick committed suicide in an attempt to avoid being jailed by the British authorities for misappropriating client funds. It was also reported that over 800 million pounds was pilfered from the foundation and this did not include real estate and other tangible assets. Investigators were having a difficult time apprehending officers of the company because most of them seemed to have disappeared off the face of the earth! Ernest smiled. He knew Lerwick wasn't dead. Lerwick would never commit suicide. All he did was execute his plan of escape. "Long Live Lerwick!" Ernest mumbled to himself. He recalled that he met Paola while in Geneva conducting business for Lerwick. Ernest hung his head and bit his lower lip until he tasted blood.

"I need a drink!" Ernest grumbled.

"Brother!" Jeffrey greeted Ernest at long last. He realized that Ernest was in distress and acted quickly.

"Hey…you don't look so good. Let me get you out of here!" Jeffrey declared.

"Nice to see you man." Ernest cried and hugged his brother. Jeffrey led his troubled brother out of the airport and ushered him into the car. He was anxious to find out what troubled his brother so.

"Ernest, what's wrong?" Jeffrey asked, and drove in the direction of his apartment. He had never seen Ernest so distraught.

"Paola is dead!" Ernest cried and put his hands to his face in anguish.

"My God! What happened?" Jeffrey asked. He was alarmed by the news.

Ernest recanted the heart-wrenching story of her untimely passing. He was grief stricken and could not believe she was gone forever. Ernest wished he could turn back the hands of time and relive the day they met. Paola was sunshine on a cloudy day. The sound of her voice and her vibrant aura always revved his engine. He loved her sense of humor, her sexuality, her selfless desire to please him. Ernest respected her loyalty to him when she had no reason to be loyal at all. Now, there was a void in his life that he had not felt in years. Ernest confided to Jeffrey his marriage to Corine was over and Jeffrey was saddened by the news. Jeffrey realized that Ernest was close to having an emotional breakdown, and took charge of his brother's care. At Jeffrey's insistence, Ernest brushed his teeth, showered, and ate a morsel of food. Jeffrey put Ernest to bed and encouraged him to get some sleep. While Ernest slept, Jeffrey removed all the liquor from the bar in the living room and hid it from Ernest. Jeffrey took the day off work to keep a watchful eye on his brother. He cooked dinner and hoped his two-year-old son, Omar, would lift Ernest's downtrodden spirits. Sisi and Omar would soon be home and Jeffrey didn't want them to see Ernest at his worse.

Sisi arrived home with Omar in her arms and greeted her husband with a kiss. She was impressed that Jeffrey prepared dinner ahead of time and seemed to have everything under control. Jeffrey advised Sisi that Ernest wasn't feeling well and may not be his usual upbeat self. Sisi made a mental note not to let Omar play with noisy toys that would certainly disturb his rest. Ernest awoke from his nap, thirsty for a drink. He made a beeline straight to the bar in the living room in search of liquor. Ernest was annoyed and suspicious when he realized the bar was stocked with nothing but soda pop.

"Ernest, what are you looking for?" Jeffrey yelled from the kitchen. He overheard Ernest fumbling around the bar in the livingroom.

"I need a ..." Ernest stopped in mid-sentence when his nephew, Omar, tottered into the room, eager to play.

"Omar! Come to Uncle Ernie!" Ernest exclaimed. He picked up the toddler and placed him on his shoulders.

Jeffrey hoped Omar would monopolize so much of Ernest's time that he would forget about booze. Ernest ran around the flat imitating a "Chu Chu" train, eliciting squeals of excitement from Omar. He spent the evening being a big kid, and Jeffrey felt compelled to laugh. Ernest doted on Omar. He fed him, bathed him, and read him a bedtime story. Sisi observed that Ernest was pale and at times wore a haggard expression on his handsome face. His rigid posture was now slightly bent. She sensed more was going on in Ernest's life than what Jeffrey chose to share with her. Sisi smiled as Ernest put Omar to bed. Ernest was exhausted and went to bed after Omar fell asleep. Jeffrey did the same while Sisi tidied the apartment. Sisi finished putting everything back in place and joined her husband in the bedroom, where she found him relaxing in bed.

"Jeffrey, your brother seems depressed. What's going on?" Sisi asked and lay next to Jeffrey.

"Oh, he'll be alright. Turn out the light." Jeffrey replied. He yawned deliberately in an effort to thwart Sisi's questions. Sisi ignored Jeffrey and pressed on.

"Jeffrey, I want to know what's wrong with Ernest!" Sisi insisted. Jeffrey exhaled an exasperated sigh and stretched his arms above his head. He confided Ernest's marital woes to Sisi, leaving out the part about Paola, whom she knew nothing about.

"Why didn't you tell me earlier?" Sisi complained in a betrayed voice.

"I didn't think my brother wanted his personal affairs publicized!" Jeffrey replied nonchalantly.

"So, now I'm the BBC?" Sisi huffed.

Jeffrey laughed. It wasn't his intention to offend her. "Sweetheart, I was just joking! Um...you smell delicious... can I have a taste?" Jeffrey whispered in Sisi's ear and lavished kisses on her neck.

"You like that?" Sisi asked breathlessly.

"Um...yes, what's that fragrance you're wearing?" Jeffrey asked in a throaty voice.

"I don't think the creator wants it publicized!" Sisi teased.

"Come on woman, tell me!" Jeffrey begged, and Sisi laughed.

Jeffrey removed Sisi's panties and kissed her stomach and her warm, chocolaty, thighs. Sisi surrendered to the feel of his cool tongue on her body and her heart raced in anticipation. She reached for the light and switched it off as Jeffrey immersed himself in her love. Sisi forgot to share the wonderful news she received today with her husband. A local chemist was willing to work with her to create a fragrance from Lady of the Night petals. But, the good news could wait until tomorrow. Sisi had no idea this flower would transform her life from that of a struggling fashion designer to one of fame and fortune.

Chapter Twenty

It was with a heavy heart that Ernest returned home to Barbados. Beulah was at the villa, sweeping the porches and airing out the cushions for the patio chairs. She greeted him with a warm smile. To Ernest, Beulah was a sight for sore eyes.

"Ernest, yuh get back?" (Ernest, you're back!") Beulah exclaimed. She was concerned about his sudden departure.

"Yes, I am! I'm happy to be back in the land of sunshine and turquoise seas!" Ernest stated in an exuberant manner. He tried not to chuckle at Beulah's Bajan dialect.

"Wait, boah, yuh doan luk too good! Wuh happen tuh yuh boosie?" ("Wait, you don't look too good! What's wrong?") Beulah asked. She stopped sweeping the porch and studied him intently. Beulah wanted to run her hands through his silky hair and massage his broad shoulders, but she realized how inappropriate that would be.

"Beulah, I just lost someone that was very special to me, and I'm having a tough time dealing with it." Ernest explained. Beulah sensed that Ernest was talking about a woman. She didn't want to pry, and offered words of support instead.

"Well, dem things does happen in life. Doan worry man, yuh gine be awrite. Uh gine mek sure dat muh Ernest awrite!" ("Well, those things happen in life. Don't worry, you'll be alright. I'll make sure that my Ernest is alright!") Beulah stated in a protective manner.

Ernest was touched by Beulah's emphatic words and nodded in agreement. They stared at each other for a long time, and Ernest couldn't peel his dark eyes away from Beulah's intense stare. Beulah clutched the broom handle to her chest and breathed deeply. Her bosom heaved, as if beckoning him to seek comfort there. She looked away in shame, and remembered who she was, and what her purpose was in this house. Beulah blinked her eyes and cleared her throat.

"Anyting yuh wan muh tuh get fuh yuh?" ("Is there anything I can get for you?") Beulah asked nervously. She hoped the treble in her voice wouldn't betray how she truly felt about him. It was a hot day, and perspiration trickled down her face.

"Gin and tonic." Ernest replied. His eyes smoldered like hot embers, igniting a passion in Beulah.

Beulah retreated into the house, swaying her hips. Her ass jerked when she walked, and Ernest was mesmerized by her rhythmic body, which seemed to walk to the beat of drum that only she could hear. He swallowed hard. This couldn't be happening. Here he was envisaging about Beulah again. He needed that drink!

Work became Ernest's other addiction, and he continued to toil at the hotel long after the administrative staff had gone for the day. He delved into his role as resort manager for

Wynter Haven with such zeal, that it became his obsession. Only Beulah knew how emotionally fragile he really was. Aside from his alcohol dependency, the hotel was a means of escape from the turmoil he was feeling inside. He mourned Paola's passing day and night, and hid his feelings well from family and friends. Evenings at home were spent enjoying Gezzy's chatter or reading business magazines. Other times he drove to one of the many beaches and stared at the vast sea that seemed to have no end. He watched the crimson sun disappear beneath the horizon until it was no longer able to soothe his wounded spirit. But, Paola, unlike the setting sun, would never rise again to brighten up his days.

Corine naturally assumed that her husband's melancholic demeanor was the result of their shattered consortium. His attitude gave her some satisfaction because it was proof that he was taking the reality of divorce seriously. At times when the lack of affection between the two of them was too much for her to bear, she reached out to him with a passionate kiss or a soothing touch. She wore revealing lingerie to entice and tempt him. Ernest responded by admiring her alluring silhouette beneath the flimsy fabrics, but that was as far as the seduction went. He was no longer interested in bedding his wife. Ernest wanted to be left alone.

Ernest frequented bars and lounges around the island because it was in these fun-loving places that he found commonality with other habitual drinkers. The atmosphere was always festive, and all were encouraged to eat, drink and be merry. When the merriment took control of Ernest, he slept in his vehicle until he was able to drive home. Oftentimes, that was not until eight or nine a.m., much to Corine's displeasure.

Months past, and Corine noticed negative changes in Ernest's personality. He took to brooding, and seemed frustrated. Ernest indulged in frequent mood swings and rejected Corine's attempts to keep the lines of communication open. Family dinner for three became family dinner for two as Ernest busied himself with other activities outside of Villa Coral. Corine voiced her concerns to the family and they tried to intervene, but, the more they pried, the more hostile his mood swings became. The family decided it was best to back off, and allow Ernest and Corine to work through their marital issues by themselves. The couple became engrossed in daily verbal attacks, and perpetual shouting matches. Corine was disillusioned by the constant arguing, and tried to focus on work, Gezzy, and her small network of friends.

A visit from Corine's parents to the island was cause for joy in the household. Their arrival at Villa Coral triggered a waterfall of tears from their daughter who hadn't seen them in three years. Her parents were thrilled to visit, and stay at Villa Coral with Corine and her family. Having never traveled outside of the U.K., the warm sunshine and picturesque beaches made them think of paradise. Corine took her parent's on informal tours, and introduced them to local cuisine prepared painstakingly by Beulah. Ernest introduced Corine's father to the bar scene where they indulged in rum cocktails and talked politics. Corine confided to her mother that her marriage to Ernest was in trouble because of his affair. She also expressed reservations at associating with Estele's dark family. Corine's mother understood the culture shock her daughter experienced at having to accept Estele's black ancestry. She advised her not to be overly concerned because Ernest looked white, and Gezebel was white. That's all that mattered. Her parent's month long vacation in Barbados came to an end and they promised to visit again.

Chapter Twenty-One

Life in the household of Villa Coral was mundane and tense. Gezebel was the only source of laughter and light-heartedness in the home. She was the reason Ernest returned home, and the reason Corine tolerated Ernest's absence at night, long after operations at the hotel had ceased for the day. Corine had finally had enough of the unpleasant side of married life. She was unhappy and emotionally defeated. It was time to accept the truth. Ernest was not going to put any effort into reviving their connubiality. She had done all that she could possibly do, and there was no point in delaying the inevitable. Corine filed for divorce in 1991 and it was finalized in 1992. She signed the divorce papers with a heavy heart and a ton of regret. Their marriage was officially over.

Villa Coral remained in the hands of the St. John family and Corine sought alternative living arrangements for herself and Gezzy. Ernest was generous in their divorce settlement and agreed to a five-figure payoff to conclude their twelve-year marriage. Corine enlisted the services of an architectural firm to design her dream home in the lush parish of St. Thomas. Architects designed a modern two-story house with lots of windows and a marbled foyer. The home had four bedrooms, three bathrooms, and pretty gardens. They moved into the

palatial house in 1993, and Corine welcomed a new life as a single woman.

She and Ernest shared custody of thirteen-year-old Gezzy, but Gezzy missed Villa Coral and her father. Villa Coral continued to be her favorite place because it was where they were once a family. Her new home was huge, and lacked the warmth and coziness of Villa Coral. Gezzy spent lots of time alone, while Corine busied herself climbing the career ladder and socializing. At times, Gezzy felt ignored, isolated and alone. There was no Beulah to make her laugh, no daddy to play with, only Corine, and he.

Clyde became an integral part of Corine's life after her divorce was finalized. Romance blossomed between the two, and he became a permanent fixture in the home after Corine moved in. Corine's prejudice against Estele and Estele's family was tolerated by Clyde because he didn't approve of interracial relationships. Corine no longer had to tolerate Estele's relatives if she didn't want to. She was no longer obligated to take Gezzy to visit them. Ernest could do that when Gezebel was in his care. What a relief it was! She confided these things to Clyde and he understood. Clyde couldn't fathom why Ernest would let a beautiful woman like Corine, go. He adored her with all his heart, but that was as far as the doting went. Clyde found Gezzy to be a rude and uncouth child. He constantly pressured Corine to discipline her, time and time again.

Clyde's presence in their lives proved an irritant to Gezzy. She loathed him. Clyde had a habit of ignoring her, and he treated her as though she didn't exist when Corine wasn't around. Gezzy complained to Corine and Corine accused her of making up stories. Corine's relationship with Gezzy disintegrated as months went by. Gezzy felt betrayed by Corine and no longer trusted her mother. Corine chastised Gezzy whenever Clyde bought an "issue" to Corine's attention, regardless of how minor the "issue" was. This angered Gezzy so much that she took to physically shoving her mother during these disciplinary sessions. A mean spirited monster reared its vile head in Gezebel, and aimed its need to destroy at Corine and Clyde. One such incident occurred in the home that changed the course of their lives forever…

Corine luxuriated in a few hours of extra sleep on Saturday mornings with Clyde by her side. Outside, the birds in the trees were chirping musicals that lulled her into dreaming of sunny days and cool ocean breezes. Gezzy was always the first to wake on Saturdays. The first thing she did on this particular Saturday was switch on her stereo to listen to rap music. Gezzy pumped up the volume just for the fun of it, and Clyde stormed out of the bedroom to have a word with the inconsiderate child.

"Can't you see we're trying to sleep?" Clyde yelled at Gezzy.

"No, how can I? I'm in here, and you were in there, remember?" Gezzy replied. She sucked her teeth and rolled her eyes.

"You know what? I've had just about enough of your nonsense! That stereo is coming out right now!" Clyde informed Gezzy in an impatient manner.

"You better leave my stuff alone!" Gezzy hollered in an agitated tone. Clyde angrily entered the room and unplugged the stereo. He carried the stereo and speakers out of the room and pelted the equipment out the front door!

"No! That's mine! My daddy got it for me!" Gezzy cried. The sound of glass and steel being shattered to pieces roused Corine out of her sleep. She rushed out of the bedroom and demanded an explanation from Clyde.

"Clyde, what have you done?" Corine shouted.

"i've had enough Corine! I asked her to turn the music down, and she insulted me! I threw that piece of junk out the door where it belongs!" Clyde curtly informed Corine.

"What? You had no right to throw it out. It was a gift from her father!" Corine admonished Clyde in a shrill voice.

"Well, Ernest has deep pockets. I'm sure he can buy her another!" Clyde responded nonchalantly. Gezzy flew into a violent rage and shoved Corine in the chest.

"Mummy, tell him to get out! Look what he did to my stereo!" Gezzy pleaded with Corine. Corine stood with a blank expression on her face while Gezzy cried.

"I hate you Corine! I hate your guts!" Gezzy screamed and ran back to her room.

Gezzy picked up the phone and called Ernest. Ernest answered, but could barely understand what his daughter was trying to communicate because her words were confounded with tears and sobs. Ernest hung up and immediately drove to Corine's house to see about his little girl.

"You shouldn't have done this, Clyde! Why didn't you wake me?" Corine asked.

"I didn't want to disturb your rest! Gezzy doesn't rule this house!" Clyde stated vehemently.

"You're too hard on her and now she hates me! She has never hated me before!" Corine cried.

"Well, if I were you, I would stop crying! It's high time some-one teach her black ass a lesson!" Clyde replied with aversion. Corine was incensed by Clyde's brutal words. She stared at him with apathy and her body shook. She was at a loss for words. Ernest arrived to find the stereo broken into pieces at the bottom of the steps. He rang the doorbell and Clyde answered.

"Where's Gezzy?" Ernest demanded.

"In her room!" Clyde replied and fidgeted from one foot to the other. Ernest marched into the home and brushed past Clyde. Clyde was no match for 6 foot 3 Ernest, and he moved aside to let him in. Ernest stormed through the house, and bee lined to Gezzy's room where he found Corine knocking on the door, begging her to come out.

"What's going on, Corine?" Ernest asked in a testy voice.

"Clyde and Gezzy had a disagreement!" Corine replied nervously.

"And?" Ernest pressed her to continue.

"And, he threw her stereo out!" Corine responded with her head down. Ernest looked at her in disgust, and attempted to coax Gezzy out of the room.

"Gezzy, its daddy. Pack an overnight bag and come on out." Ernest pleaded with his child.

"Ok, daddy." Gezzy tearfully replied. Ernest angrily made his way toward Clyde and found him standing by the front door. Clyde looked at Ernest with fear in his eyes. He was suddenly ashamed of what he had done, and didn't want to have a physical altercation with Ernest.

"Clyde, my daughter's emotional well being is paramount to me! That stereo was worth five hundred dollars and I expect to get every penny back! Is that understood?" Ernest spoke in measured tones.

"Yeah, i'll pay for it. Man… I lost my temper! You know how kids can make you do that." Clyde replied in a tight voice as he attempted to establish camaraderie with Ernest.

"i'll be back tomorrow for my money!" Ernest advised Clyde in a haughty tone.

"Daddy!" Gezzy ran to her father and jumped in his arms.

"Are you ready?" Ernest asked her.

"Yes Daddy, and I don't want to come back to this stupid house!" Gezzy replied.

"Gezzy, please don't say that, this is your home. You live here." Corine begged, and wrung her hands together.

"I don't want to live with you, and that foolish man!" Gezzy uttered those words with such conviction, Corine was taken aback.

"Gezzy…" Corine stammered.

"Let's go!" Ernest stated and they left the house.

They drove away from the house that Saturday morning, and Gezzy had no intention of going back. She thought about how much she hated Clyde. She knew that Clyde didn't like her and she didn't like him. Her mother had changed so much since she started dating him. It was because of Clyde that she spent so much time alone at the house. It was because of him that Corine no longer spent quality time with her. She was happy to be away from that place.

Ernest drove a reluctant Gezzy back to Corine's the following afternoon. Gezzy arrived at her mother's doorstep in a rebellious frame of mind. Clyde handed Ernest five hundred dollars to replace the stereo, and Ernest snatched the money out of his hands. The afternoon passed quietly and uneventfully. Gezzy ate dinner and entertained her self in her room. Corine tried to spend time with Gezzy, but Gezzy was having more fun playing with her dolls, so Corine left her alone. Corine was concerned about Gezzy's aloof disposition and cold eyes. No amount of coaxing or warm hugs could alter Gezzy's detached emotional state. Corine could not chisel through the wall of emotional fortitude her spirited thirteen-year-old had encased herself in. Exasperated, and at a loss of understanding over the change in her daughter, Corine insisted that Clyde apologize to Gezzy. She also insisted that Clyde cease all attempts to discipline the child because his tactics proved more harmful than beneficial. He was advised to do as she asked or pack. Clyde argued over having to apologize, but Corine refused to let him off the hook, and he finally relented. He grit his teeth, and clenched his fist, trying hard to contain his frustration as he stood outside Gezzy's bedroom door. Clyde was peeved by Corine's ultimatum. He plastered a fake smile on his face and knocked on the door.

"Yes?" Gezzy asked sweetly.

"Gezzy, its Clyde. I want to talk to you." Clyde stated.

"About what?" Gezzy asked sarcastically. Clyde clenched his teeth, and tried hard not to let his temper get the best of him.

"I want to apologize for what happened." Clyde pressed on, this time softening the tone of his voice hoping that she would let her guard down.

"Come in." Gezzy answered sweetly. Clyde hesitated. He was suddenly gripped by a sense of trepidation, but couldn't figure out why. He pushed the feeling aside and entered the room.

Gezebel sat in bed braiding her silky hair. Clyde hated the fact that Gezzy was so beautiful. Even though Gezzy's great grandmother was black as dirt, Gezzy, as far as the eye could see, was white. But, he knew better. He thought Gezzy was a stuck up little witch, and all he wanted to do was take a belt to her behind and run her out of the house. This way, he and Corine could start their own white family. Clyde sat on the edge of Gezzy's bed, and looked into her reproachful gray eyes that were fringed with the longest, darkest lashes he had ever seen. Her eyebrows were naturally arched, giving her face a poised, porcelain look. Her pouty lips boasted natural color. Gezzy was arrogant like her father, and entitled to the finer things in life, simply because she was a St. John. There was an old joke among those who knew of the St. John's family, and it went like this. *"If you ever want to know what old money smells like, just sidle up to a member of the St. John clan!"* Gezzy's presence was a daily reminder to Clyde that his family history was not quite so impressive. In fact his descendents were poor white servants.

"Gezebel, I'm sorry about the stereo. I don't want to argue with you or get you in trouble with Corine. All I ask is that you do what I say at all times, and your living experience here would be so much better. Also, keep in mind that your father has no control over what happens in this house! Is that clear?" Clyde informed Gezzy, and waited for her affirmation.

Gezebel's radiant complexion turned deathly pale. Her steely eyes changed to an ugly tint that seemed devoid of color. Gezebel leapt out of bed and faced Clyde with defiance. Clyde was confused by her actions and had no idea what she was up to. Suddenly, he felt something wet and slimy on his face, and in his eyes. Clyde was horrified! Gezebel had spat in his face repeatedly! He jumped up, seized her shoulders and shoved her aside. Gezebel screamed for help, and ran to the dresser! She picked up a wooden hairbrush, and hurled it at Clyde, knocking him in the forehead! Corine heard the racket coming from Gezebel's room and ran from the kitchen to see what was going on. The spit in Clyde's eyes clouded his vision and he wiped the stinking mess off his face. He rubbed his forehead where the hairbrush landed and was angered by the bump that started to form. While Clyde was engrossed in wiping his face, Gezebel crept under her bed and remained quiet. Clyde walked around the bed while Gezebel pinpointed his position by watching his feet. He stood right in front of her face, and shouted for her to come out of her hiding place! Gezebel crawled out on the opposite side from where Clyde stood, and picked up a chair. She hoisted it in the air. Gezebel waited stealthily for him to sense her presence behind him, and when he turned around, she hurled the chair at him, hitting him in the face, and breaking his nose! Clyde chased a screaming Gezebel around the room with a fury! He grabbed her by the arm and Gezebel sank her teeth into his hand! Clyde winced and slapped Gezebel's face with such force that she fell to the floor screaming for Corine!

Corine made it to Gezzy's bedroom, and Gezebel rushed into her mother's arms. Corine was aghast at the red welts on her daughter's face. Animosity for Clyde brewed inside her like a cup of percolating coffee.

"He hit me for no reason! He said he was going to kill all of us, including daddy, and then he was going to burn the house down!" Gezebel lied.

"You blasted liar! You little liar! Corine, she spat on me, threw a hairbrush at me, and hit me with a chair! Can't you see my nose is bleeding?" Clyde defended himself.

"Get out! Get out!" Corine wailed at Clyde.

"Corine, please, she's a liar!" Clyde pleaded.

Gezebel wrenched free from Corine, and bolted into the kitchen. She called Ernest and repeated the same story about Clyde. Like a superhero, Ernest was on the road in less than five minutes to save his daughter from Clyde, the villain! He placed a call to his father, Daddy St. John, who notified police. Daddy St. John briefed Estele about the drama at Corine's and hurried out, leaving her behind. Estele contacted Bella who immediately left her estate to pick her mother up. Together, they made haste to Corine's.

Corine's household was a beehive of activity. The police were the first to arrive on the scene and questioned Gezebel about the incident and the welts to her face. Ernest arrived and rushed at Clyde, punching him squarely in the jaw, only to be tackled by police who succeeded in breaking up the fight. Daddy St. John arrived soon after, and was furious at the sight of red welts on his granddaughter's face. Ernest insisted on having Clyde arrested for striking his daughter, and for making threats! Due to Gezebel's harrowing account of her ordeal at the hands of Clyde, he was hauled away in hand-cuffs to spend the night in jail! The squad car darted off in the direction of the precinct by the time Bella and Estele arrived on the scene.

"Corine, how could you let this happen?" Bella asked accusingly.

"I didn't let anything happen! I asked Clyde to apologize for throwing out the stereo. I wanted them to make up. I'm just as shocked as you are! I never expected something like this to happen!" Corine replied defensively.

"When do you intend to take Gezebel to the hospital? Look at her face!" Estele uttered in a stern voice. Corine was taken aback by the severity of angst in Estele's voice and the expression of disdain on her face. Estele was always the mild mannered one in the family, the reasonable one, the one who forgave all ills committed by the people she loved. Corine felt vulnerable, like a child being reprimanded. She was rebuked to tears.

"I'm sorry." Corine cried helplessly.

"Stop that foolish crying woman, and take Gezebel to the hospital!" Daddy St. John yelled in a gruff impetuous voice.

"Corine, I don't think you're in any position to take care of this child. It's best that Gezebel lives with me from now on." Ernest stated decisively.

"Like bloody hell Ernest! You're not taking her away from me!" Corine snarled.

"And who's going to stop me?" Ernest asked defiantly.

"I don't want to live here! You can stay with ugly Clyde, and i'll live with my father!" Gezebel spoke up.

"What? Gezzy, I'm your mother. You belong with me." Corine tearfully beseeched her daughter.

"No!" Gezebel shouted her refusal.

"i'll take Gezzy to the car." Daddy St. John announced. He was obviously irked by the entire situation.

"Ernest, you're in no position to care for her! You don't cook, you don't clean, you're hardly home… and you probably have lots women going in and out of the house!" Corine responded accusingly.

"Corine, you never did any of those things either, while living at Villa Coral. For your information, the only woman coming in and out of my house is Beulah!" Ernest replied stoicly.

"Beulah?" Corine shrieked with scorn. "All she's good for is teaching my daughter how to mop floors and cook grub! I'm really gutted that you would suggest something that absurd! Beulah will never raise my child!" Corine stated firmly.

"Well, by the looks of things, she'll probably do a better job than you!" Estele lashed out. Her words scorched Corine's pride like a hot iron branding soft skin. "Corine, I'm so deeply disappointed in you. You allowed this man to hurt your child and make her life miserable! Are you that desperate for a man? Look at you! Look at what you've become! You don't take care of yourself the way you used to! You've become a different person! Are you going to sacrifice Gezzy's happiness for a roll in the hay? You're a lousy mother, and a disgrace to our family!" Estele remarked icily.

Corine flinched at the verbal beating she received from Estele and hung her head in shame. She cried openly because the sting of those words was almost too much for her to bear. Estele was right. She did allow Clyde to wield too much control in the house, and now Gezzy was hurt. How could she win back her daughter's trust? Corine wanted to lay her head on Estele's lap and beg her forgiveness. She now understood why Estele was the matriarch of this family. She was a strong, determined woman. To be shamed by Estele was a rarity, and when it happened, it was well deserved.

"Look, why not let Gezebel live with me? I have lots of room and she'll be well taken care of." Bella offered and winked at Ernest. "Corine, you need time to get your house in order and Gezebel doesn't want to be here anyway. If she lives with me, you and Ernest wouldn't have to fight about whom she lives with. I'll be the neutral party. The two of you can work out visitation, but Gezebel will reside with me. Corine, I think this arrangement is for the best. You don't want my niece getting slapped around by your man again, do you?" Bella stated nastily.

Corine ignored Bella, but weighed the impact of her words. A chill ran down her spine. It frightened her to think what the consequences would be if Clyde ever raised his hand to Gezebel again. Bella manipulative efforts worked. She superimposed the practicality of her solution at a time when Corine was outnumbered, and vulnerable.

"Well?" Ernest shouted at Corine.

"Bella, i'll agree to it for now, but, I expect to see my child whenever I want! Is that understood?" Corine stated. She struggled to regain footing on the shifting Teutonic plates in her personal life.

"You're in no position to make demands or requests. You'll spend time with Gezebel when Bella says it's appropriate for you to do so!" Estele interjected harshly. Corine flinched.

"I promise to be fair, Corine. It's not my intention to keep you and Gezzy apart." Bella stated in a kinder tone.

"Good, then it's all settled, from now on, Gezzy lives with Bella." Estele reiterated.

"I can't ask for a better remedy to this volatile situation." Ernest responded. Corine dabbed her eyes with tissues, and vacated the house with the St. Johns to get medical treatment for Gezebel.

Estele was seated next to Deighton as he maneuvered the Mercedes on the winding roads on the way to the hospital.

"I hope Gezzy's jaw isn't broken. If it is, Clyde will pay in more ways than one!" Deighton quipped angrily.

"The nerve of that man!" Estele huffed and shook her head.

"He's lucky Ernest didn't take a cutlass to his head! Good thing my boy called me, otherwise there's no telling what he would have done to that bastard!" Deighton stated to his startled wife.

"I noticed something about Corine." Estele remarked.

"What's that?" Deighton asked in a reckless fashion.

"She's pregnant and I don't think she's aware of it!" Estele mused.

"All the better to get my grandchild out of there! She'll never live in that house again!" Deighton ascertained.

"Praise the Lord!" Estele agreed, and clapped her hands above her head for emphasis.

Chapter Twenty - Two

B ella's estate was situated on an acre of land in the vast Barbados countryside. Nestled on this land was a sprawling five bed room, four bath, Victorian house. The two storied home rested comfortably on nine hundred square feet of land with an attached two-car garage. Its main level contained a home office, laundry, living and dining areas. French doors in the gourmet kitchen revealed expansive grounds in the rear of the home. On the grounds of the estate, Bella had a pool built with showers and changing rooms. The upper floor of the home maintained four bedrooms with walk in closets, and adjoining baths. Hardwood floors, imported rugs, and local artwork added a quiet sophistication to the home. There was contemporary, chic furniture throughout the house, and crystal vases accentuated the beauty of fresh picked flowers from the gardens.

Daddy St. John, (Deighton) insisted on erecting security gates around the property to ensure her safety and security. In the evenings, Bella relished sitting on the porch at the rear of her home admiring the golden sunset and all that she owned. An elegant replica of the main house was erected on the estate with identical spindle work and lacy ornamental detail that was used for the main house. This was reserved as a guesthouse. Estele cultivated lush gardens around Bella's home to foster a sense of tranquility around the estate. She planted sugar pink begonias, desert roses, red hibiscus and yellow orchids. Palm trees and pinkish beefsteak shaped heliconias were hauled in and replanted beautifully around the property. Bella's love for animals drove her to have a mini farmhouse constructed on the grounds. The farmhouse was home to birds, ducks and rabbits, which were kept as pets. The pets were given free reign over the property during the day and locked in the farmhouse at night.

Ground provisions such as sweet potato, carrots, yams, and breadfruit thrived on the land. Sugar apple, avocado, and fig trees sprung from the fertile grounds. When the produce was "in season," it was harvested and sold in local markets. Bella was not above digging in dirt with tools to unearth wild yams or sweet potatoes, and she expressed joy at doing so. Bella created a lively atmosphere outside the estate and a serene atmosphere inside the home. The estate was her private retreat from the demands of the family business. It was here that she could literally let her hair down, and tramp around barefoot, appreciating country life. She looked forward to coming home after her grueling days as CFO of St. John's Real Estate and Business Services had come to an end.

Bella developed an intimate friendship with a local country man in the area named Dwight. His family lived in the community for three generations, and he earned a living manicuring lawns and performing odd jobs. He worked steadily for Bella maintaining lawns, gardens, overseeing crops, and conducting repairs around the property. He was Bella's personal handy man, and she admired his work ethic. In the beginning, Dwight was just another worker on Bella's payroll and she treated him as such. With skin the color of the blackest blue, teeth as white as snow, and a winning smile, Dwight's

talent as a highly skilled worker never ceased to amaze her. Dwight wasn't book smart, but he was assertive and wise. He was a highly intelligent being that learned all he knew from his elders. There was nothing refined about Dwight. He was a rugged, weather beaten man with large callused hands who preferred to work outdoors. Bella grew to depend on Dwight and he became an indispensable part of her life as their business relationship evolved into friendship and love.

The sun was mercilessly hot, and beat down on Dwight like a torrential downpour. He spent most of the morning and early afternoon hammering, painting, and working on the farmhouse. Perspiration rolled down his black face and trickled down his beefy chest. Bella called him to join her inside for homemade lemonade and roti. At first, Dwight was hesitant to join Bella because she never invited him to lunch in the three years he had been working for her. He assumed something needed repairing inside the home, and entered through the French doors of the kitchen.

"Dwight, let's have lunch." Bella stated. She was pretty in a flowery summer dress that showed off bowlegs with shapely calves.

"Lunch? I thought you had a job for me. So, what's on the menu?" Dwight asked.

"Chicken-roti and lemonade." Bella replied and laughed.

"Umm... I didn't know you could cook! Smells good and looks real good too!" Dwight drawled.

He was referring to Bella in the latter half of his response. She sauntered past him to retrieve the lemonade from the refrigerator, and the scent of her perfume aroused his senses. Dwight had always fantasized about holding this bow-legged, mixed raced woman in his arms. Feeling inadequate and totally out of her league, he dismissed the notion of something like that ever happening. He was the handyman, fit for nothing but yard work. The two of them sat at the kitchen table and ate heartily. Bella enjoyed Dwight's companionship immensely, and studied the dark complexioned man that sat across from her. Dwight's six foot stature, with a body seemingly built of bricks, was strong, strapping, and intimidating. His tightly coiled hair glistened from pomade, and she longed to run her fingers through it. Bella tried not to notice how his biceps curled into well-developed muscles every time he put the roti to his mouth and took a bite. Perspiration made his cotton shirt cling to his body, and her eyes roamed over his Pecs, down to his muscled abs. Bella shamefully looked away when Dwight caught her admiring his body-builder physique. He smiled boyishly at her.

"Sorry, I didn't mean to stare. It's just that you're so fit. Do you work out?" Bella asked innocently.

"No, not really. I get lots of exercise from my day to day work. Bella, there's no harm in looking. It's about time you noticed me." Dwight replied.

"Excuse me?" Bella responded. Her eyelashes fluttered in feigned astonishment. Dwight chuckled.

"i've been wondering if and when you were ever going to say anything more to me, other than. "When can you start this project? Or here's your check!" Dwight joked.

"It was just business. I know, I know, you've been working here a long time and our relationship should've been more relaxed. That's why I switched gears and invited you to lunch. This way I can get to know you a little better." Bella explained sheepishly.

"Well, what do you want to know pretty lady? My life is an open book." Dwight offered.

The more they talked, the more Bella liked what she heard. Dwight lived with his elderly mother in a quaint chattel house about a fifteen-minute walk from where Bella lived. His father was deceased and he had two older sisters, with homes of their own. Dwight was thirty-six, one year shy of Bella. He dated occasionally, and had a twelve-year-old son from a previous relationship. Bella confided in Dwight that she dated occasionally but her dates were infrequent because her parents were known for trying to arrange dates on her behalf. She resisted, and insisted that her love life was her business. Bella snickered when she recalled secret admirers that sent flowers and invitations for romantic getaways. She refused them all because she suspected her parents were the driving force behind most of them. Out of rebellion, Bella remained the spinster of the St. John clan, and relished the victory of defying them when it came to matters of the heart. Dwight was a good listener and Bella was comfortable baring her soul to him. They talked well into the afternoon until the sun went down.

"Dwight, it's already eight o'clock! I can't believe time flew by!" Bella exclaimed. She stood up and proceeded to clear the table.

"Whoa, it's that time already? I'll help you clean up." Dwight offered, and got out of the chair.

"No, that's ok. I have a dishwasher for that." Bella interjected.

"Yes, I know, and a housekeeper who comes in and cleans for you twice a week!" Dwight joked.

They laughed in unison at how well Dwight had come to know the inner workings of Bella's household. Bella stared into Dwight's charcoal eyes and he tipped her chin toward his lips with his hand. Dwight used his tongue to pry open her lips. Bella froze! She was uncertain of what was transpiring between them, but threw caution to the wind and returned his ardent kiss. Embers of passion that smoldered within her for years, begged to be released! He drew her close, and Bella felt his organ stiffen with excitement. Dwight massaged her firm buttocks, and wished her body would melt into his. The woman he desired her for so long was now in his grasp. Dwight unpinned Bella's hair and kissed her neck. He unbuttoned her summer dress and it fell softly to the floor. Dwight gasped at the sight of her rosy nipples, perched on her beautiful breasts. He kissed her stomach and thighs with his molten lava tongue. Dwight removed his clothes and stood naked in front of her. Bella gasped at his brawny physique and erect manhood. He picked her up with minimal effort, and whisked her up the stairs to the master bedroom. Dwight placed her on the comfy four poster bed and his thirsty eyes drank in her unveiled beauty. His fingers probed her moist insides and he parted her thighs. Dwight stroked her powerfully with his love. Bella was snagged in the throes of lust, and shuddered in his arms that night, and many other nights. He became her lover and companion for life.

Bella tested Dwight's honesty and loyalty by refusing to let him into her bed for weeks at a time without so much as an explanation. She left hundreds of dollars in conspicuous places to see if he would steal. Dwight was stupefied by Bella's apparent carelessness, scolded her, and returned every penny! She confided tidbits of information about important business deals to see if the information would be relayed to gossip columnists or local newspapers. Dwight passed all these check points with flying colors. Dwight didn't care about her money, family background or influence. He loved the astute businesswoman that loved country life, who sometimes worked side by side with him in the grounds to plant and reap.

Dwight was Bella's best kept secret. Privacy, in terms of personal relationships was of utmost importance. She guarded their relationship from watchful eyes and malicious lips. The happy twosome was scrutinized by acquaintances whenever they attended social functions, but Bella never felt obligated to explain her association with this attractive, yet uneducated man. Dwight felt special because he was romantically linked to Bella but he remained humble. He loved Bella. He respected Bella, and was comfortable being there to support her emotionally whenever she needed him to. They kept their relationship so private that family and friends became frustrated in their efforts to infiltrate and assess the mismatched pair. A year into the relationship, family and friends of the couple refrained from meddling. They were unwilling to subject themselves to anymore of Bella's and Dwight's insolent verbal expressions.

At Bella's insistence, Dwight moved in, and their commitment to each other was sealed. Bella wanted Dwight to be accessible to her at all times. He filled a void in her life that had been there for so long. She wanted him to embrace her in his strong arms, and kiss her with his warm, hot-chocolate lips, after a long day at the office. Two years passed, and Dwight placed an engagement ring on Bella's finger. He wanted her to be his wife, but the family business was her priority, and it was not yet where she wanted it to be financially. Bella's vision was to build a Wynter Haven Hotel franchise across the Caribbean. She wanted to marry Dwight, but that ceremony would just have to wait.

After the induction of Gezebel into Bella's household, life was once more sunny and bright for the fifteen-year-old. Bella wanted instant motherhood without the inconvenience of pregnancy, childbirth, and the constant care required by an infant. She didn't want these responsibilities to intrude on her busy lifestyle and interfere with her post as commander in chief for the family business. Gezebel's arrival was just what she needed to entertain and delight her. No diapers to change, no getting up at odd hours in night, no bottle-feeding and no wiping snotty nose either! Gezebel filled the motherless void in Bella's life. Bella enjoyed watching Gezebel play in the grounds, and making a mess in the kitchen when she tried to cook. She relished Gezebel's idle chatter about things that piqued her interest or amused her.

Gezebel befriended a girl in the neighborhood that was the same age. Joi, the daughter of successful attorney, resided with her parents less than a five minute walk from where Bella lived. Bella was familiar with the couple since their paths crossed at social functions or when conducting business. The girls became instant companions and formed a tight bond of friendship. They were so close; they could read each other's thoughts.

An amicable relationship was forged between Dwight and Gezebel after he resigned himself to the role of "friend" instead of officiating like a father figure. Attempts by him to parent Gezebel were resented by the child, and she responded to those attempts in the most disagreeable ways. Gezebel would laugh at him, ignore him, or sing loudly to drown out his voice. His complaints to Bella resulted in her encouraging him to brainstorm solutions for a win/win situation. She suggested he read up on child rearing techniques, and this baffled him. Bella handled the situation in much the same way she managed conflicts between employees of her father's company. He was curtly advised to find an amicable solution to solving his parenting issues with Gezebel. Bella refused to be a pawn in the power struggles that ensued between the two of them, and Dwight decided to leave the child rearing to Bella and the family. The three of them lived in peace and contentment in Bella's household.

Chapter Twenty-Three

In the coming weeks after the incident with Gezebel, Clyde's performance at work was heavily scrutinized. He became the target of a professional witch-hunt that culminated in job loss. Daddy St. John's hoodwinked connections in the business world bared their teeth, and Clyde was caught in a strangle hold. Clyde suspected his misfortunes were the handiwork of the St. John Clan, but he couldn't prove it. Ernest bought suit against him for assaulting his fifteen-year-old daughter and threatening to slay the entire family. Clyde's relationship with Corine suffered tremendous emotional strain, especially after Corine informed him that she was pregnant. Corine viewed her pregnancy as nothing short of a miracle since she never conceived for Ernest after having Gezebel. She decided to forge ahead with the newest addition to her family; after all, her financial portfolio was sound, and Clyde would get another job. But, his resources were being taxed in order to compensate attorneys for handling his case during this domestic crisis. Clyde believed that Corine's pregnancy was his only chance out of this legal mess. He persuaded Corine that should Ernest continue with the case, he would be ruined financially, and probably jailed. Corine agreed with Clyde and visited Bella at her Bridgetown office to plead Clyde's case.

Corine signed herself into the three storied building and rode the elevator to Bella's office on the upper floor. She waltzed pass Bella's secretary, and ignored her queries about who, what, and where she was going. Corine pushed open the door to Bella's spacious office, and found a surprised Bella sitting behind her polished desk reviewing a stack of papers.

"Bella, we need to talk!" Corine announced, as if it was the most natural thing in the world to enter Bella's office without being invited. She plopped herself into the empty chair opposite Bella's desk.

"We do?" Bella asked quizzically, and wondered why Corine didn't call to let her know she was stopping by. She had a meeting in the next thirty minutes and it was imperative she spot-check the documents on her desk in order to be properly prepared. She hoped Corine wasn't about to ask her to bring Gezzy back.

"Yes, we do!" Corine replied in an irritated voice.

Bella's beleaguered secretary buzzed her on the telephone and stated that Corine entered without permission. Bella hung up and pursed her lips. She sucked her teeth and saved the last entry into the computer database before riveting arrogant eyes on Corine. Now that Corine had Bella's full attention, she wasted no time getting to the point.

"Clyde and I are having problems because of this court case! Ever since this incident with Gezzy, he's experienced job loss and can't seem to get hired! Bella, I'm pregnant with Clyde's baby and I can't raise this child on my own! I won't! I met with Clyde's attorney before coming over here, and it's possible he could go to jail! Bella, I don't have the stomach for this! This situation is stressful and stress is not good for the baby!" Corine implored Bella anxiously and wrung her hands in an agitated manner.

"Ok, I agree with you! Stress is not good for the baby!" Bella reiterated icily.

"Bella, have a heart!" Corine yelled fervently but Bella remained silent. Frustrated in her attempts to score Bella's empathy, Corine quickly lost control.

"Do you want me to spell it out for you?" Corine yelled nastily, and a scowl surfaced her attractive face. Bella remained silent and stared at Corine with a blank expression. Corine, in fit of rage, got to her feet, and addressed Bella sternly.

"Alright! Perhaps its better this way so there can be no misunderstanding! I want you to tell Ernest to drop all charges against Clyde! You already have my daughter so locking him up would be an act of vengeance against me! The depression and stress heaped on me because the father of my child is left to rot in a stinking jail is enough to make me have a miscarriage! The St. John's wouldn't want the blood of my baby on their hands!" Corine promised.

Bella remained silent but the ferocity of Corine's words unnerved her. Pleased that she had finally cracked Bella's frozen demeanor, Corine whirled around with her nose in the air, and walked calmly out of Bella's office. She slammed the door on her way out and stopped at the secretary's desk for a little fun.

"Oh, excuse my manners! I'm the former Corine St. John, and I'm here to see Bella!" Corine stated sarcastically and laughed.

Bella sighed, and got to her feet. She felt old and tired as she walked to the window behind her desk, hating the fact that she was being coerced by Corine to have Ernest drop the case. What should she do? Corine would blame them all if she lost the baby due to being stressed over Clyde. Then what? Corine would be bitter and definitely fight to get Gezzy back. Bella gazed out the office window, and looked down at the busy street teeming with people and passing cars. Losing Gezzy was a chance she was not willing to take. Throwing Clyde in jail wasn't worth the trouble. Ernest would have to drop all charges. Bella walked over to her desk and sat on top of it. She called her parents and briefed them on the squalid details of Corine's visit. They agreed with Bella that it was in the family's best interest to drop the charges against Clyde immediately. Ernest eventually complied.

Gezebel's visitations with her mother were uneventful and calm. Clyde stayed out of her way whenever she spent the weekend or he went elsewhere. On those rare occasions when their eyes locked, he was rebuked with the most spiteful stare that he had ever witnessed in his life. In his opinion, Gezebel was the physical embodiment of the green-eyed monster!

Chapter Twenty-Four

Gezebel and Joi hopped into Joi's vehicle, and drove away from Bella's country estate into Bridgetown. They were on their way to join friends for lunch at a local eatery. The girls hadn't had time to talk about Gezebel's romantic escapade with a fitness trainer.

"Gezebel, Come on! Tell me what happened last night! I want details!" Joi pleaded with her friend.

"Alright, alright!" Gezebel responded. She was impatient to spill her guts to her best friend, but wanted to tease her first.

"Last night, Kendrick took me to the beach!" Gezebel stated and stifled a giggle.

"Yes, yes, and?" Joi asked with alacrity.

"The water felt so goood!" Gezebel responded playfully.

"Ok, ok, and? That's it? Come on!" Joi pleaded, and laughed hysterically. Gezebel doubled over in laughter at her friend's desperation to know more.

"Ok, ok! Yes, we did "the nasty" several times last night!" Gezebel boasted with a grin on her face. The girls high fived each other, and snickered all the way to the eatery, while Gezebel filled Joi's imagination with the intrinsic details of her sexual encounter with Kendrick.

They were seated at a table enjoying their food when Kendrick walked in, and spotted Gezebel with her sidekick, Joi. He tapped himself on the back for scoring with Gezebel. Gezebel was an eighteen-year old knockout that towered six feet, with long, jet black hair, and eyes fit for an ice princess. Kendrick lusted oved her gorgeous breasts, and tight, round buttocks. She was a stunning, intimidating beauty whose poise was often mistaken for snobbery. Kendrick observed other guys in the eatery casting hopeful looks at the girls, so he sauntered over to their table quickly. He wanted Gezebel to demonstrate her affection for him in public, for all to see.

"Gezzzy!" Kendrick drawled and gave her a kiss on the lips. "Joi, what's up?" Kendrick asked.

"Is that a trick question?" Joi teased, and Gezebel giggled.

Kendrick realized that Joi was informed of his tryst with Gezebel and was a little embarrassed. Why did girls have to tell each other everything?

"Kendrick, when can I visit you again? Gezebel asked and fluttered her eyelashes. Joi burst into laughter.

"Anytime you want!" Kendrick responded. These young ladies made him feel powerless and unsure of him self.

"I'm ready now!" Gezebel replied decisively and Joi guffawed.

"Now?" Kendrick asked. He was taken aback by her response.

"Yes, now!" Gezebel replied affirmatively.

Joi tried hard to stifle her hysterics but the laugh in her belly threatened to tear her lips apart. Kendrick was confused. He felt as though he were being ordered around and seduced at the same time. Was Gezebel serious? He looked at both girls, and then focused on Gezebel. She continued to eat in silence, waiting for him to respond. Gezebel sensed his bewilderment but managed to keep a straight face. She shoved the last forkful of shrimp salad into her mouth, and chewed like a contented cow in a green meadow.

"Ok, let's go!" Kendrick agreed. He wanted to appear as though he had some control over the situation, and walked out of the eatery. He waited for Gezebel outside.

Gezebel flung her handbag over her shoulder, and promised Joi she would call later. She ventured outside the eatery and found Kendrick seated on his perilous black and red motor bike. He motioned for her to get on, and handed her a helmet. They zoomed away from the eatery, and Kendrick was the envy of all the guys. Joi remained in the eatery mingling and drinking with friends. She caught up on the latest gossip to share with Gezebel later.

Kendrick rode to the impoverished neighborhood where he lived with his mother. He steered the noisy motorbike expertly through a maze of haphazard gaps and alleys. They passed sheets of galvanize some residents erected around their property for privacy. The crowded community was rammed with homes built too close together, and some of them rested on foundations created from various sized rocks, and concrete blocks. Gezebel even observed a public bathhouse, which was still utilized by some members of the community. Barebacked young men lounged on the steps of homes, playing dominoes, cards, or gambling. Some huddled in small groups and debated with each other over social issues. They halted their activities to gawk at the 'white girl' seated on Kendrick's motorcycle. The guys whistled their jealous approval, and jokingly threatened to steal her away. Some of the guy's belligerently wisecracked about Kendrick liking "milk in his coffee," and berated him publicly for being a sell out. Kendrick ignored the fellas, and steered the motorbike into a narrow, needlelike gap.

Two stray dogs ran after the motorbike, looking for something to eat. Kendrick referred to the strays, as "pot starvers." He explained to Gezebel, that the strays were too hungry to attack, so she had nothing to fear. Kendrick parked in front of a small gray house supported on a foundation of large stones. At the front of the house was a window on the right, and a window on the left. The front door separated the right window from the left window. This was where Gezebel spent a few hours with Kendrick last night. In the daylight, she noticed the exterior of the home was in desperate need of a paint job and minor repairs. But, at least, it was neat and clean. Kendrick put his arm through one of the open windows at the front of the house and unlatched the front door. He held it open for Gezebel, and she stepped in.

"Kendrick, dah's you?" ("Kendrick, is that you?") A woman's voice bellowed from somewhere in the home.

"Yeah, mummy, is me." ("Yes, mummy, it's me.") Kendrick responded.

"Wait, uh taut yuh wen wuk! Sumtin happen?" ("Wait, I thought you went to work. Is everything alright?") His mother asked worriedly.

"No, uh off today. Mummy, uh got somebodie fuh yuh tuh meet." ("No, I was off today. Mummy, I have someone for you to meet.") Kendrick informed his mother.

"Oh! Wuh yuh ain suh so?" Gimmuh a minute dey." ("Oh! Why didn't you say so? Give me a minute.") She replied.

Gezebel's eyes scanned the entire layout of the house in less than a minute. She stood in the living room furnished with a sofa and love seat. The upholstery had lost its rich color and the fabric was tattered. Kendrick's mother had tried to preserve the furniture by sewing some of the open patches with needle and thread. A newly purchased twenty five-inch television set modernized the ancient room, and gave those that lived in the house, hope for a better life. An archway guided her eyes to a compact dining room, which had an enormous dining table decorated with flowery, plastic tablemats. The dining table hoarded most of the space in the room and Gezebel couldn't help but wonder if the small house was built around it. Last night she had to suck in her stomach and squeeze around the table, in order to access Kendrick's room in the rear of the house. Gezebel glimpsed the faded picture of Jesus Christ on the wall partition in the dining room. He was eternally poised to reprimand all those that forgot to say grace before dinner. Kendrick's mother startled Gezebel by emerging through a make shift door built into another partition that separated her bedroom from the living room. She was a bulky figure with braided hair. Gezebel thought she was probably in her early-fifties. She walked with a stiff gait, as if her formidable bulk was a burden to carry. The woman took one look at Gezebel and smiled at the scent of money.

"Kendrick, wuh yuh dine tell muh yuh wuz brinin sech ah pretty girl ova?" ("Kendrick, why didn't you tell me you were bringing such a pretty girl over?") His mother exclaimed.

"Mummy, this is Gezebel." Kendrick stated with a sense of pride, and stuck his chest out like a rooster.

"Geze wha?" ("Geze what?") Kendrick's mother asked with her hands on her hips. Her eyes bulged from their sockets.

"Gezebel! It's spelled with a G instead of J." Gezebel explained, and giggled. Kendrick's mother burst into fits of laughter.

"Well, well, well! Uh taut uh did hear um all! Wuh anybodie would give ah beautiful gurl ah name like dat?" ("Well, well, well! I thought I heard it all! Why would anyone give a beautiful girl a name like that?") She stated jovially.

"Wuhloss! Looka dem eyes! Uh neva see nuhbodie wid eyes like dat in muh life! Yuh culd see muh doah?" ("Oh my goddness! Look at those eyes! I've never seen anyone with eyes like that! Can you see me?") She guffawed and peered closely into Gezebel's face. She relaxed her pudgy hands on jelly-like hips.

"Just call me Gezzy. Everyone else does." Gezebel suggested kindly.

"Awright den, uh gine call yuh Gezzy but de name Gezebel is mo sport!" ("Alright then, i'll call you Gezzy but the name Gezebel sounds like more fun!") Kendrick's mother laughed.

Kendrick's mother offered Gezebel a cola and Gezebel accepted it. She watched in amazement as his mother squeezed her considerable bulk through the small entryway that separated the living room from the dining room. She disappeared into the kitchen, and within a few moments called Kendrick to assist her.

"Kendrick, who dis gurl is? She's ah Bajan? She sweet fuh days doah!" ("Kendrick, who's this girl? Is she from Barbados? She's sweet!") His mother fired off a barrage of questions.

"She's a member at the fitness club where I work. She's cool!" Kendrick explained.

"Oh! Well, wuh bout Sharon? Miss Green's daughter from down de gap? Yuh ain had she fuh de pas year?" ("Oh! Well, what about Sharon? Miss Green's daughter? Haven't you been dating her for the past year?") Kendrick's mother asked.

"Man, She still dey!" ("She's still around!") Kendrick informed her.

"Well, lemmuh tell yuh dis! Dis gurl is high class! She famalie mussee got nuff, nuff, money an ting! Yuh ain see how propa she does talk? If dis gurl fancy you, fuhgit bout Sharon! All Sharon gine do is sik yuh wid chile! She caan do nuffin fuh we, atall, atall, atall! Stick wid dis wun an mebbee we cuh get new house wid indoor bath and toilet. Uh tired going out in de yard tuh bade, man!"

("Well, listen to me! This girl is high class! Her family must have a lot of money! See how proper she talks? If she fancies you, then forget about Sharon! Sharon will get pregnant and hold you back! She can't do anything to make our lives better!

Stick with this one, and maybe we could get a new house with indoor bath and toilet. I'm tired of going out in the yard to bathe!") Her words cracked like a cruel whip against his back.

"Mummy, how can you tell me to use her like this?" Kendrick berated his mother and shook his head.

"Wait, Kendrick, yuh like she fuh trute?" ("Kendrick, you really like this girl?") His mother asked in wonder.

"Let's just say… I can't refuse her!" Kendrick replied sheepishly.

"Den doan look at it as if yuh using she! Evabodie does help those dem love! Dah's all uh sayin! Uh wun steer yuh wrong an uh ain tellin yuh nuttin bad. Sumtimes people need a helpin han in life an we ain gine get anoda chance like dis! Yuh hear wuh ah telling yuh Kendrick?"

("Don't look at it as if you are using her! We help those we love! That's all I'm saying! I won't steer you wrong, and I'm not telling you anything bad. Sometimes people need a helping hand in life, and we'll never get another chance like this! Do you hear me, Kendrick?") His mother asked sternly.

"Yeah! I hear you loud and clear!" Kendrick snapped.

"Good!" She snapped back, and shoved two glasses of cola in his hands.

Kendrick returned to the living room and handed Gezebel her drink. She was grateful for the refreshing beverage because the humidity in the house was overbearing. The words of

Kendrick's mother resounded in his head and he started to wonder, if, in time, he could persuade Gezebel to provide things for him that seemed out of his reach. Even though he had a great body, a smooth toffee complexion, owned a motorcycle, and had a part-time gig, finding an outlet from poverty seemed impossible! What he wanted more than anything was to break out of the ghetto.

"Gezzy, it wuz nice tuh meet yuh. I gine in town an pay some bills so mek yuself at home an visit offen." ("Gezzy, it was nice to meet you. I'm going into town to pay bills so make your self at home, and visit often.") Kendrick's mother advised Gezebel. She hoped she made a good impression on the girl.

"Thank you." Gezebel replied, and watched with interest as his mother heaved her heavy body down the concrete steps.

"Kendrick, lock back!" (Kendrick, lock the door!") His mother yelled from outside the house.

Kendrick knew his mother purposely left so they could be alone. As soon as she was gone, Gezebel walked over to him, and kissed him. He led her to his confining bedroom, which was located through the dining room and opposite the kitchen. In the bedroom sat a twin-sized bed, a small dresser, and, thankfully a window, to let the breeze through. They wasted no time undressing each other. Kendrick remained standing, while Gezebel traced sexy kisses down his chest, to his navel, and lingered on his manhood. Kendrick moaned with pleasure. He lay back on the firm twin-sized bed and said to Gezebel. "Sit on me baby!" Gezebel complied and rocked his world with a ton of energy! Great sex and fun times were her goals in this association with Kendrick. They threw caution to the wind, and he satiated her body relentlessly with raw passion. Kendrick's mother successfully sowed the seeds of deception in his heart, and those seeds took root in his psyche. He enjoyed Gezebel with abandon, and envisioned a future paved with the finer things in life.

Chapter Twenty-Five

Kendrick and Gezebel soon became an item, and dated steadily that year. Kendrick was a hustler. Even though he worked at the gym part-time, he also dabbled in the sale of illegal narcotics. He was leading a double life. At work, he was a clean-cut fitness trainer that preached about the benefits of exercise and healthy eating. He promoted the doctrine of living a healthy lifestyle. But, when he was off the clock, he was a small time drug pusher. Gezebel heard the rumors about Kendrick's illicit activities, but they never talked about such things in each other's company. She didn't care what he did when they weren't together, so long as he kept her happy.

Gezebel and Joi graduated high school, but chose to remain in Barbados to study at the University. They bounced ideas off each other about owning a fashion boutique, and selling the trendiest gear on the island. Joi was blessed with creative talent while Gezebel inherited business smarts. Aunt Bella put her in charge of maintaining the household account, and she was responsible for paying the housekeeper, gardeners, and any one else that performed a service at the estate. This arrangement afforded Bella time to focus on a new business ventures she and Dwight wanted to embark upon.

Dwight built an impressive roster of clients that he had serviced over the years, and Bella thought it would be a good idea to capitalize on this solid customer base. He traveled abroad, and earned certificates in a variety of trades before returning to Barbados fully armed to run his first professional enterprise. Dwight saved a tidy sum of money, and purchased the heavy-duty equipment needed for professional work. He managed all this without financial help from Bella. The start up venture was run from Bella's home, and Bella advertised the business as one offering a variety of services such as landscaping, home repairs, painting, plumbing, and other blue-collar services. No job was too small. Dwight hired assistants to help with big jobs when requests for his services poured in. Bella was the brains behind the operation while Dwight managed the workload. D & B Professional Services was off to a rousing start. "D & B" was short for Dwight and Bella, of course!

During that summer, at the request of Bella, Gezebel reported to the family's business headquarters to perform various jobs within the company. Bella was grooming Gezebel to assist her and Ernest with running the company. Gezebel was invited to sit in on confidential meetings, and participate in business making decisions. While Gezebel groaned under the tutelage of her iron-fisted aunt, Joi toiled at her parents law office, running errands to the courts, and preparing litigation papers. When the girls were off duty, they relaxed at the beach, shopped, gossiped, and hung out with friends. They pored over fashion magazines, and made sure they were in sync with the latest trends in hair, make up and fashion. It was on one of these afternoons at the beach that Joi took the opportunity to share news with her friend.

"Gezebel, I have something to tell you and it might be upsetting." Joi stated meekly. She sat cross-legged on the gritty sand in a rum colored bikini, and gathered her long braids in a ponytail. Joi secured the ponytail in place with an elastic band, and stretched out her legs. She leaned back on her hands and turned her attention back her friend.

"What's up?" Gezebel asked in a concerned voice. She sat cross-legged on the sand, and leaned back on her hands.

"Yesterday, I overheard a conversation at the gym. It was about Kendrick." Joi stated cautiously. Gezebel furrowed her brow in anticipation of what Joi had to say. She drew her legs to her chin and hugged them. The breeze blew her hair away from her shoulders, and accentuated her high cheekbones. Her eyes reflected the turquoise hue of the Atlantic Ocean.

"Kendrick has been dealing drugs at the gym! That's why he's so damn popular!" Joi informed Gezebel in a dry tone.

Gezebel remained silent. This was definitely bad news and no doubt true, otherwise Joi never would have mentioned it. The idea of having to forfeit his sexual prowess put a damper on things, but her association with him could cause her family scandal and public embarrassment. Kendrick wasn't worth the risk. Aunt Bella would question her judgment, and hesitate to promote her within the company. Summer was coming to a close and she would use her studies at the university as a reason to break the relationship off.

"Joi, I'm going to miss his good loving!" Gezebel yelled playfully. They high-fived each other in a spirited fashion.

"I bet your skinny ass can't beat me to the water!" Joi quipped and challenged Gezebel to a race for the waves.

"Oh yeah, ms. Dimply butt? Try me!" Gezebel smirked and accepted the challenge.

They hastily got to their feet and made a mad dash for the water, when Gezebel doubled over and stumbled on the sand. Joi realized her friend was no longer running by her side and looked back. Gezebel sat on the sand with her knees drawn to her chest. She clutched her stomach and laid her forehead on her knees. Joi quickly forgot about the waves, and raced toward her friend.

"Are you alright?" Joi huffed. She was out of breath and alarmed at Gezebel's blotchy complexion.

"I don't know. Everything started to spin out of control and my stomach is queasy! Lately, i've been feeling dizzy!" Gezebel replied with her head down. She wanted to throw up.

"Are you ok?" Asked a man with a British/American accent.

Both girls looked up and peered into the blue eyes of a chestnut haired stranger that appeared to be in his late forties or early fifties. He assisted Joi with getting Gezebel to her feet.

"Uh, I don't know." Gezebel responded and continued to clutch her stomach.

"Help me get her to a chair." Joi pleaded with the stranger.

"Yes, of course!" The kind man replied.

They guided Gezebel to a beach chair so she could sit down. The stranger signaled a passing waiter for a glass of water.

"I saw you collapse moments ago. How do you feel?" The stranger asked.

"I feel better now. I don't know what came over me." Gezebel responded in a shaky voice and rubbed her forehead.

The waiter returned with a glass of water and Gezebel sipped it. The nausea subsided and the cool ocean breeze made her feel much better.

"My name's Jack Chagall. I'm a visitor to the island." The stranger introduced himself.

"Hi, I'm Joi, nice to meet you." She extended her hand out to him.

"What a pretty name!" He replied and shook her hand.

"I'm Gezebel."

"Did you say Jezebel?" Jack reiterated. He was astounded by what he heard.

"Yes. It's spelled with a "G" not "J." Gezebel replied. Jack laughed profusely! It was rare to meet someone with such a name!

"Are you a visitor to the island?" Mr. Chagall asked her.

"I live in Barbados." Gezebel responded. She took note of the twinkle in his eye and the dignified manner in which he spoke.

"I would like both of you to join me in the restaurant for a bite to eat. Perhaps a little nourishment will help you feel better." Mr. Chagall stated eagerly.

"Uh, I don't know." Gezebel started to refuse his invitation because she wasn't in the mood to socialize.

"Come on girl! I'm hungry!" Joi interjected. Her enthusiasm was contagious and Gezebel agreed to take Mr. Chagall up on his offer.

Gezebel was taken aback by Joi's willingness to give this stranger the time of day. Joi was always on guard for tourists out to have a good time with local girls. Maybe she sensed that Jack was different. Gezebel and Joi wolfed down fish cakes and fries while Jack captivated their interest with stories about his life as a self-made businessman of British descent. His home was in America, where he owned an adult entertainment company. He also owned an adult magazine which was a spinoff of his company. Mr. Chagall resided on the Upper East Side of Manhattan where he lived the life of a bachelor after his four-year marriage ended in divorce. Gezebel found Jack intriguing and attractive. He invited them to dinner the next evening, and they readily accepted. They soon parted company with Jack because Gezebel was ready to go home. As soon as they were in the car, Joi dialed the contact number he gave them. A housekeeper answered and informed her that Mr. Chagall was not available. Joi declined the housekeeper's invitation to leave a message but asked for the address. They were able to discern from the address provided, that Mr. Chagall was vacationing in a villa not too far from The Wynter Haven Resort. Villas in that area ranged from five hundred to a thousand dollars per night, and that was in U.S. dollars! Jack was no ordinary tourist!

Gezebel contacted Jack the next day and confirmed dinner plans. Joi cancelled at the last minute because her boyfriend demanded she spend the night with him. Gezebel prepared for an evening out on the town with Jack. She selected a black, backless, knee length dress and red heels. Diamond studs sparkled in her ears, and a matching bracelet complemented the ensemble. She spiral curled her hair, and tendrils danced sexily about her shoulders. Gezebel painted wine colored gloss on her lips, and smiled in the mirror at her reflection. She sailed downstairs, and fished the keys to Bella's Mercedes out of the drawer where she kept them. Gezebel waltzed out of the house looking like a million bucks, and sped away from the estate in anticipation of her dinner date.

When she arrived at the restaurant, Jack was already seated and waiting for her. He smiled his approval when Gezebel appeared and thought she looked more beautiful than he remembered. Jack accurately calculated her measurements at 36-24-36, and envisioned her alluring beauty splashed across the pages of fashion magazines. He was determined to win her over. Jack stood up, and planted a soft kiss on her cheek. He held out the chair for her to sit, and was impatient to learn more about her. He gazed into Gezebel's bright eyes, and was smitten by her lively personality as she rambled on about her life over a sumptuous seafood dinner and white wine. Jack felt like a lucky pirate who discovered a priceless jewel on a remote white washed beach.

After dinner, Gezebel joined Jack at the luxurious villa he rented for his two-week vacation. The housekeeper greeted them at the door, and Jack ushered Gezebel to the rear of the villa to show her the spectacular panoramic view of the sleepy sea. Gezebel was given a tour of the property, which housed a private tennis court, and a theater room with reclining leather seats. Afterwards, they lounged outside by the pool, and sipped champagne. Brightly lit private yachts and the twinkling lights of other marine vessels cast a kaleidoscope of color on the brimming sea. They gazed at the stars in the sky, and listened as soft waves returned to the shore just to whisper goodnight. Jack tore his eyes and ears away from the tranquility of the night, and admired lithe Gezebel as she lounged beside him.

"Gezebel, I have a proposition for you." Jack stated casually and looked up at the sky.

"A proposition?" Gezebel asked.

"I think you have what it takes to become a super model. I have contacts in the entertainment business and I can make it happen for you!" Jack stated.

"Me? A super model?" Gezebel quipped in disbelief.

"Yes, you! I know talent when I see it! I'll get you properly trained, and, in no time you'll be on the cover of top fashion and beauty magazines!" Jack stated in a hopeful manner.

"Me?" Gezebel asked again, and touched her thumb to her chest. She turned down offers to model on the local circuit but modeling on an international stage was entirely different.

"Gezebel, I have a confession to make. I had my eyes on you from the moment you arrived on the beach, and the opportunity presented itself when you fell." Jack confessed. Gezebel blushed.

"Jack, how do I know I can trust you?" She asked doubtfully.

"Well, you've been with me all evening and I haven't tried to seduce you! I'm a man of my word. Look, you can always research my company on the Internet." Jack advised her.

"That's true. Jack, I'm being trained to assist my aunt in running our family's real estate business. The business is expanding and she's spent her whole life working with my grandfather to build the company. I don't want to disappoint her." Gezebel somberly explained.

"My dear, don't you think your Aunt would've liked to follow some of her own dreams? Gezebel, don't live your life to please others, and don't let your beauty go to waste. Share it with the world!" Jack stated with emphasis.

He leaned over and cupped Gezebel's face in his hands and was smitten by her bewitching beauty. Jack touched his lips to hers and tasted the bittersweet champagne. He nibbled her lower lip enticingly and slipped his tongue into her mouth. Gezebel ran her fingers through his sparse chestnut hair and returned his kiss. She unbuttoned his shirt and unzipped his trousers. Jack stood up and removed his clothes. He wasn't built precociously like Kendrick, but he had a strong body. Gezebel kissed his receding hairline when he leaned over to taste her nipples. She found this older man amorous and appealing in every way. Jack took Gezebel's hands in his and she got to her feet. He slipped the dress off her body

and massaged her firm breasts with his lips. Jack reached for the bottle of wine and splashed it all over her feverish body. Gezebel moaned in delight as he licked the wine off her neck, her breasts, her stomach, and her thighs, before immersing himself in his wildest fantasies.

As usual, Gezebel met Joi at the gym for a vigorous work-out after a long day at the office. After her work out routine, she frolicked with Kendrick in the massage room where they satisfied each other's carnal desires. After her sessions with Kendrick, Gezebel drove home, packed an overnight bag, and spent her evenings with Jack. Kendrick was baffled by Gezebel's disappearing act after they frolicked with each other at the gym. She never answered her cell phone, and Joi remained tight assed over the issue. He convinced himself that no other man could compete with him for Gezebel's affections but remained mystified by her behavior. Kendrick's demands for an explanation from Gezebel were met with denials and insinuations that he was insecure and paranoid. Gezebel set the stage for an inevitable break up.

Jack visited the family's business headquarters in Bridgetown and Gezebel introduced him to Bella. Bella questioned Jack's interest in her niece since he was a visitor to the island, and, was significantly older than Gezebel. But, there was little she could do to stop them from seeing each other. Gezebel was eighteen and could date whomever she wanted. She didn't care about Bella's reservations, and Bella was grateful Ernest wasn't in the office to meet his daughter's latest fling! Jack showered Gezebel with expensive gifts and ritzy nights out on the town. Throughout it all, Gezebel experienced bouts of nausea, and realized it was time to visit the doctor.

Jack's extended stay in Barbados came to an end, and he begged Gezebel to accompany him back to the United States. She balked at the idea because they were just getting to know each other, and she wasn't ready to leave her family. Jack insisted Gezebel consider a career in modeling and she agreed to do so. They promised to keep in touch, and Gezebel was truly sad to see him go.

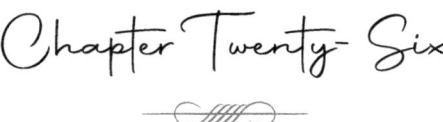

Chapter Twenty-Six

Gezebel drove away from the medical office building in her new SUV with Joi by her side. Her worst fears were confirmed. She was seven weeks pregnant! Her mind reeled from the reality of being a mother. Gezebel felt confused and afraid. Motherhood was something she never dreamed would happen so soon in her life. Kendrick was the father of her child.

"You need time to think about your options." Joi stated as they waited for the red light to turn green.

"Um, Hum." Gezebel murmured.

"When are you going to tell him?" Joi asked.

"Now!" Gezebel replied.

"Ok, let's do it! There's no time like the present!" Joi stated, and Gezebel sped away in the direction of Kendrick's house.

This was the first time Joi had ever visited the impoverished ghetto where Kendrick lived. Her eyes darted nervously around the neighborhood as she observed bare backed young men gambling and chatting with each other in gaps, and street corners. Gezebel tried to steer the SUV into the narrow gap where Kendrick lived, but it was too big. She resorted to parking on the side of the street in front of a pink chattel house. A dreadlocked woman that wore a red, gold, and green Rastafarian scarf around her head peeked out the window to see who was parked outside. She noticed the stylish young women exiting the shiny vehicle, and construed they must be visiting someone in the area. The dreadlocked woman poked her head out the window, and offered to keep an eye on the car for a small fee. Joi thanked the woman and gave her a ten-dollar bill. Gezebel led Joi by the hand through the winding gap until they reached the dilapidated gray house where Kendrick lived. One of the stray dogs she encountered on previous visits was resting under the shade of an ackee tree. The animal raised its head and wagged its tail to greet her.

"Shoot! I hope that mangy dog doesn't bite me! He might have rabies!" Joi stated apprehensively. She stepped carefully on jagged rocks bridging the pathway from the gap to the house. Joi prayed she wouldn't break her ankle and threaded precariously in platform shoes.

"Don't worry, he's harmless." Gezebel reassured her friend. The dog wandered lazily over to them and sniffed their ankles. The animal yawned and stretched its pot marked body before returning to the shade provided by the ackee tree.

"Okay, this is it!" Gezebel informed Joi and pointed to the gray house.

"You're not serious!" Joi exclaimed in an implausible manner.

"I told you he was piss poor!" Gezebel hissed.

"You weren't kidding!" Joi snapped. She stared at the huge slabs of rocks thrown together with chunks of concrete blocks that served as the foundation for the home.

Gezebel had already informed Kendrick she and Joi were on their way to his house. This was a good omen to Kendrick because it meant his relationship with Gezebel was back on track. His mother straightened up the house and anxiously waited for the girls to arrive. She was delighted that Gezebel was bringing a friend. She hadn't seen Gezebel in two weeks, and questioned her son about Gezebel's scarcity. The woman was so elated by the news of the impending visit she turned on the radio and danced a jig to calypso music.

"Kendrick, dis is it, muh boy! You gine mek dis ting wuk fuh we! We gine get outta hey an live in de parks and terraces!" (Kendrick, this is it, my boy! Make this relationship work so that we can get out of the ghetto and live in a fancy neighborhood!") She sang at the top of her lungs in a jubilant manner.

"Mummy, please don't embarrass me!" Kendrick pleaded. He wore denim cargo shorts, and walked around the house barebacked with a gold chain dangling around his neck. The chain was a gift from Gezebel two months prior. Gezebel rapped on the door, and bits of peeling paint flaked off and fell to the ground. Joi sneezed. Kendrick flexed his Pecs and contracted his abdominal muscles to impress Gezebel before opening the door.

"Hey, beautiful girl!" Kendrick drawled and kissed her lips.

"Joi, welcome to my humble abode!" Kendrick announced brightly. In his mind, he cursed his impecunious roots. His home life was a vast contradiction to the flashy image he portrayed at the fitness club, and it shed light on his desire to make easy money.

"Sit down and make yourself comfortable. Mummy, this is Gezebel's best friend, Joi." Kendrick stated graciously.

"She suh prettie! Wuh wunna does use pon wunna skin tuh mek um suh smood boah?" (She's so pretty! What do you girls use on your skin to make it flawless?") Kendrick's mother asked with envy.

"Uh…soap?" Joi answered sarcastically. The smell of poverty unnerved her and she looked down on Kendrick's mother for not being able to speak the Queen's English.

"Ohh!" Kendrick's mother replied slowly. Joi's blunt response made her feel foolish. She wanted to kick herself for being simple-minded, and not capable of speaking proper English. The woman quickly formed an opinion of Joi as a stuck up snob!

"Kendrick, this is not a social call. I have something important to share with you." Gezebel stated in a business like tone.

"Well, I hope its good news." Kendrick replied. He hoped she hadn't found out about his drug dealing activities at the gym.

"Dis soun like young people bizness, so lem muh guh lon!" ("i'll leave you young people to talk in private!") Kendrick's mother interjected. She delayed leaving the room by picking at lint on her shirt, hoping they would invite her to stay. Since no one encouraged her to stay, she squeezed past the dining table, and disappeared into the kitchen. She pressed her ear to the partition that sectioned off the kitchen from the dining room, and eavesdropped on the conversation in the living room.

"Ok, so what's up?" Kendrick asked staunchly.

"I'm six weeks pregnant with your child!" Gezebel replied coolly.

"What? Girl, you have the wrong man! Gezebel, we haven't been together long enough for you to get pregnant! That kind of stuff takes years to happen! And, what about the disappearing acts you've pulled? You might be pregnant, but it ain't mine!" Kendrick avowed and rejected the idea of a baby.

"The only man she was sleeping with six weeks ago was you!" Joi fumed at Kendrick.

"Look Kendrick, I'm not thrilled about this either! It not exactly an honor to carry your seed!" Gezebel quipped.

"Oh yeah? You seemed to like the honor of receiving it just fine! How come you don't answer my calls at night woman? I know you've been giving it up to someone else! Tell me who he is!" Kendrick yelled viciously and grabbed Gezebel by the arm!

"Get your hands off my friend!" Joi screamed at Kendrick. She balled her fists, prepared to pummel him at any moment!

"Shut up and mind your own business!" Kendrick hollered at Joi.

"Let me go!" Gezebel yelled and wrenched free from his grasp. "Don't put your hands on me!" She shouted in a defiant voice and shoved her forefinger in his face. Kendrick backed away. He put his hands up in the air with palms facing forward, furious with himself for acting like a jealous lover!

"Kendrick, what are your intentions as far as this child is concerned?" Gezebel demanded.

"Why don't you find the real father of your baby and ask him the same question!" Kendrick scoffed at her.

Gezebel was incensed! The grayish pupils of her eyes resembled the clouds of a category five hurricane! She lunged at him and clawed his face with her sharp nails! Kendrick grabbed her wrists and Joi jumped into the fray! She pummeled his muscled back with her small fists and Gezebel kicked him in the knee! Kendrick buckled in pain! Gezebel was about to knee him in the groin when his mother rushed into the living room and forced her sizeable bulk between them. She swung her backside forcefully against Kendrick's stomach and he stumbled backward from the powerful thrust. Kendrick's mother listened maliciously to the heated discussion and couldn't be happier!

"Stop dis fightin in muh house! All uh dis ain call fuh! Wuh happen wid wunna nuh? Uh leff wunna in hey good, good, good!" ("Stop fighting in my house! This is not necessary! What happened? When I left, you were all getting along!") Kendrick's mother lamented in mock ignorance.

"I'm pregnant and he's denying that this baby is his!" Gezebel informed his mother heatedly.

215

"Fuh trute? Yuh having muh granchile?" ("For real? Are you having my grandchild?") Kendrick's mother implored Gezebel and held her breath. Gezebel remained silent and refused to answer. Kendrick's mother pursed her lips and fixed smoldering eyes on her son.

"Kendrick, uh raise yuh betta dan dis! Yuh must tek care yuh responsibilities! She ain mek dis chile by sheself, yuhno!" ("Kendrick, I raised you better than this! You must take care of your responsibilities! She did not make this child by her self!") His mother admonished him and tried to be a voice of reason in the midst of drama!

"Mummy, uh ain got nuh money fuh nuh chile! You caan see how we living hey han tuh mout? A chile gine only keep muh back! She can do it alone! Afta all, she's de wun wid all de money! She famlie got hotel an ting!"

("Mummy, I don't have money to support a child! We're living paycheck to paycheck! A child will prevent me from getting what I want out of life. She can do it alone! After all, she's the one with money! Her family owns a hotel!") Kendrick shouted at his mother. He ran his fingers over his scratched face and his knee throbbed.

Gezebel was humiliated by his harsh words and punched him in the jaw! She winced in pain because her knuckles were bruised in the process.

"Ow!" Kendrick howled and balled his fists! He was determined to inflict a few blows of his own to Gezebel, but his mother stood protectively in front of her.

216

"Uh ain gine stan hey an leh yuh hit she! Yuh gine gaw com thru muh! She carryin muh granchile!" ("I will not stand here and let you hit her! You will have to come through me! She's carrying my grandchild!") Kendrick's mother stated in an alarmed voice and blocked him with her impressive bulk. Kendrick was outnumbered and defeated.

"You an yuh stinkin fren get outta dis house befo uh chop wunna up wid muh cutlass!" ("You and your stinking friend get out of this house before I chop you with my cutlass!") Kendrick hollered at Gezebel in a dreadful voice.

"Gezebel, leff he out! He ain nuh use! He jus like he ignant fada! Yuh culd cum hey anytime darlin! Doan mine he! He ain nuh good! He foolish an own way!"

("Gezebel, forget him! He's no use! He's just like his ignorant father! You are welcome here anytime darling! Don't listen to him! He's foolish and stubborn!) Kendrick's mother defied him.

"Gezebel, let's go!" Joi snapped in an irritated voice. She feared the situation would further deteriorate.

Gezebel kicked the rickety door open and marched down the steps. She stormed through the narrow gap leading to the opening on the side of the road with Joi in tow. The charismatic persona perpetuated by Kendrick was a smokescreen for the selfish user he really was! She unlocked the SUV with the remote car key, and they got in. The automatic seat belts secured them, and they zoomed away. The dreadlocked woman in the pink chattel house poked her head through the window, and opened her mouth in awe as the shiny vehicle made its way out of the ghetto. Clouds of dust and exhaust were stirred up when the SUV raced away at top speed. The dreadlocked woman coughed and sputtered from the polluted air.

Chapter Twenty-Seven

G ezebel sat in her room and mulled over the situation. She opted to refrain from frequenting the same places of entertainment Kendrick visited in order to avoid a public confrontation. Gezebel changed her cell number and refused to take his calls. She despised the shameless brute, and devised a plan to make him suffer. She solicited Joi's assistance in her plan of revenge. Joi's task was to seek information about Kendrick's drug selling activities at the gym. Gezebel planned to use that information against him. Her relationship with Kendrick was purely physical, and not once had she given any thought to what she would do, should she ever get pregnant. But, now that she was, Gezebel realized the thought of having a baby appealed to her.

Gezebel reclined on the comfy chaise in her bedroom, and looked out the window. She caressed her tummy and smiled about the new life forming inside her. Her thoughts settled on Aunt Bella. When Gezebel informed her about the pregnancy, Bella cried profusely. She pleaded with her not to go through with it because Kendrick was a broke, uneducated bastard! She couldn't fathom why her niece would sleep with such a low life when other promising young men pursued her. After an exhausting round of arguments, Bella had no choice but to accept Gezebel's decision to forge ahead with

the pregnancy. Bella agreed to support Gezebel, and that's what she intended to do.

The doorbell chimed and roused her out of her thoughts. Gezebel got up from the chaise and left the bedroom. She crept down the carpeted stairs and joined the others inside the family room. Bella summoned Corine, Ernest, Daddy St. John, and Estele to the estate in order to deliver the news about Gezebel's pregnancy. The group entered the family room, anxious about Bella's mysterious announcement. After everyone was accounted for, Dwight closed the door so the housekeeper couldn't eavesdrop on the discussion that was going to take place.

"I guess you want to know what this is all about." Bella stated hesitantly. She stood in the middle of the room wearing an oversized white shirt and black leggings. Worry lines invaded her brow overnight; a testament to how stressed she really was. She cleared her throat and continued. "Gezebel has important news to share, so i'll turn it over to her!" Bella announced as though she were conducting a business meeting. She moved aside so that everyone could focus on her niece.

"Well, I don't know how to start or where to start, but I must start." Gezebel started as she took her aunt's place in the middle of the room. Her words elicited jittery laughter from everyone, but Bella. She glanced nervously at their curious faces and wished Bella hadn't invited them all at once. These people meant more to her than anything in the world, and she was about to drop a bombshell.

"I have to get this off my chest so here goes! I'm seven weeks pregnant! The baby's father is Kendrick Sealy who lives in

Nelson Street! He's disowned the child and wants nothing to do with it! I know that this…" Gezebel's vocal chords were constricted by nervousness and her voice trembled with fear. She was interrupted by her father's angry outburst before she could finish!

"Have you lost your blasted mind girl? You're about to enter the university or have you forgotten that? I'm going to belt your little ass!" Ernest ranted in an infuriated manner. He stood up and proceeded to remove his belt!

"Don't you touch my niece! She wants this baby and I have given her my full support!" Bella yelled at Ernest. She stood in front of Gezebel, prepared to protect her from Ernest's fury.

"Oh, and you're going to stop me Bella? You need a belting too, for allowing something like this to happen!" Ernest lashed out at his sister.

"You better think long and hard about laying a finger on my woman!" Dwight addressed Ernest in a sinister tone.

"And what the hell are you going to do about it? By the way, what's your name again?" Ernest asked sarcastically. He thought Dwight was as gold-digger and was happy Bella had sense enough not to marry him. Dwight crossed his beefy arms against his chest and ignored Ernest.

"Bella, what kind of role model are you? I never should have trusted you with my child! She would've gotten better guidance from me instead of you! This must be some kind of sick joke!" Corine ranted. She wasn't going to miss the opportunity to throw a bucket of cold water in Bella's face!

"If you were an attentive mother, Gezebel wouldn't be living here in the first place!" Estele quipped and jumped to Bella's defense.

"Oh hush up, old woman!" Corine snapped at her.

"Shut your stupid mouth Corine! This is just as much your fault as it is Bella's!" The elderly Daddy St. John reprimanded Corine.

"My fault?" Bella asked! She was stunned at being blamed for Gezebel's transgressions.

"Damn right it's your fault! Look at the example you're setting Bella! You've been shacking up for years in this house with that hard foot, yard man!" Ernest yelled in disgust.

"I can do whatever I want in my house!" Bella hollered nastily.

"Ernest is right, Bella! You haven't set the best example for our child!" An embittered Corine interjected sourly.

"My God, Gezebel! You slept with a man from Nelson Street? That place is full of pimps, whores, drug dealers and hustlers! I'm going to belt you right now!" Ernest riled rabidly. He wrapped the buckle end of the belt around his hand and stormed toward Gezebel.

"Daddy, please! Don't!" Gezebel pleaded in a terrified voice. Ernest had never doled out corporal punishment before.

"Ernest, I'm warning you!" Bella shrieked. Gezebel hid behind her aunt.

"Just make sure you don't strike Bella in the process!" Dwight seethed at Ernest between clenched teeth.

"Get out of here man! You're not family!" Ernest shouted in disdain.

"Ernest, why don't you leave?" Bella shouted tersely.

"Son, put that damn belt away! Gezzy is pregnant!" Daddy St. John ordered Ernest. Estele hastily got up from the leather sofa and wrenched the belt away from her stupefied son. She flung the belt on the floor and addressed everyone in the room.

"The only person who needs belting is Corine!" Estele remarked bitterly.

"It's always my fault, isn't it?" Corine challenged Estele.

"Since you had that other child, Gezebel seems to be an afterthought in your scheme of things! Bella has loved and cared for Gezebel as if she were her own!" Estele denounced Corine.

"I resent every word, Estele! How could you say such horrid things? I may not be with Gezebel everyday, but I make lots of bloody time for my daughter!" Corine replied. She bristled with tears.

"Bella did an outstanding job raising Gezebel to be the young lady she is today. This is a set back for you, Gezebel, because we wanted you to attend the university. You probably won't enjoy college life much if you're tramping around campus barefoot and pregnant!" Estele spoke harshly to Gezebel.

Gezebel hung her head and averted her eyes from Estele's hard stare. The forgiving, indulgent, grandmother she knew and loved was transformed into an iron fisted, steely witch! Estele approached Gezebel and fixed a foreboding stare on her grand daughter. She appeared to be ten feet tall as she stood rigidly in front of Gezebel and looked right through her.

"I'm disappointed in you but i'll respect your decision! Be prepared to live with it for the rest of your life!" With that said, Estele raised her hand, and slapped Gezebel's face with such force that Gezebel lost her balance and crumpled to the floor. Bella rushed to Gezebel's side and consoled her.

"Get up Bella!" Estele hollered. She prodded Bella in the ribs with her shoe, forcing her to stand up. Bella recoiled in pain, and hurriedly got to her feet, fearful of inciting her mother's wrath. Her mother's fiery temper was legendary in the St. John household. Estele was the matriarch of the St. John clan, and she was about to decree how the family was going to handle the situation.

"Gezebel is pregnant and no amount of punishment will make it go away. What's done is done, and I suggest we prepare ourselves accordingly. I won't tolerate anyone stressing Gezebel about being pregnant, and I won't tolerate anyone in this family starting trouble with that loser from Nelson Street! This baby will get all it needs from us! Is that understood?" Estele asked.

Everyone in the room nodded in agreement. Estele extended her hand to Gezebel and helped her to her feet. Gezebel searched her grandmother's face for forgiveness, and was appeased when Estele's steely grain softened. The sweet grandmother reappeared and the old witch who slapped her was gone! Gezebel threw her arms around her grandmother and hugged her. Bella cried and hugged them both. Ernest retrieved his belt off the floor and secured it around his waist. Estele's word was as good as law. Hushed silence filled the room as three generations of St. John women stood in the center crying, in support of each other.

Chapter Twenty-Eight

Ernest drove back to Villa Coral after meeting with the family at Bella's estate. The news of Gezebel's pregnancy filled him with anxiety. His little angel was about to be an unwed mother. The father of the child? An irresponsible bum! Was Gezebel crazy or dumb? He parked his car under the mahogany tree close to the villa. Ernest sat in the car and watched fire flies reveal their hiding places by flashing specks of light in the darkness. Gezebel skipped down the front steps with her dark hair bouncing about her shoulders, impatient to greet him. Ernest beamed with pride as he opened the door of the vehicle, and stepped onto the pebbly drive. He was eager to lift her up in his arms and spin her around until she had a giddy head.

A male frog expressed his desire to find a mate and called to attract a female. The gurgling, throaty sound jolted Ernest from his fantasy, and he blinked his eyes. Gezebel was not there. The little girl who bounded down the steps to greet her daddy was gone forever! He sighed and held his face in his hands. He had no choice but to love the little bastard that was going to make him a grandfather. Ernest walked dejectedly up the steps and unlocked the door. The mouth-watering aroma of roast lamb and the "clink" of wares in the kitchen welcomed him. Beulah was busy preparing dinner. Ernest followed his nose into the kitchen and sneaked up behind Beulah. He put his arms around her waist and planted a kiss on her neck. Beulah was startled by Ernest's embrace because she didn't hear him come in.

"Ernest, yuh friten muh!" (Ernest, you scared me!") Beulah exclaimed with her eyes wide open. "Yuh doan luk too happy! Wuh happen wen yuh went by Bella?" (You don't look too happy! What happened at Bella's?) Beulah asked in a concerned voice.

"Beulah, this afternoon we were informed that Gezebel is pregnant and I guess I'm still in shock!" Ernest informed Beulah and proceeded to help her set the table.

"Pregnant?" Beulah blurted out. She put her hands to her mouth and her eyes bulged from the surprising news.

Ernest dished out rice and peas, and vegetables, into serving bowls and placed them on the table. He seated himself and waited for Beulah to join him.

"I caan balieve this!" ("I can't believe this!") Beulah cried out and seated herself.

Ernest slammed his fist on the table and the silverware rattled! Emotional pain and mental anguish distorted his handsome features. Beulah's heart went out to him! Over the years she had resorted to calling him "Ernie" whenever she wanted a favorable reaction out of him or whenever he needed to calm down. It usually worked.

"Ernie, doan be suh vex wid she! Gezebel is a good girl an uh help raise she from small. All uh we does mek mistakes! Uh know she let yuh down but doan fret! Be glad she ain went tuh nuh doctor tuh botch up she insides! Dese is tings tuh be tankful fuh! Relax, man. Gezzy gine mek it through dis, awright?"

("Ernie, don't be so upset with her! Gezebel's a good girl and I helped raise her. We all make mistakes! I know she let you down but don't worry! Be thankful she didn't go to an incompetent doctor to botch her body! These are things to be thankful for! Relax! Gezzy will make it through, alright?") Beulah reasoned and tried to calm him down.

Ernest took a bite of the roast lamb, and chewed thoughtfully. He savored the spicy seasonings Beulah marinated the tasty meat in.

"Wait, tell muh sumting doah, whose de chile fada?" ("So, who's the father of the child?") Beulah asked out of curiosity and sipped fruit punch.

"A punk from Nelson Street!" Ernest stated dryly.

"Wuh?" Beulah shouted and the glass fell from her hand onto the kitchen floor.

Ernest got up and wiped the spill with paper towels. He swept the broken glass into a dust pan and threw it into the trash. Ernest poured Beulah another glass of fruit punch before taking his seat at the table again.

"Yeah, that's the worst part!" Ernest stated in a gruff voice.

"Wuh wrong wid she? Nelson Street! Of all places? She musse mad entrute!" ("What's wrong with her? Nelson Street! Of all places? She must be crazy!") Beulah ascertained and sucked her teeth in annoyance.

"Don't let your food get cold." Ernest reminded Beulah to eat. Beulah sucked her teeth again. She was unable to come to terms with the information Ernest shared.

"The family has decided to support Gezebel's decision." Ernest informed Beulah coldly, and shoved a forkful of rice and peas into his mouth.

"Wuz dah boah?" ("And, what's that?") Beulah asked.

"Gezebel is going ahead with the pregnancy even though the low life from Nelson Street doesn't want any part of it!" Ernest added flatly.

Beulah resumed eating in silence. Gezebel being pregnant was one issue but she was worried about her association with a man from such a lurid part of the island.

"She head ain good! Dah's all uh culd suh!" ("She's crazy! That's all I can say!") Beulah replied adamantly and finished eating. The food was cold.

After dinner, Beulah followed Ernest to the master bedroom he once shared with Corine. She peeled off her clothes, and stepped into the shower wearing nothing but panties. Ernest entered the shower after Beulah, and watched as the warm water cascaded over her dark skin, and trickled between her ample breasts. He was aroused. Ernest worked the soap into a rich lather and washed Beulah's shoulders. He rolled the panties off her hips and massaged her generous backside with soapsuds. Beulah shampooed his wavy hair and lavished passionate kisses on his lips. Ernest drew her close, and was stirred by her breathlessness as he washed between her thighs. He gripped Beulah's ample derriere, and hoisted her plump legs around his hips. His rigid manhood sizzled inside her throbbing body and he fervently made love to her in the steamy bath. Beulah grabbed his shoulders, and Ernest guided her vulva over his engorged organ, until both of them reached that crescendo of sexual fulfillment.

Ernest remained awake while Beulah slept soundly in his arms. Never in a million years did he imagine that Beulah would be the love of his life. After his divorce from Corine, Beulah was there to pick up the pieces of his shattered existence. He talked candidly with her about his life in England and how he managed to secure a tidy fortune for himself. They were best friends and Ernest valued her companionship. She fulfilled her dream of becoming an R.N. and was employed at a local hospital. Ernest was so proud of her accomplishment. Their easygoing friendship blossomed into romance two years after his divorce. After many women had come and gone.

Ernest mellowed with age and proved himself a kind and generous man. He was an incredible lover. He encouraged Beulah to move in with him and she did. Her son was now in his teens and preferred to reside with Beulah's mother but visited Villa Coral on a regular basis. The arrangement worked beautifully. Beulah didn't care about networking with any of Ernest's influential friends because she was content to live in peace and harmony with the man of her dreams. At social events, Beulah felt out of place and incredibly shy. She was hesitant to speak at length in certain social circles because of her strong dialect, but Ernest chided her for being silly. The man she secretly desired when she worked in his household as a maid was finally hers. They looked forward to celebrating three years of happiness and love.

Chapter Twenty-Nine

As agreed, the St. John family supported Gezebel's pregnancy, and the thought of having a baby in the family drove them to feverish excitement. Gezebel was fussed over as though she was an invalid, especially now that she was fast approaching her due date. Her diet was scrutinized, and her wardrobe assessed to make sure she was giving the baby room enough to grow! The constant hen pecking annoyed Gezebel, and she avoided her family whenever she could. Grandmother Estele made frequent visits to Bella's home, and randomly stuck a thermometer in Gezebel's mouth whenever she felt it was necessary to do so. She ordered Gezebel to the doctor if she had the slightest cough or the tiniest sniffle. Corine converted a guestroom at her house into a nursery so the baby could be properly pampered and cared for when Gezebel visited. She refused all of Gezebel's decorating suggestions and referred to them as "hideous!" Kendrick's mother almost drove her self mad with the thought of her grandchild being born into a wealthy family, and bombarded Gezebel with phone calls four to five times a day. She begged Gezebel to stop by and visit but Gezebel refused. Kendrick's mother wouldn't take 'no' for an answer, and swore that Gezebel's absence was making her blood pressure rise! The incessant calls aggravated Gezebel, but she refused to be manipulated. Gezebel finally advised the woman she wouldn't set foot in her house until after the baby was born! She complained to Joi these women were driving her bananas. Joi laughed and agreed that they were overbearing bunch, but soon, she started reading parenting magazines, and became an overnight expert in child rearing! She schooled Gezebel about pregnancy, childbirth and bringing up baby! Poor Gezebel, the situation was hopeless!

The telephone in Gezebel's room rang, and the caller id identified Joi as the caller. Gezebel picked up the phone and was pleased to learn that good 'ole Joi had information about Kendrick's activities at the gym. Gezebel perked up and listened intently to every word. Joi found out from a reliable source that Kendrick was going to make a significant narcotic sale at the gym later that evening. Gezebel hung up and dialed the police. She informed the detectives and they assured her they would act on the information provided to them. Gezebel hung up, and fell asleep waiting for the trap to register the catch.

At 7:01pm that evening, Joi informed Gezebel the police stormed the gym and Kendrick was caught selling illegal drugs! A befuddled Kendrick was arrested and carted off to jail! Gezebel received the news with a joyfull heart! Revenge tasted so sweet! She left the estate and drove to the gym to meet Joi. Gezebel arrived and observed Joi chatting with other members about Kendrick's arrest. She joined the group and feigned dismay over the unfortunate incident. It was difficult for them not to laugh at their devilish handiwork! Gezebel, Joi, and one of their peers strolled away from the gathering of people and talked in hushed tones among themselves. Gezebel glanced around, and made sure no one was watching as she stealthily removed a white envelope from her handbag. She handed it to the associate that acted as Joi's informant. The envelope contained one thousand dollars! It was payment for critical details about Kendrick activities which led to an arrest. The trio rejoined the huddled groups of people, and speculated about Kendrick's future.

Gezebel smiled cunningly to herself, and pulled into a gas station to purchase a pack of cigarettes and a lighter. She detested cigarette smoking but felt inclined to have one. Gezebel drove to a nearby beach and parked her vehicle on the sand. She rolled down the window and removed the pack of cigarettes from her bag. She opened the box and took a cigarette out. Gezebel flicked the lighter, and passed the flame over the tip of the cigarette. She took a long drag. Gezebel reclined the seat, put her legs on the dashboard, and admired the majesty of the magnificent sea. She took another drag of the cigarette, and smirked at the thought of Kendrick having to spend his nights in jail! Gezebel puffed on the cigarette and laughed. It would have been nice to witness the horror on his face when the police stormed the gym! Serves his ass right! Gezebel thought. Did he really think he was going to walk away from his baby so easily? Was he really that stupid? Gezebel dragged on the cigarette again and tossed the butt onto the sand. She fished the pack of cigarettess out of her bag and threw it out the window. The lighter suffered the same fate. Gezebel searched her bag for chewing gum, and popped a few pieces into her mouth to camauflage the nicotine on her breath.

Chapter Thirty

Gezebel birthed a seven pound, two ounce, baby boy, whom she christened Baron. Childbirth was an ordeal for Gezebel because it rendered her helpless and emotionally vulnerable. She was unable to control the discomfort of labor, and grunted for 21 hours until Baron was born. At the age of nineteen, Gezebel became a mother. Gezebel arrived home at Bella's estate with Baron in her arms, and was surprised by the presence of her Uncle Jeffrey, his wife Sisi, and their two sons, who flew from England to meet the newest member of the family. Sisi swept the sleeping infant out of Gezebel's arms and cooed at the adorable baby. As the afternoon wore on, Bella's house filled with family and friends who were eager to see the newest member of the St. John clan.

An hour or two later, Sisi seized the opportunity to share exciting news with the group, and everyone huddled into the spacious family room for a special announcement. Jeffrey decided to get the ball rolling.

"Most of you know that my wife, Sisi, is a fashion designer. But, for the past twelve years or so, she's been working on a fragrance. Sisi, i'll let you take it from here!" Jeffrey stated, and Sisi took over.

"As my husband was saying, I made a slight detour from fashion and delved into the art of fragrance! The fragrance was grafted from a local flower found in Barbados, known locally as "Lady of the Night," but the scientific name for the plant is Brunfelsia Americana. This plant releases a beautiful fragrance at dusk, but stops emitting the fragrance at dawn. My team has spent years, and a considerable amount of money capturing the elusive scent in a bottle so that women all over the world could enjoy its fragrance not only at night, but also during the day! We added essential oils, glycerin, and tested various aroma groups until we created perfumes worthy of being introduced to the world! Three scents were created from this plant. The original fragrance has oils of Brunfelsia Americana blossoms, oils of grapefruit and ylang-ylang. We call it, "Lady of the Night." The second has oils of Brunfelsia Americana blossoms and oils of clove. We call it, "Lady Clova." The third has oils of Brunfelsia Americana blossoms and bergamot. We call it "Lady Berga." Sisi stated breathlessly to her captivated audience.

She whisked perfume samples out of a case and distributed them to guests. The women dabbed drops on their wrists and behind their ears. Sisi beamed at their nods of approval, and fielded inquiries as to when they would be able to purchase the real thing from stores. Corine sidled coyly over to Sisi and shot her an appraising look. She always liked Sisi but felt that Sisi was a backward African with lofty dreams. Corine couldn't figure out how Sisi managed such an ambitious project all by herself! How come she was the one to capitalize on this silly flower, taking root in everyone's garden? As a matter fact, she had this plant in her backyard, and the scent was sickening! It was nothing special! Out of curiosity, Corine dabbed a drop of the original fragrance on her wrist and turned up her nose in the most disagreeable way! She disliked it immensely! Corine sniffed the other fragrances and thought they were just ghastly! These perfumes would never sell! Sisi was wasting her time! She should focus on cutting patterns and stitching kinte! She initiated small talk with Sisi, hell bent on letting her know exactly what she thought!

"Sisi, you look fantastic! How've you managed to keep that girlish figure after having two handsome boys?" Corine asked demurely.

"Thank you, Corine! I eat right and exercise!" Sisi replied exuberantly.

"Do you think these perfumes will actually sell?" Corine asked slyly and stifled a giggle.

"Of course! Testing has gone remarkably well in London!" Sisi replied and Corine sneered at her.

"Sisi, I don't think so! You're underestimating the market! Even though testing went favorably, it doesn't mean the perfumes will sell in the real world! Don't make a fool of yourself trying to push this! These things can't compete with the top fragrances of the world! I'm telling you this because I care!" Corine advised Sisi in a compassionate voice. Sisi was at a loss for words and Corine drew satisfaction from that. Corine pursed her lips and her face hardened.

"Look, if you go ahead with this ridiculous idea, consider placing an aspirin or two into the box with these perfumes! The little bit I dabbed on my wrist gave me an instant headache!" Corine added dryly. Sisi placed a hand stylishly on her hip and shook her head. She eyed Corine with disgust! Hurt emotions convened in her throat and prevented her from spitting out a suitable rebuttal. "You're in over your head and I'm surprised Jeffrey hasn't talked some sense into you!" Corine added flatly.

"Corine! We haven't had a chance to talk!" Jeffrey exclaimed and embraced her warmly.

"Sisi, are you alright? Jeffrey asked his wife. He noticed the displeasure on her face and was concerned.

"Oh, I'm great!" Sisi replied and forced a smile.

"Jeffrey, we have lots of catching up to do but first let's go see my grandchild." Corine suggested quickly and whisked Jeffrey away. Sisi couldn't wait to fill Jeffrey in on all Corine had to say.

"Sisi! I love it! I love it! This smells just like the flower!" Gezebel gushed excitedly.

"Gezebel, I'm glad!" Sisi replied and pitied her for having such a trifling mother. The sting of Corine's words diminished and she was determined to have the last laugh. Her signature fragrance was going to be a success and Corine would have to eat her words!

Chapter Thirty-One

Gezebel's son was christened Baron St. John in a church ceremony surrounded by family and friends. Joi was chosen as godmother and promised to love Baron as her own. Soon after the christening, Gezebel relented, and took the baby to visit Kendrick's agitated mother. The woman fussed over the baby with such vigor, Gezebel was afraid she would kidnap the child! Baron was the only source of Joy in Kendrick's mother's life since Kendrick was serving a four-year sentence for selling illegal narcotics on private property. Kendrick's mother pleaded with Gezebel to help Kendrick get out of prison, but Gezebel turned a deaf ear to her pleas, and the frustrated woman eventually gave up. Kendrick was destined to do the time.

Gezebel kept in contact with Jack and he proved himself a sincere friend. She kept Baron's birth a secret, and he had no idea she was even pregnant. Gezebel stalled his attempts to visit by blaming her course load at the University, and working full time, as reasons why he should wait a little longer to see her. He proposed visiting after the spring semester concluded and Gezebel readily agreed. This gave her plenty of time to get back in shape.

Family life was stressful for Gezebel as Bella, Estele, and Corine insisted she commit all her time to her college, the family business, and Baron. A rebellious spirit raged within her and refused to be caged. Why did her life have to come to a screeching halt just because she had a baby? Who gave them the right to limit her options and plot the course of her life? Gezebel resented the authority they wielded over her existence, and she felt stifled. To make matters worse, Daddy St. John and Estele were up to their old tricks, and assembled a string of suitors from affluent families for Gezebel to date. But, like her Aunt Bella, Gezebel turned a stone face to these young men and sent them packing!

Gezebel sat at the kitchen table feeding Baron when Bella frantically rushed downstairs, shrieking about Daddy St. John being hospitalized! Gezebel contacted Joi and asked her to babysit Baron while she accompanied Bella to the hospital. They arrived to find Daddy St. John in critical condition, suffering in a hospital bed! A distressed Estele hovered over her frail husband as he breathed with difficulty. The doctor entered the room, and communicated to the family that Daddy St. John was ill with pneumonia, which was probably caused by a bought with the flu he battled weeks ago. His lungs were inflamed and full of fluid, and he breathed with difficulty. X-rays revealed several abscesses on his lungs which were treated with antibiotics.

Days passed, and Daddy St. John's condition deteriorated. Further tests were ordered by the attending physician, and the results indicated that bacteria from his lungs spread to his bloodstream. He suggested they hope for the best, but prepare for the worst! Jeffrey and his family flew to Barbados to spend as much time with Daddy St. John during this uncertain time. Family members took turns keeping vigil at his

bedside so that Estele and the children could rest, and take care of business.

Deighton's physical demise weakened Estele emotionally and physically. He was her champion, the man who made her transition from a poverty-stricken mulatto girl to that of a wealthy woman of high social standing, possible. He provided her, and the children with the best life, and wonderful opportunities. Deighton was a giant among men who crushed obstacles in order to gain personal enrichment. Estele read to her husband, and sang his favorite songs as he lay on the bed and wheezed. Deighton opened his eyes and managed a feeble wink at Estele. She told him how much she loved him, and smiled at his attempts to flirt with her at this sorrowful moment in their lives. Estele reminisced about the early stages of their love affair when she peered into his intelligent gray eyes and laughed at his silly jokes. He was the only man she had known intimately. She remembered when her mother scrubbed the floors in his family's house and cooked their meals. Her mind reeled back to their very first date, and Estele wept.

Bella and Ernest worked doggedly to build the Wynter Haven hotel franchise. Wynter Haven Resort opened its doors to tourists in the neighboring islands of St. Lucia and Grenada. The family had planned a huge celebration to commemorate these events, and Daddy St. John was so very proud of all Bella and Ernest had accomplished. But now, the celebration would have to wait.

Deighton wheezed fitfully, and in a frail voice, asked to see his children, and his family. A high strung Estele summoned everyone to the hospital, and refused to leave his side. Family and close friends stood somberly at either side of the bed.

Ernest and Jeffrey cried openly as their father told them how proud he was of the men they had become. The two sons hugged and kissed their father. Deighton praised his daughter, Bella, for her strength and commitment to the family, and she threw herself across his body, and cried woefully. Ernest and Jeffrey removed Bella, and escorted her out of the room. She collapsed in the corridors, and wailed at the thought of losing her icon. Ernest and Jeffrey helped Bella off the floor, and cried with her. Deighton managed to hug Gezebel and made her promise to raise Baron as a strong "St. John" man. Gezebel cried, and promised she would. He ruffled the hair of Jeffrey's two sons, and Gezebel told the boys it was time to leave their grandfather. Deighton's siblings hugged and kissed the dying man, and tried not to break down emotionally. Friends of Deighton shared colorful tidbits about their friendship with him through the years, and ordered him out of bed. Deighton chuckled feebly, and promised them he was going to do just that! Everyone left the room so Estele could be alone with her husband. Loud sobs and dispirited wails echoed throughout the corridors as death loomed near.

Estele lay next to Deighton in the hospital bed and kissed his lips. Deighton put his arm around his wife in an effort to comfort her. She closed her eyes and listened with dread as his breaths became more labored. Estele drifted off to sleep. Death floated through the corridor where the others stood crying, and passed through Deighton's hospital door. He recognized death when it entered the room, and said a final prayer. Death floated closer to him and his life's experiences played out like a movie before his eyes. He was satisfied with the conclusion. Deighton had committed no significant wrongs and he was not afraid. He nodded at death with confidence, and it took his breath away. A few minutes later, Estele opened her eyes and screamed in horror! Deighton was dead!

Chapter Thirty-Two

For Gezebel, the passing of Daddy St. John signified the importance of getting as much as you could out of life. She studied hard at the University, and worked under Bella's guidance at the family's corporate headquarters in Bridgetown. Bella was a kind and loving aunt but she was a tough act to follow. In her position as CFO, Bella was a demanding tyrant and she ran the outfit with a manicured iron fist! Gezebel exploded at Bella dozens of times as they argued over business related issues.

Bella treated Gezebel like a naive junior executive that was still wet behind the ears. Gezebel resented being scoffed at by Bella and officers of the company when she tried to implement an idea that in their estimation, lacked practicality. Turning to her father for advice was pointless because he supported Bella's management style. Ernest was not interested in petty squabbles between Gezebel and Bella. He was busy managing on site operations for the family's hotel franchise in Grenada and St. Lucia. He traveled back and forth between these islands once or twice a month to make sure quality standards were being adhered to. In time, Gezebel was able to separate her personal relationship with Bella from her business relationship with her. She asserted herself in business meetings and demonstrated maturity by agreeing with hard lined decisions drafted to benefit the business. Study, work, and motherhood monopolized Gezebel's life. It wasn't long before these pressures started to take their toll. Jack's visit to Barbados was fast approaching, and she welcomed his distraction from the drudgery of her responsibilities.

Jack arrived by private jet, and Gezebel welcomed him with open arms. He was more attractive than she recalled, wearing white trousers, a matching blazer and an aqua colored polo shirt. The scent of aftershave lingered on his skin when she hugged him, and it reminded Gezebel of long it had been since she made love. Jack rented an intimate two-bedroom villa with an outdoor pool, nestled in the northwest coast of the island. Tall palms caressed the villa and gave them the ultimate in privacy. Behind closed doors, he wasted no time, and lavished her with kisses. Gezebel grasped Jack's shoulders, and reciprocated his kiss. Jack slipped her bra off and tasted her tanned skin. Gezebel removed her shorts, and teased him with black thongs, which he ripped off with his bare hands! Jack kissed her body until she was impatient with desire. She tore off his shirt, and unbuckled his belt. His trousers fell to the floor, and he kicked them out of his way! He led Gezebel to the heated outdoor pool that was constructed in the center of a lush garden, in the rear of the property. Gezebel wrapped her legs around his firm buttocks, and Jack eagerly satisfied her carnal desires. She relinquished her frustrations to electric currents that besieged her core. Gezebel moaned with pleasure as Jack squeezed her buttocks, indicating that he too had relinquished all he had. Her evenings were spent with Jack, and she arranged for Bella and Estele to babysit Baron. She offered no explanation for the change in her routine other than she was in the company of a friend vacationing in the island. Gezebel dismissed their suspicions about the individual she was spending her time with, and remained aloof, determined to keep them out of her business.

Gezebel's exotic features photographed remarkably well, judging from the amateur photos Jack took of her. Jack knew she had the makings of a star. She was tall and elegant, in full control of her body instead of appearing tall, gawky and awkward. Jack recognized her potential, and she was exactly what he was looking for. His entertainment company focused on adult movies and magazines, but he was ready to branch off into mainstream entertainment. He needed talented, clean cut artists, looking for that big break. He was poised to finance a number of budding superstars, and Gezebel was an example of the fresh talent he was looking for. His pleasurable retreat on the sunny island was going to end in two days, and he wanted Gezebel to accompany him back to New York. Jack pondered how best to persuade Gezebel to grab the opportunity as they dined at a seafood restaurant built atop a rugged, sandy beach. The red, strapless mini dress worn by Gezebel showed off tanned, flawless skin, and a shapely physique. He admired her immensely. Her eyes twinkled mischievously, and he decided to broach the subject again.

"Gezebel, i'll be leaving the island in two days." Jack remarked cautiously.

"I know. Jack, i'll miss you a lot." Gezebel replied and smiled.

"Come with me Gezebel! You have what it takes to become an international super model! I can make it happen for you! Gezebel, you stand to make millions in a short space of time!" Jack stated with emphasis.

"Jack, not this supermodel fairy tale again!" Gezebel blurted out and laughed.

"Gezebel please take this seriously! Haven't you realized how heads turn when you walk into a room? Not every woman has the ability to command that kind of attention! With the right coaching you can become a millionaire in your own right, but first, you have to leave this island!" Jack advised Gezebel.

"Jack, I don't know. I've never been away from my family. I don't want them to think I'm shirking my duties at the family business. Don't you understand?" Gezebel pleaded for understanding.

"No, I don't understand!" Jack replied in an exasperated manner.

The hardness in his voice caused Gezebel to wince. She realized she sounded like a country girl afraid of living in a big city with bright lights but she didn't care! She was thinking about her son. Leaving with Jack would mean leaving Baron behind.

"Jack, I'm an island girl at heart, and I'm not used to being in the spotlight. Pretty girls are a dime a dozen in America. I'm not that special!" Gezebel quipped demurely. Jack stared at Gezebel hard. Was she playing hard to get or was she serious? He had to get through to her.

"Ok, Gezebel, what do I have to do? Kidnap you?" Jack asked in a frustrated voice and Gezebel laughed.

"Jack, I just don't know what else to say about your proposal. I promised my family I would study, and work with them to grow the business my grandfather started. You're asking me to renege on those promises. What if this brilliant idea of yours doesn't work? They would never forgive me for being so stupid and I would have to start all over again!" Gezebel stated testily.

"Gezebel, you can complete your studies in the United States while you model! That should be a great selling point for you to make with your family." Jack reasoned with her.

Gezebel was silent. She was caught between wanting fame and fortune, and wanting to be there for her son, and her family. If she left with Jack, they would raise Baron until she returned. Is that what she really wanted? Baron was a year old and taking his first steps. She was tormented by thoughts of Baron crying for her while she was halfway around the world chasing her dreams. A solitary tear rolled down her cheek.

"Gezebel please don't cry. I'm sorry if I pushed too hard. I know the idea of leaving all you have here is incomprehensible. I purchased this in case you agreed to go." Jack stated and handed Gezebel an envelope. She opened it, and inside was an airline ticket departing Barbados on the same date and time as Jack.

"Jack, I can't believe you did this!" Gezebel exclaimed in disbelief and wiped a tear from her cheek.

"Let's not discuss the issue anymore. I want to toast to life, liberty, and the pursuit of Gezebel!" Jack shouted merrily and Gezebel touched her glass to his.

Jack wasn't accustomed to being turned down or having to beg a woman to accept an offer for the possibilities of riches beyond her wildest dreams. If Gezebel didn't take advantage of this opportunity, he would never broach the subject again. Gezebel felt the pressure of his demands, and knew that she wasn't exhibiting the independence needed to take that big leap into the unknown. The night before Jack's scheduled departure, Gezebel was at home with her family. She bathed her son, and read him a fairy tale before putting him to bed. She was burned out from dividing her time between Baron, work and Jack. Gezebel was grateful for a night of uninterrupted rest. She went into the bath and filled the tub with hot water. Gezebel sprinkled mineral salts into the water, and soaked her achy body. She closed her eyes, and emptied her mind of clutter that accumulated during the busy day. The tepid water soothed her limp body, and her muscles relaxed. Gezebel was lulled to sleep by the calming water. Gezebel shivered and opened her eyes. Bella called out to her, and knocked gently on the bathroom door. Gezebel looked at the clock and realized she had dozed off for more than an hour. The bathwater had cooled off considerably and she leapt out of it. She wrapped a thick bath sheet around her shoulders and opened the door. Bella stood there, looking flustered.

"You fell asleep in the tub didn't you?" Bella asked in a reprimanding voice.

"Yes, I was exhausted!" Gezebel replied and yawned.

"Hum! You should be! The way you've been running around these last two weeks." Bella remarked snidely. "So, what time will you be leaving tonight?" Bella quipped.

"I'm staying home. My friend is leaving in the morning." Gezebel informed Bella in a weary tone.

"I see. Has Baron been fed?" Bella asked.

"He's been bathed and fed. Now that he's asleep, don't wake him." Gezebel added dryly.

"Oh, what a shame! I was looking forward to playing with him for a while. Ok, i'll let him sleep but if he wakes up bring him to my room. Dwight prepared steak, baked macaroni, rice, and salad for dinner." Bella informed Gezebel and left.

"i'll be down soon." Gezebel promised and dried off. Gezebel changed into a t-shirt and shorts. She pulled her tangled hair into a ponytail and was walking down the stairs when the doorbell rang. Gezebel opened the door, and welcomed her grandmother, Estele.

"Gezebel! You're the last person I expected to see!" Estele exclaimed.

"Grandma please! I still live here!" Gezebel replied. She was a little embarrassed. "Grandma's here!" Gezebel hollered to Bella and Dwight. They were already seated in the dining room.

"Mummy, you're just in time for dinner." Bella stated.

"Well, that's what I came for!" She replied jokingly and seated herself. "Where's Baron?"

"He's asleep!" Gezebel informed her grandmother and heaped baked macaroni on her plate.

"So early? It's only 7:30! Bella lets him stay up late so I can play with him." A disappointed Estele remarked. "Well, let's say grace." Estele concluded grace with a resounding "Amen" and everyone started heaping food on their plates.

"Dwight, this steak is delicious! It's so succulent!" Bella whispered sexily and slipped her foot out of the bedroom slipper. She tickled his leg with her toes under the table. Estele glanced at Bella flirting outrageously with Dwight at the dinner table, and cleared her throat to remind her daughter that she should refrain from such behavior in her presence. Bella snickered at her uptight mother.

"Grandma, Baron's normal bedtime is eight o'clock, but he fell asleep afther his bath, so stop spoiling him!" Gezebel scoffed at Estele.

"That's my job young lady! You make the rules and I break them!" Estele retorted defiantly. Everyone laughed and mocked Gezebel.

"That makes it harder to get him back to his regular routine!" Gezebel pointed out.

"Oh, poor Gezzy! Well, you should've thought about that before you rode off into the sunset with that mystery man of yours!" Bella interjected and chuckled.

Dwight sipped juice and cleared his throat. "It is a man, isn't it? I mean we don't want any surprises!" Dwight joked and the others laughed hysterically.

"Of course it's a man!" Gezebel answered defensively.

"Hal le lujah! Hal le lujah! Hal le lujah! Praise the Lord!" Estele sang and clapped her hands together. Dwight and Bella guffawed and tears streamed down Bella's face. Estele coughed from laughing so hard.

Gezebel decided it was best to join the mirth at the dinner table. She stuffed her mouth with meat and her cheeks bulged. Gezebel crossed her eyes, and Estele and Dwight hollered with laughter. Bella stumbled out of her chair and held her stomach because her muscles ached from laughter! She laughed fervently at just how silly her niece could be! Gezebel chuckled, and almost choked as she tried to swallow the food in her mouth. They wisecracked at each other for the rest of the night. Laughter is so good for the soul! Estele decided to stay overnight and slept in a guestroom close to Baron's.

It was past midnight and all was quiet at the estate. Gezebel tossed and turned in bed as the clutter returned to her mind with a vengeance. She gave up trying to sleep and checked on Baron. Gezebel watched lovingly as her son lay in the crib sucking his thumb and playing by himself. She picked the toddler up and hugged him. Gezebel sat in the rocker and fed the hungry child. Baron played with his mommy until he fell asleep and Gezebel whispered in his ear how much she loved him before kissing him goodnight. Gezebel returned to her room and lay in bed. She closed her eyes but attempts to sleep were defeated by insomnia, so she sat up in bed, and switched on the light. Gezebel snatched the handbag off the night table and recovered the airline ticket. The flight was scheduled to depart Barbados at 7:30am and the time was now 2:07am. She dialed Joi, who kept an ear out for her call.

"Joi, it's me." Gezebel whispered hoarsely into the phone.

"How are you?" Joi asked in a shaky voice. She closed her eyes and squeezed back tears. Her best friend was about to embark on a risky journey.

"I'm leaving with Jack!" Gezebel informed her.

"i'll drive you to the airport." Joi replied.

"i'll be outside the gate by 5:45." Gezebel stated.

"i'll be there." Joi cried and hung up.

Gezebel glanced around her room and cried profusely. Was she choosing the right path? Hell, it was now or never! She packed a suitcase and got dressed. Gezebel had about fifteen thousand dollars in her account and this small sum converted to six or seven thousand United States dollars. She secured the bankcard in her purse in case she needed emergency access to cash. Gezebel threw on blue jeans, a chic blouse and wedged heels. She brushed her hair away from her face and placed a bandal over it. Gezebel picked up the suitcase and tiptoed out of the bedroom. She crept down the stairs. Her heart pounded as she entered Bella's home office and retrieved a pad and a pen. She wrote a brief note to Bella and Estele explaining her decision to move to New York with Jack Chagall. Gezebel scribbled a separate note to her parents, and placed it under the one for Bella and Estele.

The time on the kitchen clock read 5:41am, and Gezebel slipped out the front door of the Victorian estate, to walk the two minute trek toward the iron gates. The dewy grass clawed at her ankles when she walked, as if trying to hold her back, but she opened the gate and slipped outside. Joi was already waiting for her. They drove to the airport and

Joi prayed Gezebel would be safe. Gezebel observed Jack checking in when they arrived at the airport. She chose to surprise him on the plane because she wanted to spend a few moments with Joi. The best friends hugged and tears rolled down their cheeks. They promised not to let distance come between them. Passengers were boarding, and it was time for Gezebel to go. She was the last of the queued passengers waiting to board the jumbo jet. Gezebel entered the departure gate without looking back, and Joi broke down in tears. She refused to leave the airport until the plane was airborne. Gezebel nervously walked up the steps leading into the aircraft and entered the first class cabin where Jack sat and leafed through a magazine. He had a pained, frustrated expression on his face. The seat next to his was hers and Gezebel approached it apprehensively.

"Excuse me, but I think that seat is mine." She said quietly. Jack looked up and couldn't believe his eyes.

"Gezebel! I didn't expect you to show up but I was hoping you would! What made you change your mind?" He asked exuberantly.

"I thought about all the things you said. This is a once in a lifetime opportunity and I don't intend to miss out!" Gezebel replied and gazed at Jack with tears in her eyes. She took her seat and fastened her safety belt.

Gezebel laid her head on his shoulder and tried to suppress the tears that barreled through the levees of her eyelids. The plane roared down the tarmac at 7:31am. Estele arose and went downstairs to make breakfast. She scooped coffee into the filter of the coffee maker, and started the brewing process. Estele got the eggs and bacon out of the refrigerator and turned on the range. She cracked the eggs into the frying pan and scrambled them in butter. The coffee was already brewed by the time Bella appeared.

"Good morning mummy." Bella chirped like a beautiful songbird.

"Good morning." Estele replied.

"What's this on the counter?" Bella asked.

"Oh, I don't know! You know I can't see too well without my glasses." Estele replied.

It was 7:45am and the plane knifed through the air, shooting far above the clouds. Gezebel used tissue to soak up the torrential downpour flowing from her eyes.

The serenity of the morning was shattered by Bella's horrible screams.

"Oh my God! I can't believe this! Oh my God!" Bella wailed and put her hands to her head in agony.

"Bella, what's wrong?" Dwight shouted. He rushed downstairs clad in nothing but shorts when Bella screamed.

"Bella, what is it? Tell us!" Estele stammered and clutched her breast. Bella shoved the letter at Dwight and he read it out loud.

"Dear Aunt Bella and Grandma,

By the time you receive this letter, i'll be long gone. I've accepted an offer by Jack Chagall to live with him in New York. Jack has a lot of contacts in the entertainment business and believes I have what it takes to be a supermodel. I trust him. Please take care of Baron for me. I love him with all my heart. I have to strike out on my own and Baron needs to be in a stable environment while I pursue this opportunity. I will resume my maternal responsibilities at a later date. Look for me on the cover of every fashion magazine because that's where i'll be. I trust that you will not interfere and let me do this my way. I love you with all my heart.

Gezebel

It was 8:00am, and the jet cruised through the air. Gezebel laid her head back on the headrest and Jack reached for her hand. Estele collapsed on the kitchen floor, unable to get back up! Bella sat on a kitchen stool with her face in her hands. There was nothing Dwight could do to console mother and daughter. He helped Estele off the floor and walked her upstairs to the guestroom. Dwight encouraged her to lie down. He rushed back to Bella. She was the love of his life and it hurt him so to see her so despondent. Baron awoke and cried for Gezebel. Estele heard the child cry and went to him. She picked him up in her arms and held him close. How could her granddaughter be so selfish? She asked herself. Last night they were joking around, having fun. Gezebel gave no indication, no hint, as to what she was about to do. She had never felt such remorse and worry. Dizzying sensations fluttered in her head, a signal that her blood pressure was on the rise! She sat in the rocker and soothed Baron. Dwight held Bella in his arms until she could cry no more. In a voice drenched in sorrow, she telephoned Ernest and Corine and asked them to come over. Bella hung up the phone with a trembling hand. Her eyes were swollen from crying.

"Lord, how could she? First she gets pregnant for some low life and now this? Was I such a sorry excuse for a parent? I gave that girl everything and this is the thanks I get? A Dear John Letter?" Bella cried out in anguish.

"Darling, its ok. We still have Baron. At least she left him with us instead of taking him with her. That's something to be grateful for." Dwight reasoned. He wanted Bella to look at the bright side of things and embraced her. She buried her face in his chest and cried.

The housekeeper answered the doorbell when it rang and Ernest walked in. She advised him that Bella and Dwight were waiting in Bella's office. Ernest entered the room looking handsome and smelling of woodsy cologne. Bella threw her arms around her brother and cried. Ernest was taken aback by Bella's show of emotion and knew that whatever was going on was serious!

"Hey, what's wrong?" Ernest asked in a concerned voice. Dwight handed him the note from Gezebel.

Dear Mum & Dad,

I've decided to leave Barbados with Jack Chagall. Jack lives in New York and intends to make me a supermodel. I trust and believe in him. Dad, please don't come searching for me. I need to do this my way. Mum, please don't blame Bella for my actions. This is not her fault. Help the family take care of Baron. I love you both.

Gezebel

Ernest read the hastily written note over and over again, and grinded his teeth. He could not understand how his nutty daughter could take such a risk. He grappled with images of Gezebel left for dead in a New York slum and shuddered!

"i'll hire a private investigator to track her down and keep an eye on her! This way, we'll know where she is and what she's doing. If she's in a bad situation, I will personally remove her from it, and crush her with my bare hands!" Ernest shouted in a hoarse voice. "How could she?" He wept and hugged Bella. The doorbell rang and the housekeeper let Corine in. The sound of her heels stomping on the hard wood floors as she made her way to Bella's home office was silenced when she entered the carpeted room.

"My goodness! Whatever is the matter?" She asked with a strong British accent. Corine was taken aback by the distraught expressions that welcomed her. Ernest handed her the letter and the color drained from her face.

"Bella… is this a lark? What have you done?" Corine asked in disbelief.

"Corine, I'm not in the mood for your bullshit!" Bella snapped.

"If anything happens to her, I'm holding you responsible! Where's my daughter?" Corine shrieked with fear.

Ernest comforted Corine as they agonized over their daughter's welfare. Questions abounded, telephone calls were made, coffee was sipped, but lunch refused. No one could stomach food at this miserable time. Estele remained in bed for the rest of the day, unable to get up. She was growing sick from worry. Ernest tended to his mother, and was a pillar of strength for Corine, but he needed consoling himself. Corine clung to him like never before because Gezebel was the only reminder of the life they shared. They reconciled their differences and vowed to support one another through this nightmare.

Chapter Thirty-Three

In 2001 Gezebel arrived in New York. She was greeted by tumultuous grey skies on a humid summer day. The limousine cruised through the busy streets of Manhattan, and jostled for position with yellow cabbies and buses. Diverse throngs of people were out and about enjoying the rain, and walking the water logged streets. The vehicle sped over potholes of water filled to the brim by the torrential downpour and splashed passerby's who walked or stood close to the pavements. They were angered by the splash of cold water that drenched their clothes. Some cussed, and others angrily stuck their middle fingers at the limousine!

They arrived at Jack's home in the pouring rain. The sun shunned Gezebel by refusing to come out and lift her spirits with its warm, sunny rays. Jack resided in what was a three-storied apartment building on the Upper East Side of Manhattan. He renovated the entire building into a 21, 000 square foot town house. The upscale urban home was built of brick and surrounded by steel gates. Gezebel was ushered into the foyer of the elegant home as the skies crackled ominously with thunder and lightning. Grey clouds blanketed the atmosphere and darkened what would otherwise be a bright and cheerful day. Outdoors resembled late evening instead of early afternoon, and dampened Gezebel's spirits.

A uniformed housekeeper greeted the couple as they entered through heavy oak doors. They entered a foyer with medallion styled tiles that piqued Gezebel's interest. Jack introduced the housekeeper to Gezebel. He explained that Inez hailed from the Dominican Republic, and she took care of anything that was related to the household. Inez directed the chauffeur as to where the luggage should be placed while Jack gave Gezebel a tour of his grand home. He led Gezebel down a stairway located to the left of the foyer and entered the lower quarter of the townhouse. They entered a black and white ceramic tiled kitchen loaded with professional grade appliances and black granite countertops. A huge stone island stood in the center of the kitchen surrounded by four wrought iron stools with cushioned seats. There was a set of doors that separated the kitchen from the other half of the lower level and Jack opened them. He walked down a marbled hallway and it opened up into a beautifully decorated studio apartment with carpets the color of a vanilla milkshake. Jack informed Gezebel that this was where Inez lived.

They returned to the first level of the stately home, and passed the foyer to gain access to a magnificent white marbled room that resembled a ballroom. This was where Jack entertained guests. Gezebel walked into the room and was awed by the two twenty-four Swarovski Crystal Chandeliers from the Schonbek Trilliane collection. Interesting artwork collected by Jack over the years adorned the walls of this dazzling showroom. Artifacts and statues collected from his travels abroad stood in unassuming positions at either side of the windows or in the corners of the room. A fireplace with white marble surrounds commanded the attention of guests, and elegant chairs were strategically placed in the wide-open space, leaving lots of room for guests to dance, and enjoy themselves. Gezebel walked through an archway, and entered a formal dining room with a wooden trestle table that seated eight. It was complemented by leather back chairs, a buffet, a hutch, and sideboard.

They walked back to the foyer, and headed up the grand staircase. Jack stopped on the second level, and explained that the two apartments on this floor were used to accommodate guests. There was a one bedroom apartment with a cozy study, and a two bedroom, two bath apartment. Both were elegantly furnished, and equipped with full kitchen facilities because Jack preferred for guests to have their own space instead of sharing his private quarters. He continued up the staircase to the third level of the home. This floor had a more relaxed feel with deep grained hardwood floors and a carpeted hall. Jack punched a security code into a panel attached to the wall, and entered his private penthouse. Gezebel gasped at the white lacquered spiral staircase in the penthouse apartment. The lower level of the penthouse apartment contained living and dining areas, a study, and a private terrace that overlooked tree tops in the distance. An onyx colored baby grand piano was placed near one of the windows in the living area, and this, along with the remarkably high ceilings, gave the room a relaxed contemporary feel. Jack promised to teach Gezebel to play in his spare time, and she was ecstatic at the opportunity to learn.

Plush wall to wall carpets lined the floors of the penthouse, and Gezebel's toes sank into the luxuriant fibers as if it were quicksand. A rustic leather sectional snaked around the living area as if it were still in a retailer's showroom and teased Gezebel's tired body with its rich leather. Gezebel trailed Jack up the spiral staircase, and gaped at the two master bedroom suites with marbled roman styled baths. The bedrooms lacked naught, in terms of furnishings, style and ambiance. White roses were placed in vases atop the stone fireplace mantles in the bedrooms, and reminded Gezebel of her Aunt Bella, who loved having fresh picked flowers in her home. Gezebel was overcome with emotion, and choked back sobs. Jack drew the drapes over the windows in the bedrooms to block out the wretched damp and darkness that hovered outside. He noticed the tormented expression on Gezebel's face and his heart went out to her.

Just when Gezebel thought the grand tour was over, Jack had one more surprise in store. They exited the penthouse and went up another set of stairs located in the hall. Jack entered a security code into another panel on the wall and pushed open a steel door. Gezebel's breath was taken away by the enclosed rooftop swimming pool, Jacuzzi and sundeck! Surrounding the enclosed swimming area were rooftop gardens in full bloom! Gezebel had never seen anything like this before, and it blew her mind! Jack, the trip to New York, this house, was overwhelming and almost surreal! Gezebel's head was spinning from all the excitement and Jack suggested they return to the penthouse for a bite to eat. Instead of taking the stairs leading down to the penthouse, Jack pressed a button in the wall close to the stairwell, and doors opened up to reveal an elevator! This was too much! He chuckled at the stunned expression on Gezebel's face and explained that the elevator worked on all floors so there was no need to take the stairs unless one wanted to. They rode the elevator to the third floor and ventured back to the penthouse.

Gezebel sought out the leather sectional, and Jack activated the reclining mechanism. She laid her head on the deluxe headrest, and relaxed, while Jack buzzed Inez on the intercom, and ordered something to eat. Gezebel sighed and peered at her watch. It was 6:02pm and she wondered how Baron was

holding up without her. Her heart ached at not having him there to rest against her bosom. She cursed herself for worrying so much. Gezebel's head sank into the headrest, and in her mind, she rounded up her personal demons, bound them to a stake, and lit their souls on fire! She smiled cunningly as they hollered in pain, and was reduced to nothing more than foul smelling ash!

After they ate, Jack took Gezebel by the hand, and led her up the spiral staircase to one of the master suites. He undressed himself and gazed lustfully at her. She removed her clothing and laid back on the king sized bed. Gezebel readily received Jack as he thrust himself eagerly inside her. She was taken aback by his callous approach, and raised her hips to meet his volatile thrusts until he lost the battle to dominate her sexually. Jack was spent and quickly fell asleep. Gezebel got out of bed and walked in a dazed fashion into one of the bathrooms. She filled the tub with hot water, and poured bath oil into it before stepping in. Gezebel winced when the steamy water scorched her skin as she immersed her languid body. Here she was, at age twenty, living in New York City with a man old enough to be her father! Gezebel pinched her nose and took a deep breath. She slid her head under the water and reminded herself that she was here for all the right reasons!

Chapter Thirty-Four

━━━━◦≪◈≫◦━━━━

Gezebel's ravenous stomach refused to let her sleep a minute longer and gnawed at her insides. She tossed and turned fitfully in bed. It was 10:01am, and Jack was already out of the house. Gezebel was upset with herself for having slept so long and attributed her lethargy to jet lag. Images of Baron crying out for her flashed through her mind and Gezebel was anxious about not being there for him. She forced herself out of bed, brushed her teeth, and took a quick shower. Gezebel brushed her mangled hair into a ponytail, and donned well-worn jeans, and a while t-shirt. She skipped the stairs, and rode the elevator down to the kitchen where she found Inez chopping cucumbers. Gezebel entered and plastered a cheerful smile on her face.

"Good morning Gezebel, did you sleep well?" Inez asked. Her English was colored with a heavy Dominican accent.

"Yes, I did! I'm starving, mind if I make myself breakfast?" Gezebel asked.

"i'll make it for you. What would you like?" Inez asked.

"Something New Yorkish!" Gezebel replied and giggled nervously.

Minutes later, Gezebel sat at the stone island in the kitchen, and devoured two eggs, three pancakes, and a toasted sesame seed bagel with cream cheese! Her voracious appetite was finally satiated, and she felt more alive. Inez seemed easy to get along with, and Gezebel hoped the housekeeper would help her get acclimated to Jack's way of life.

"Inez, how long have you been working here?" Gezebel asked curiously.

"I here seven years." Inez replied and clipped the stems of flowers picked from the rooftop garden. She arranged them adroitly in crystal vases to place on various mantels and tabletops throughout the house.

"I guess you like working here?" Gezebel asked.

"I have no problem. Jack is good man." Inez replied curtly.

"Yes, he is!" Gezebel agreed.

"I wouldn't work for anyone else!" Inez stated firmly.

The doorbell rang.

"Excuse me." Inez apologized and left to answer the door. Gezebel overheard the animated voice of a young woman conversing in Spanish with Inez. Their voices grew louder as they descended the stairs and entered the kitchen.

"Lizette, this is Mr. Chagall's girlfriend from Barbados. Her name is Gezebel. Gezebel, this is my sister, Lizette." Inez introduced the girls.

"Nice to meet you… Gezebel? Now, that's a unique name!" Lizette exclaimed with her Spanish/English/New York accent. Gezebel snickered and outstretched her hand to Lizette for a handshake. Lizette laughed and clasped Gezebel's hand firmly. The two girls chuckled. Gezebel had a feeling she and Lizette were going to get along.

"Yo! Yo motha actually name you that?" ("Hey, your mother actually gave you that name?) Lizette stated and waved her hand in the air for dramatic effect. She popped chewing gum between her teeth and drew attention to her pink glossy lips. Lizette's hair was tinted the color of a bloody mary, and she maintained it religiously in the Dominican beauty shops. Gold hoop earrings matched perfectly with the gold belt that hugged the waist of the skintight jeans she wore. The jeans emphasized Lizette's pear-shaped derriere which she was very proud of. Lizette was a "tell it like it is, in your face New Yorker" who thrived on the everyday experiences of city life. The Dominican lass viewed Gezebel with interest and found her mysterious beauty rather captivating. She was envious of Gezebel's tall stature and natural poise, since she, herself, was much shorter at 5'4" and a little rough around the edges. But, there was something about Gezebel's haunting eyes that caught her attention.

"You wearing contacts mami?" Lizette asked boldly. Gezebel didn't understand why Lizette referred to her as "mami" so she remained silent just in case Lizette suspected her of being a mother.

"Aye! Lizette, please!" Inez hissed at her sister. She thought Lizette was going too far.

"Never!" Gezebel replied and smiled. She wasn't offended because she answered similar questions dozens of times.

"Honey, if I had your height, and gorgeous face I would quit my job and work as a model!" Lizette stated as if she were making a revelation of some sort.

"Maybe I will!" Gezebel murmured. She enjoyed being scrutinized by Lizette. Lizette didn't know what to make of her. It was obvious the girl wasn't one of Jacks' adult entertainment models. What Lizette saw was someone who enjoyed a life of privilege; someone that was sheltered from birth.

"Gezebel, if you need someone to show you around, give me a call. I know New York better than anyone else, and girl, I know how to shop! Jack knows I'm good people!" Lizette boasted about her tour guide abilities and personal character. She liked Gezebel and wanted to know her better.

"Ok, i'll keep that in mind." Gezebel assured Lizette. Lizette withdrew a pen from her handbag and scribbled her number on a piece of paper.

"Here's my number. I'll be your first friend in New York, ok mami?" Lizette stated, and appointed herself Gezebel's personal mentor. Gezebel accepted the piece of paper, and stuffed it into the front pocket of her jeans.

"Why do you call me mami?" Gezebel asked. She needed clarification.

"Oh! Honey, that means you've got it going on!" Lizette exclaimed and laughed. Gezebel breathed a sigh of relief.

The doorbell rang.

"Excuse me." Inez excused her self to answer the door. She was grateful her sister did not offend Gezebel. Some people were turned off by Lizette's bold nature. Inez returned to the kitchen followed by a young blond with a chic haircut. She looked at least twenty-four years old of age and stood five foot ten. Loads of foundation masked pimpled skin, and the bright red lipstick worn in conjunction with jet black mascara, and green eye shadow, caused her to resemble a circus clown. Her nail extensions were devilishly long, and painted bright red. Gezebel thought she wore them like lethal weapons! The contorted look on the young woman's face signaled aggravation, and she stormed into the kitchen with a hard gait. Inez was suddenly on edge and busied herself with frivolous duties around the kitchen. The sides of Lizette's mouth turned down with displeasure at the sight of the young lady.

"Not this witch!" Lizette muttered under her breath but loud enough for Gezebel to hear.

"Inez, are you having a party down here or are you working?" The girl asked in an authoritative manner.

"Yes, I work! I always work! You know Mr. Chagall doesn't mind Lizette visiting!" Inez reminded the young lady in a respectful tone.

"And, who's this?" The girl asked and nodded towards Gezebel. Inez remained silent so Gezebel spoke up.

"I'm Gezebel. I moved in yesterday." Gezebel answered and wondered how this girl was connected to Jack.

"I remember Jack mentioning something about that!" The girl stated in a flat voice. Disappointment surfaced in her face.

"I see!" Gezebel replied dryly.

"Do you? Do you really see?" The girl asked Gezebel in a sarcastic manner.

"Told you she was a witch!" Lizette whispered to Gezebel and picked a grape out of the fruit bowl. She tossed it into her mouth. Gezebel was caught off guard by the resentful tone in the girl's voice. She had a feeling this girl was linked to Jack romantically.

"Who are you by the way?" Gezebel asked and crossed her arms over her chest.

"It's obvious she ain't shit, otherwise, he would've mentioned her stupid-ass!" Lizette sneered and Gezebel giggled.

"You got something to say, la nina?" The blond challenged Lizette in a hostile manner. Lizette turned her back and refused to acknowledge her. Inez breathed a sigh of relief when Lizette didn't respond. Lizette had a previous run-in with this girl and she didn't want it to happen again, because it could jeopardize her job. The young woman directed her attention back to Gezebel.

"I'm Lynn! Some people refer to me as Jack's girlfriend!" The young lady quipped.

"And, some people say, she ain't!" Lizette hissed and Gezebel giggled.

"Ladies! Good afternoon! Lynn, I see you've met Gezebel!" Jack announced with a relaxed air and entered the kitchen.

"Is this what you've bought back from the islands?" Lynn asked contemptuously.

"As a matter fact, she is! Isn't she lovely?" Jack quipped, and stoked Lynn's jealousy.

Lizette stifled her impromptu chuckles by covering her mouth with her hands. Gezebel's face remained expressionless and she successfully camouflaged her mirth beneath a cool exterior. Lynn struggled to remain calm but her body shook with rage. She wanted to slap Jack's face for humiliating her, and claw Gezebel's eyes out!

Gezebel was perfectly poised and well spoken. Not what she was expecting from someone originating from a third world country! Gezebel possessed the flair that she herself had worked so hard to mimic when struggling to make it as a super model. Lynn was a poor country girl that moved to New York from a small southern town. She worked as a waitress in between modeling assignments to keep a roof over her head. Modeling was a competitive industry, and Lynn was nothing special. She responded to an advertisement in search of models for a special project. Her audition went well, and she was one of the lucky girls chosen to work on the assignment. It was then, that Lynn learned the project required her to pose nude for an adult magazine! Lynn was apprehensive because this type of exposure could ruin her chances of ever becoming a highly sought after top model. But, meager savings, and having to share a studio apartment with a struggling actress, fueled her decision to take the job. Lynn photographed so well for the raunchy shots that Jack's editorial team selected

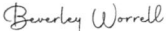

her photo for the magazine cover. She had a hard-edged style that worked well in the adult entertainment business. Lynn piqued Jack's interest with her fresh appeal, and it wasn't long before he invited her out to dinner. Over dinner, Lynn talked about her poverty stricken background, and having to hustle for every penny since she arrived in New York on a Greyhound Bus. Lynn was desperate for money, and stressed the need for it with such vigor that Jack extended an offer to Lynn to perform in adult movies. She signed a contract, and started to make money.

Lynn threw caution to the wind, and made her adult movie debut the following week. The money rolled in, and within two years Lynn earned more money than she could spend! She spiced up her on camera persona by investing in breast augmentation, and having her lips plumped up. The end result was a buxom, overly made up, oversexed blond vixen known as "La La Lynn" in the world of adult entertainment. Jack's business relationship with Lynn turned sexual, and Lynn kept him firmly anchored to her pubic area by doling out plenty sex and smothering him with her affections. She was convinced that Jack was in love with her and they would marry. Lynn already had their future planned. First marriage, and then she would work side by side with him to build his entertainment empire. Since Jack was significantly older than she, it was only a matter of time before he turned the reins over to her, leaving her in charge to call the shots! But now, her desire to snag a multi-millionaire, and live in the lap of luxury was smashed!

"Lynn, I need to speak with you privately." Jack addressed her in a business like tone.

"Time for me to go!" Lizette announced. She pecked Inez on the cheek before exiting the kitchen.

"Gezebel, excuse us." Jack stated and left the kitchen with Lynn in tow. Gezebel and Inez chatted until Jack returned with a red faced Lynn, hot on his heels!

"Gezebel, I have wonderful news! Fashion week in New York kicks off in September, and that's when you'll make your modeling debut! I've met with a couple agents this morning and they were excited by your photos! They forwarded your shots to two famous designers, and they can't wait to meet you! I've put Lynn in charge of chaperoning you to modeling, acting, and dance class so you can get properly trained. This means you two will be spending a lot of time together so make the best of it. We have two months until fashion week and I want you to hit the ground running! Your first modeling class starts in forty-five minutes so I suggest you two get moving! I've got other business to attend so i'll see you later." Jack informed Gezebel excitedly. He kissed her forehead and left. Lynn stared resentfully at Gezebel. Gezebel folded her arms across her chest and returned an ominous stare. Lynn decided to break the stony silence.

"Are you ready?" Lynn growled.

"Let's go!" Gezebel replied and they departed.

Modeling, acting, and dance consumed Gezebel's life for the next two months. These activities kept her focused on the future, instead of the past. Instruction in these classes focused on communication, perfecting that runway walk, makeup, working under diverse conditions, and being patient with demanding designers. Gezebel, at six feet in height, was the

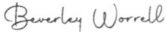

envy of her class. Instructors used her as an example of what students should try to emulate. Gezebel enjoyed the dance class because it helped her to move more fluidly when she modeled. She was free to be whoever she wanted to be. Lynn dutifully chaperoned Gezebel to various commitments, and for weeks they sat next to each other in the car without saying a word. Dialogue between the young women was for informative purposes only.

The month was August and the year was 2001. Lynn indignantly drove Gezebel to her final modeling class, and this marked the end of her chaperon duties. She couldn't wait to give this anorexic slut that stole her man, a tongue-lashing!

"You think you're hot shit don't you?" Lynn railed at Gezebel. She parked in front of the building where the class was held.

"What?" Gezebel quipped. She was surprised by Lynn's premeditated verbal attack.

"You think you've got what it takes to be a top model in New York? Competition is tough bitch, and if I didn't make it, you sure as hell won't!" Lynn yelled hatefully.

"You're failures in life don't have a damn thing to do with me!" Gezebel replied nastily.

Lynn was aghast at the truth of Gezebel's words and was unable to come up with a tactful response. Her mind reeled because she had to have the final word. She hadn't spent one night with Jack since Gezebel moved into the house and he treated her as just another employee. She wanted this witch to jump on her broom and fly back to the Caribbean!

"The only thing I failed at is running your anorexic ass out of town! What the hell does Jack see in you anyway?" Lynn yelled at Gezebel with disgust.

"At least my anorexic ass doesn't have to screw on camera just to make a buck!" Gezebel's words hit Lynn below the belt! Lynn had no idea Jack told Gezebel that she was a porn star!

"You're nothing Gezebel! You don't have what it takes to be a top anything! Jack belongs to me! Understand?" Lynn screamed dementedly at Gezebel.

Gezebel got out of the car and held the door open. She stuck her head inside the car and screamed at Lynn.

"Kiss my ass you belligerent whore!" She slammed the door of the red Mercedes and calmly walked to class.

Chapter Thirty-Five

Fashion week in New York kicked off during the second week of September, and fashion houses paraded their frocks and latest collections on the backs of stunning models. Gezebel was propelled into the dizzying world of fashion on a global scale. Couture, vintage, exotic, avante garde, eccentric, and luxury creations graced her elegant body. Beauty and glam dominated these fashion extravaganzas and excitement filled the air. Gezebel stalked the runways with confidence, and remained oblivious as photographers dazed her with the blinding flash from their cameras. The feeling was surreal, and Gezebel felt as though she was Alice in Wonderland. She rubbed elbows with renowned designers, and posed for photos with famous entertainers. Jack's money and influence catapulted Gezebel to the front line of every show, ensuring her maximum exposure.

Gezebel's calendar was booked solid with commitments to model during fashion week in London, Hong Kong, Paris and Milan. Photos of the Caribbean beauty appeared on the cover of fashion and beauty magazines all over the world. Gezebel traveled with Jack and worked hard to become the brightest star on the modeling scene. She saved magazines in which her face appeared on the cover, and mailed them to her family and friends in Barbados. Gezebel hoped the magazines would serve as proof that she was in America pursuing her goals and earning big money. The demand for Gezebel to make appearances at international events was tremendous and Jack had no choice but to hire an agent to manage her whirlwind career.

Gezebel and Jack returned to New York for much needed rest and reprieve. She had never been so mentally and physically fatigued in all her life. The glitz and glam of modeling was personally rewarding but like anything worth having in life, sacrifices had to be made. Modeling wasn't all about glamour. She worked long hours and some days functioned on not more than three or four hours sleep. Her feet and back ached from wearing stilettos for more than ten hours a day, but she performed like a pro, and smiled through it all. She was grateful to Jack for accompanying her as she traveled around the world to work. His guidance and protection from the gossip mongering press was necessary, as demand to know more about the exotic model with the mysterious eyes intensified. Inez welcomed the couple home when they arrived from their grueling journey. She heeded Jack's request not to be disturbed for the rest of the evening as he and Gezebel retired to bed. Gezebel awoke the next morning, and reached for Jack but he was already gone. She looked at the clock in the dim room, and the time was 11:02am. She was still groggy and started to snooze when the telephone rang.

"Yes?" Gezebel answered in a sleep-filled voice. She glanced at the caller id. It was Lynn.

"Oh, shut up! You think you're something special, don't you? I'm amazed at how you've brainwashed Jack! Everyone's talking about how he's bewitched by the mysterious island princess! It won't last Gezebel! I'll get him back and that's a promise!" Lynn declared angrily over the phone.

"Everyone's also talking about how Jack prefers real boobs to that imitation stuff you serve up!" Gezebel replied icily.

"You bitch!" Lynn cried and Gezebel hung up. The telephone rang again but Gezebel ignored it when the caller id registered Lynn. Gezebel sat up, and decided to leaf through her appointment book. Her calendar was booked solid with appointments for fittings, rehearsals, meetings with designers and agents, photo shoots, and auditions for a variety of skin care products. The rigorous schedule overwhelmed her, and she tossed the book on the floor. Gezebel quickly fell asleep.

Chapter Thirty-Six

"*Dear Family,*

It's been a year since I left and I miss all of you. As you should know by now, i've become a successful model. Life is wonderful and exciting. Jack takes good care of me and I trust him with my life.

Baron means the world to me and I think of him constantly. I intend to have him with me in the near future. Knowing that he's in good hands helps me to achieve all my goals. I've landed a sizeable contract with a beauty care line and already filmed a commercial. So now you can see me on t.v. Isn't that great?

I hope you've forgiven my sudden departure. Enclosed is a check for ten thousand dollars. Buy Baron a toy, and give him my love.

Gezebel.

"The nerve!" Bella ranted as she concluded reading the letter out loud to the family.

"Does she really expect us to buy Baron a ten thousand dollar toy?" Corine asked in disbelief.

"I'm still coming to grips with the knowledge that my granddaughter left us in the manner that she did! I didn't know she had it in her! If Gezebel thinks we're going to hand Baron over after she abandoned him, she better think again!" Estele stated with resolution and shook her head.

"At least we know she's safe. The private investigator has been keeping watch over her for the past year and reports to me on a weekly basis." Ernest stated.

"Praise the Lord!" Estele exclaimed and clasped her hands thankfully.

Chapter Thirty-Seven

"Jack, where you ever in love with Lynn?" Gezebel asked as they lounged in the living room watching a movie. His eyes pierced Gezebel's with a sharpness that made her shiver.

"Sorry! Perhaps I should mind my business!" Gezebel apologized with mock sincerity.

"No need to apologize. I'm glad you asked. The answer to your question is no." Jack replied. Gezebel was appeased by his answer and quickly changed the subject.

"You know what I'm in the mood for?" Gezebel asked spontaneously.

"What?" Jack murmured, and turned his attention back to the movie.

"French fries!" Gezebel stated and laughed.

"Are you serious?" Jack asked and rolled his eyes.

"Yes, I'm serious!" Gezebel asserted and giggled.

"It's almost midnight so take one of the cars and hurry back."
Jack suggested as Gezebel prepared to leave.

Gezebel drove out of the garage in Jack's midnight blue
sports car. Out of the three vehicles in Jack's garage, this
machine was her favorite because it was fast, and handled
perilous turns superbly. She drove at a moderate speed along
the sparsely populated streets of Upper Manhattan, appreciating the sights and sounds of city life. An occasional car
zipped past her but the streets were mostly quiet, almost
serene, which was unusual for New York. The golden arches
of the fast food chain glowed at her from a mile in the distance, and Gezebel drove on in her quest for the ultimate
midnight snack. She stopped at a red light, and waited for a
blond female pedestrian to cross the street. Gezebel thought
the blond sported a haircut similar to Lynn's, and she exam-
ined the woman closely as she walked staunchly pass the
car. The headlights of the sports car illuminated the face of
the blond, and Gezebel confirmed that it was in fact, Lynn.
She was probably heading to her condo somewhere in the
neighborhood.

Lynn clenched a cigarette between her lips, and lit up. Her
stiletto sandals clamored noisily on the pavement. She
crossed the street, walked a few feet down the block, and
disappeared around the corner. The light turned green and
Gezebel made a u-turn. She made a right turn at the same
corner Lynn turned on. The street was deserted except for
one or two night owls that were half asleep inside late night
cafes and bars. Gezebel drove at less than five miles per hour,
and switched off the headlights. Malevolence toward Lynn
ran amok in Gezebel's senses and her intentions turned
lethal. Gezebel eyed Lynn strolling down the street enjoying
her nicotine habit. Gezebel mashed the gas pedal with a fury!

The vehicle roared toward Lynn and she looked over her shoulder and screamed! She ran down the middle of the road in terror and twisted her ankle! Lynn hobbled in zigzag fashion, trying in vain to outsmart the crazed driver! The sports car sideswiped Lynn's elbow and hip. The blow knocked her off her feet! Lynn sat upright in the road, dazed, and unable to comprehend what was happening. Her elbow was bloodied either from being hit or from scraping it on the pavement when she fell. Lynn scrunched up her eyes, desperate to get a better view of the car and driver. It didn't take her long to recognize Jack's sports car and the dark haired figure behind the wheel. It was Gezebel! The sports car made an ominous u-turn in her direction, and the tires screeched demonically. The vehicle stopped abruptly, and the headlights flashed on and off as if signaling for her to get up and run!

"Gezebel, I know it's you!" Lynn screamed in anguish.

The tires screeched and the car bolted toward Lynn! She scrambled to her feet, and half-ran, half-hobbled, on the twisted ankle! Something cracked beneath the shoe she wore on the twisted ankle. The heel of her stiletto snapped in half, making it impossible for her to regain balance! Lynn panicked and staggered on the street! The vehicle sideswiped Lynn again, this time whacking her hard in the buttocks! Lynn was sent careening onto the sidewalk! The car sped away, leaving a terrified and bruised Lynn in a heap on the pavement! A trembling Lynn sought her handbag, and dialed 911 from her mobile phone. The ambulance rushed her to the emergency room, and Lynn tearfully reached out to Jack. He rushed to the hospital, consumed by concern for Lynn. She suffered a sprained ankle, a fractured elbow, and ugly bruises on her hip. The bang she endured in the buttocks caused some lower back sprain, and the doctor suggested she follow up with a chiropractor. Luckily, she suffered no broken bones. Hospital staff summoned police, and Lynn gave them information about the events that transpired that night. Jack listened in dissent as Lynn recounted that Gezebel tried to run her over with his sports car. The police visited Jack's home, questioned Gezebel, and inspected the sports car. The vehicle showed no signs of damage and Gezebel denied having driven at all that night. She claimed to have purchased a sandwich from a local deli and returned home. The police questioned workers at the deli but they were unable to confirm whether or not Gezebel was in fact there. Eventually, the case was closed due to lack of evidence, even though Lynn stoically maintained that Gezebel viciously attacked her that night.

Lynn gossiped about her ordeal to Jacks' business associates and mutual friends. She accused him of harboring a woman in his house that was capable of murder. Lynn succeeded in casting doubt in Jack's mind about Gezebel and her accusations soon began to affect their relationship. She threatened to ruin Gezebel's career by selling her story to the tabloids but refrained from doing so when Jack threatened to cancel her contract. Jack reacted to all these accusations by keeping tabs on Gezebel's whereabouts at all times. If she wasn't working or auditioning for a gig, Jack insisted she remain at home. His relentless control over her comings and goings stifled Gezebel. Gezebel's life with Jack revolved around work, lovemaking, and frequent spats. She was reduced to being an object he bought back from a faraway island to admire and enjoy. Jack continued to relish a free and active lifestyle, while Gezebel's movements were restricted. He conducted his personal and business affairs, while fame and fortune seduced Gezebel. But, once the cameras stopped rolling, Gezebel was isolated from the rest of the world. She was determined not to live her life in a fishbowl, but did she have the guts to be on her own in New York? She had never even taken the subway or the bus! All she had to do was walk out the front door, and reclaim her life. But, what price would she pay? The temptation to strike out on her own, and be independent appealed to Gezebel more, as Jack tightened the reins on her freedom. She knew that Lynn's silence wouldn't last forever, but Jack's chokehold on her liberties just might.

Gezebel turned to Lizette, Inez's sister, for support. Lizette kept Gezebel informed about what was happening in the real world outside the pampered and glamorous lifestyle she lived. Lizette resided in Brooklyn, near Flatbush, and vividly described it to Gezebel as a Mecca of Caribbean, European and Asian cultures. Gezebel's mouth watered as Lizette described restaurants serving spicy roti dishes just like the ones she enjoyed back home, and it sounded like a community where she could easily fit in. She didn't want to act out of haste and made a last ditch effort to convince Jack to loosen up. They were enjoying jumbo shrimp and coconut rice at the penthouse when a frustrated Gezebel expressed her desire to explore the city on her own. She wanted to feel a part of the city she lived in.

"Jack, can we talk?" Gezebel asked. She cut a portion of jumbo shrimp with her fork and put it in her mouth. It was delicious!

"Sure. What's on your mind?" Jack asked.

"Jack, I'm bored! I feel suffocated! I need to get out and do things on my own!" Gezebel complained.

"Gezebel, you have a famous face, and there are a lot of crazy people in this city. It's not safe!" Jack stated dryly.

"I'm not going to run wild like an animal! I just want to catch a bus, a train, shop, or simply take a stroll in a park by myself! I'm cooped up like a pigeon in here!" Gezebel retorted in an irritable voice.

"Gezebel, I'm not holding you prisoner!" Jack replied harshly.

"I never said you were!" Gezebel replied defensively.

"You almost ruined everything we worked for when you struck Lynn with the car! Do you really think I'm going to give you another opportunity to make another stupid mistake? I'll do whatever it takes to protect my investment, and that's you!" Jack stated flatly.

Gezebel's eyes narrowed dangerously and her lips twisted in an ugly grimace. She ignored his comments about Lynn and refused to implicate herself. As far as she was concerned, Lynn's tragedy was a dead issue.

"I'm your investment? Thanks for putting our relationship in perspective!" Gezebel replied and flung the fork in the plate.

"Gezebel, you're much more to me than that, and you know it. Forget about exploring this crazy city all right? Let's go to bed!" Jack suggested, and removed himself from the table.

Gezebel stood at the foot of the king-sized bed and Jack undressed her. She shivered when her nakedness was exposed in the cool room. Jack tenderly held Gezebel's head between his hands, and sucked her soft, creamy neck. He held the back of her head with one hand, and slipped his tongue between her lips, tasting her nectar. His other hand teased her nipples, and caressed her taut stomach. Jack's fingers lingered between her thighs, and caressed her body. Gezebel lay on her stomach and Jack ran his tongue along her buttocks, and buried his face between her youthful thighs. She turned over, and unzipped his trousers. Gezebel hugged his organ with her lips, and Jack cried out in ecstasy. Gezebel straddled him as he lay back on the bed, and he raised his hips every time she descended upon him. His sexual release was unlike anything he had ever experienced, and Gezebel's body tingled from the aftershocks of earth shattering sex.

Chapter Thirty-Eight

Jack awoke with Gezebel sleeping soundly in his arms. It was almost 5:30am and a feeling of sadness cloaked his heart. He had a premonition that Gezebel would not be here when he returned. Fame and fortune was not enough to keep her rooted by his side. Jack reasoned that Gezebel never thirsted nor hungered for anything, but she had proven herself to be resilient, tactful and smart. He was hopelessly in love with this twenty-one year old starlet, and for the first time in his life, he was afraid of losing a woman.

Gezebel opened her eyes to welcome a new day, and as usual, Jack was already gone. She removed her mobile phone from the drawer, and listened to a message from a realtor hired to find an apartment in the Park Slope section of Brooklyn. The realtor found a cozy one-bedroom apartment, and it was all hers. Gezebel was ecstatic! She had roughly eleven thousand dollars at her disposal, to do whatever she wanted. Jack invested the bulk of her earnings, and she decided it was best to leave that money where it was. She was determined to make it on her own, and eleven thousand dollars wasn't too shabby to start. Gezebel packed her suitcases, and took the elevator down to the kitchen where Lizette waited for her. Car service drove the ladies from Manhattan to Brooklyn.

The one bedroom apartment was on the first floor of a brownstone. Lizette grabbed the key from Gezebel and opened the door. Gezebel hurried into the apartment and screeched happily at the spacious rooms and high ceilings. There was a compact modern kitchen with track lighting, a bedroom, bathroom, and a living/dining area. Gezebel was thankful to have Lizette as a friend who understood her need for independence.

"Ok, girl, so what's next?" Lizette asked a giddy headed Gezebel.

"Furniture! Let's go shopping! Gezebel exclaimed. Lizette and Gezebel spent the better half of the day shopping for furniture, bedding, bath accessories, curtains, and anything else needed to fill her empty apartment. They returned later, and busied themselves hanging curtains, decorating, and putting items in place.

"Gezebel, what was it like?" Lizette asked curiously. She removed the newly purchased dishware from boxes.

"What was what like?" Gezebel quizzed Lizette. She hammered a nail into the wall to hang a framed picture of furry puppies with colorful hats on their heads.

"Sleeping with Mr. Chagall! Gezebel, he's so much older than you!" Lizette stated with emphasis.

"Lizette, I have no problem with his age. Jack treated me very well. If it weren't for him, I never would have become a top model this fast!" Gezebel replied. She felt it was necessary to defend Jack's honor.

287

"Then why did you leave?" Lizette asked sarcastically with a hand on her hip. Gezebel let out a long, exasperated sigh.

"I left because I wanted my life back! Living with Jack was like being locked in a prison! I was only let out to work and then it was back to the cellblock! I need control over my life!" Gezebel explained.

"I don't know! If a millionaire like Jack is going to let me live large, and all I got to do is look pretty, and give up the nookie whenever he wants it, then consider me his partner for life!" Lizette quipped and snapped her fingers.

"You go girl!" Gezebel egged her on and laughed.

The doorbell rang. Furniture deliverymen stood outside with a box spring and mattress that Gezebel ordered. They assembled the bed, and Gezebel handed the men a tip on their way out.

"Now, I want to see where you live." Gezebel advised Lizette.

"Ok, let's go, but remember, it's nothing like this beautiful apartment you have here." Lizette replied.

Lizette stood at the curbside of Flatbush and Atlantic Avenue, and hailed a passing van when the driver tooted the horn. She explained to Gezebel that vans with tooting horns were known locally as dollar vans, and they had a reputation for getting passengers from one end of Flatbush Avenue, to the next, in record time! The van drove expeditiously in the direction of Prospect Park, and Gezebel held onto her seat for dear life! The driver blasted reggae music, and Lizette laughed hysterically at Gezebel's terrified expression as the van tore down Flatbush Avenue, and zoomed past Central Library and Prospect Park! Lizette yelled to the driver, "Empire Boulevard" and handed the "conductor" a few crumpled bills. The "conductor" took the bills from Lizette and smiled at Gezebel. He was an attractive guy with strong African features, a bright smile and perfect teeth. He wore loose fitting jeans, and a short sleeved shirt, which showed off well-toned biceps. The cap on his head gave him cool look with a sophisticated urban edge. Gezebel was drawn to his dark eyes and curly eyelashes. She liked the way he flirted by winking inconspicuously in her direction every chance he got.

"Hey beautiful, what's yo' name?" He asked with an island drawl that sounded distinctly Jamaican.

"Gezebel." She responded and winked.

"You kidding me, right?" He asked incredulously.

"No mon! She serious mon!" Lizette mocked the guy's island accent and Gezebel laughed.

"Awhoa! Gary, this girl's name is Jezebel!" The conductor yelled to the driver.

"You don't need to mess with a girl who has a name like that, mon!" The driver drawled in a sugary Jamaican accent and laughed. The other passengers laughed and nodded in agreement.

"You beautiful still! Call me, ya hear?" The "conductor" scribbled his number on a piece of paper and handed it to Gezebel.

"Ok, mon, I will!" Gezebel promised.

The driver stopped abruptly at Empire Boulevard and Flatbush Avenue. Lizette and Gezebel hopped out of the van and walked to Ocean Avenue where Lizette lived. Lizette resided in a rooming house where she shared a kitchen and bath with two other people. The carpeted room was nicely decorated, and it was warm and cozy. Lizette had a TV, a small stereo, microwave, telephone, and a mini refrigerator, neatly tucked into the room. Even though it was comfortable, Gezebel didn't think it represented a real home. Lizette described previous living arrangements where she and her sister Inez shared a one-bedroom apartment with their parents and two brothers. When Lizette turned eighteen, she got a job in retail, and moved out of her parents' cramped apartment. This was all she could afford on her salary but Lizette didn't mind. She loved her room, her privacy and having peace of mind.

Lizette took Gezebel on an exploration of Prospect Park where they talked, licked ice cream cones, and listened to drummers beating out tunes. Kids rode their bikes and joggers jogged. Park goers fired up grills and enjoyed informal picnics with friends and family. Lizette was given insight into Gezebel's life in Barbados, and her reason for being in America. Gezebel didn't tell her about Baron because she preferred to keep that information private.

Later that evening, Gezebel returned to her apartment after a wonderful fun-filled day. This was her place and she was free to do whatever she liked. She picked up the phone and dialed Aunt Bella in Barbados. The voice mail answered the call, and Gezebel left a brief message, mentioning her new digs. She left her telephone number, confident that Bella would call.

Chapter Thirty-Nine

Gezebel fulfilled commitments for modeling gigs, special assignments, and personal appearances, but her agent had not secured future projects on her behalf. She was concerned about the lack of assignments, and contacted the agent to find out what was going on. Gezebel didn't want to face an economic crisis so soon after snatching her life back.

"Ms. Lanier, its Gezebel." She said when her agent picked up.

"Gezebel, it's nice to hear from you. How are you?" Ms. Lanier asked cheerfully.

"I'm doing great. Look, I noticed you haven't booked any new assignments for me." Gezebel stated.

"Um hum." Ms. Lanier murmured.

"Is there a reason why?" Gezebel asked with a sharp edge to her voice.

"Gezebel, Mr. Chagall hired me to work as your agent. He informed me that I was officially off his payroll after you fulfilled your last commitment. I understand that he's no longer managing your career." Ms. Lanier informed Gezebel apologetically.

"Oh, I see. I wasn't informed." Gezebel admitted.

"Gezebel, I suggest you give him a call. He said you left rather abruptly. Look, i'll give you the numbers for a few people who work directly with designers. Maybe they can secure some work on your behalf for a nominal fee… I don't know if you're aware of this but your contract with the beauty care line was cancelled… and… the television ad was pulled! Gezebel, a storm is brewing, and it's headed your way! I've gotta run!" Ms. Lanier advised Gezebel and hung up.

Gezebel sat in her apartment and held the telephone receiver to her ear. She listened to dial tone until her knuckles turned white. What storm was Ms. Lanier talking about? Would Jack ruin her career just because she walked out? Just because she wanted to live her own life after two years of being locked away from the rest of the world? She desperately wanted to call, but refused. The last thing she wanted was to appear emotionally weak and needy. Gezebel placed the telephone receiver back in its cradle with a trembling hand, and focused on contacting some of the people referred by Ms. Lanier. She left messages, and sent emails to photographers, designers, personal assistants, and anyone that was well connected in the business. She was confident they would respond favorably. After all, she was Gezebel. The most sought after model in the world.

Gezebel need a distraction so she called the "conductor" she met on the dollar van weeks ago. Sylvester was a proud Jamaican who uplifted her spirits with colorful stories about life in his homeland. They talked amicably for hours and he invited her to a movie later that evening. The movie was an outrageous comedy and Gezebel laughed until tears rolled down her cheeks. After the movie, Sylvester took Gezebel to a festively decorated Caribbean restaurant on Utica Avenue that played lively calypso music. They dined on fish and chips, which Gezebel doused with an outrageous amount of salt, ketchup and hot sauce. Sylvester fancied himself a natural comedian, and latched onto every opportunity to put a smile on her face. Laughter was just what the doctor ordered.

Weeks past and Gezebel did not receive offers or invitations to model in upcoming shows. Was she an overnight sensation? Never, Gezebel thought defiantly. Not in a million years! She left her apartment to grocery shop at a local supermarket, and waited in line at checkout when her eyes caught the headline of a well-known tabloid. She stood transfixed in horror when she realized her face was plastered on the cover!

The caption screamed, *"Porn Queen Accuses Top Model of Hit and Run!"* Gezebel snatched the tabloid off the rack, paid for the groceries, and hurried home. She entered her apartment, and dropped the bag of groceries on the floor. She turned to page seven, and read Lynn's damaging account about being the victim of a hit and run by top model Gezebel! A vengeful Lynn accused police of not conducting a thorough investigation into the matter, which would have resulted in the arrest of Gezebel! Lynn had finally made good on her threats! Gezebel learned that Lynn went so far as to recant the woeful tale on late night radio shows that granted her airtime. Listeners called in to console the queen of porn, and empathized with her attempt to build a public case against Gezebel. Through tragedy, Lynn finally received the international recognition she craved all her life. She used this situation to hurl her career into the spotlight as some type of porn celebrity, and DVD sales showcasing her lurid talents flew off the shelves. Gezebel was sick to her stomach! She was ruined! Lynn had single handedly reduced her modeling career to rubble, and used that rubble as a springboard to propel her own career.

Gezebel's sought support in Lizette and Sylvester. They were disturbed by the tale sold to the media by the porn queen, and believed that Lynn was a vengeful ex-lover of Jack's. Gezebel was distraught, and longed for the comfort and security of her family. She wished they were here to help her cope with Lynn's antics. Her voice mail and email was flooded with inquiries from malicious reporters that wanted her to comment on Lynn's accusations. She was in no frame of mind to defend her self on this issue and avoided the press.

Back in Barbados at Villa Coral.

"Have you seen this?" Estele shoved the tabloid into Ernest's hands.

"Of course I have, and it stinks! I got word from the private investigator that Gezebel is living alone in Brooklyn, New York." He replied.

"She's not with Jack Chagall anymore? Ernest, this situation is getting out of hand! We need to get her back home! I'm afraid for her safety!" Estele cried out.

"No!" Ernest stated obstinately and turned his back to his mother.

"And, why not?" Estele yelled in disbelief, challenging her son.

"Gezebel has made her bed, and she must lie in it! We can't rescue her every time she messes up; otherwise she'll always take us for granted! Mum, trust me on this one, I know my daughter!" Ernest pleaded with his mother.

Estele realized that she was getting too old for all this drama. She agreed to go along with Ernest and prayed that they were making the right decision. She worried about Gezebel day and night.

Back in New York

"I can't believe this!" Gezebel stated anxiously to Sylvester and Lizette. They gathered at her apartment in a show of support.

"That loco, loco witch!" Lizette quipped with hands on her hips. Lizette was dressed in a denim miniskirt, a black lace camisole that revealed maximum cleavage, a denim jacket, and black sandals. Colorful bangles adorned her wrists and "clanged" every time she moved her hands. Lizette's recently colored black hair was slicked back into a ponytail with hair gel, and showed off her smooth mocha complexion. Her lips glistened with orange colored gloss.

"Gezebel, what are you going to do? You haven't worked in months! Do you have any money left?" Lizette asked in a worried voice.

"I have seventeen hundred dollars left. That's only enough for next month's rent, and food." Gezebel informed her friend.

"i'll help you with food until you find a job." Lizette reasoned.

"And I can pay your utility bills until you get on your feet. You don't need this modeling crap mon! Just get yourself a steady gig to support yourself. It's hard out here!" Sylvester consoled Gezebel. He gave her a hug and left the apartment.

"Gezebel, Lynn was at the house last night. Looks like she's got her hooks in Jack again!" Lizette advised her friend when they were alone.

Gezebel's mouth twisted in a spiteful snarl because she was jealous and angry. She hated the thought of Lynn being cozy with Jack. Gezebel missed the security he provided now that her life was wrought with scandal and unemployment. She would have to correct these things without his intervention. Ten months ago she walked out of Jack's life, and she missed him dearly. Could she be in love with a man old enough to be her father? It couldn't be! It was the fame and fortune she was in love with, not Jack! Gezebel assured herself. She shrugged jealousy aside, and was confused as to why those feelings surfaced in the first place. Jack didn't love Lynn so there was nothing to be jealous of. After all, she was the one that walked out.

"Earth to Gezebel!" An exasperated Lizette yelled.

"What? I'm sorry I was deep in thought!" Gezebel replied, and snapped back to reality when Lizette's razor like voice sliced through her private thoughts.

"You were thinking about him, weren't you?" Lizette asked accusingly.

"He who?" Gezebel replied nonchalantly.

"Jack, that's who! You love that rich cld geezer, mama sita?" Lizette teased Gezebel. Gezebel turned away from Lizette and bit into her lower lip. She fought to stave off tears of hatred for Lynn and tears of love for Jack.

"Hey, don't worry about them ok? Listen, i'll pick up an application for you from Mayberry Department Store where I work. You're in luck because they're hiring! You'll be trained as a sales associate and as a checkout clerk. You'll also learn about inventory and stock. I've been with Mayberry's for four years and worked my way up. Next month, i'll be in training for a management position. I know people that can get you hired so don't worry!" Lizette advised Gezebel with an air of importance. She gave her a sisterly hug and left the apartment.

Gezebel collapsed on the floor and wept over the sorry state her life. She rocked herself, and lamented over the situation. Once the tears subsided, Gezebel realized she had to push on! She couldn't let Lynn win! Gezebel was too proud to accept financial help from Lizette or Sylvester, and she didn't want to call Jack. Instead, she reached out to her Aunt Bella in Barbados.

"Bella St. John!" Bella answered her cffice phone with a sharp tone.

"Aunt Bella, its Gezzy!" Gezebel spoke breathlessly into the receiver.

"Gezebel? I haven't spoken to you in almost three years!" Bella exclaimed.

"I sent you a letter, and left my number on your voicemail months ago but no one called. I sent magazines that featured me on the cover... It's not like I never initiated contact!" Gezebel reminded Bella.

"Gezebel, how could you leave us like that?" Bella asked in a pained voice.

"I made the decision at the last minute... I knew that if I told the family it would have been much more difficult to leave. Or, perhaps, I wouldn't have left at all!" Gezebel explained. Now was not the time for Bella to dwell on the past.

"And, what about Baron? He's almost four, and learning to read and write. He's the cutest little boy i've ever seen." Bella informed Gezebel. She could tell that Bella truly loved her son.

"That's wonderful! I miss him so much. Aunt Bella, I love my son." Gezebel replied. A sob traveled through her gut and lodged itself in her throat.

"We put that ten thousand dollar check into Baron's trust fund to build value instead of buying a worthless toy!" Bella haughtily advised her niece.

"Sounds good! How's the family?" Gezebel asked timidly. She wanted to keep the conversation positive.

"Let's see:
Your father is on the verge of disinheriting you,
Your mother is worried sick and would love to hear your voice,
Your grandmother has aged because of your cruel behavior,
And, your son calls me Ma Ma!" Bella retorted sarcastically.

Gezebel pursed her lips until they were colorless. The thought of her son calling someone else Ma Ma was like a fist to her stomach. Bella was getting under her skin, and she focused on the reason for her call.

"I don't expect anyone to forgive me! I know my actions were deplorable but it is what it is! Nothing can change the past! Aunt Bella, I need help!" Gezebel confessed.

"Help?" Bella repeated harshly. Her vocal chords constricted and her heart beat furiously in her chest. Her temper seethed until it reached boiling point. Bella sat behind the desk of her executive suite, and crossed her legs. She tapped her high-heeled shoe rapidly on the carpeted floor.

"Work is slow and I'm running out of money! I need a few thousand dollars." Gezebel sucked up her pride and asked for the money.

"Gezebel, I closed all of your accounts and the money was transferred to your trust fund. There's no cash available in the coffers for you! Why are you in need of money? Didn't the television ad and contract with the skin care company pay handsome dividends?" Bella asked arrogantly and sucked her teeth.

"Aunt Bella, please! I need to keep a roof over my head!" Gezebel begged.

"A top model like you shouldn't be broke! Has the well suddenly run dry my dear? Do your misfortunes have anything to do with those horrific accusations I read about in the tabloids?" Bella mocked Gezebel.

"If those accusations were true wouldn't I be rotting away in jail?" Gezebel shouted.

"I suppose!" Bella retorted dryly.

"What about the money?" Gezebel demanded.

"Sorry kid!" Bella replied.

"What? You're not going to help me just because I decided to have a life of my own instead of ending up a childless tyrant like you?" Gezebel sputtered in a rage.

"You ungrateful pig! Don't you know I would put my hands around your scrawny neck and strangle the piss out of you?" Bella hollered into the telephone receiver.

"Like hell, Bella!" Gezebel shouted and slammed down the phone.

Tears of desperation beseeched Gezebel. She needed a job. She needed an income. The world of fashion and modeling eluded her. She had to recapture it. Gezebel was tough but now she would have to hone a resilience that was suitable for survival. She pulled herself together, and made a desperate call to her best friend Joi. Joi wired five thousand U.S. dollars from her bank account in Barbados to Gezebel's account in the United States. Gezebel contacted Joi once the transaction registered successfully in her U.S. bank account.

"Joi, I owe you one." Gezebel stated.

"Gezebel, I wish I could send more. I hope this tides you over." Joi stated worriedly.

"i'll have to get a job because it looks like modeling is not in the cards for me at the moment. So much has gone wrong but i'll reclaim the throne." Gezebel promised her dearest friend.

"I know you'll find a way to make it happen. I've got some news. Bella purchased Kendrick's mother a small bungalow near Collymoore Rock, St. Michael. She wasn't comfortable taking Baron to visit Kendrick's mother in Nelson Street so she moved her out. Bella owns the house but they live in it. Kendrick is finally out of jail and he's living with his mother in their new home. He's still working as a fitness trainer, and... are you ready for this? Kendrick is a born again Christian!" Joi declared and giggled.

"Kendrick? A born again Christian?" Gezebel exclaimed and they laughed until their stomachs hurt.

"Yes! He goes into Bridgetown, holds up the bible, and preaches about heaven and hell! He even has a collection plate for donations! I hear he's planning to open up a church, and... he even has a congregation of fifteen that meets at the house every Sunday! No other preacher can deliver a hell fire and brimstone sermon better than Kendrick! Can you believe it?" Joi asked and roared with laughter.

"Oh my goodness! This is too much!" Gezebel cackled. "Kendrick has finally found himself a legitimate hustle in the name of the Lord!" She declared and both of them fell down laughing in their respective parts of the world.

Chapter Forty

L ack of income and hard times forced Gezebel to register with a temporary employment agency in Manhattan. The agency found her work in administrative capacities for major corporations. Compensation was laughable compared to the thousands of dollars she earned an hour as a super model, but she trudged on, determined to improve her lot. Gezebel successfully hid her famous looks by wearing wigs, no makeup, and black contact lenses. She made every effort to assimilate into the workforce without attracting attention. Occasionally, an eyebrow was raised or a question was posed by about whether or not she was the popular model "Gezebel" but she blew those suspicions off, and pretended to be flattered.

An up and coming fashion designer in need of models for his fashion debut placed an ad in the newspaper, and Gezebel responded. Damarco was the name of the designer and his label was christened "Simpli Fab." Damarco hired Gezebel on the spot, but his budget was so airtight, he could only afford to compensate her $200 for each show. Gezebel welcomed the opportunity for a modeling gig, and rehearsed with inexperienced and unknown models that were eager for exposure. The models were excited to work with Gezebel, and bombarded her for advice on how to make it big. They questioned her about the stories in the tabloids and Gezebel dispelled the rumors as totally false.

The first show was held in the gymnasium of a public school in Queens, New York, and the turnout exceeded Damarco's expectations. Gezebel's modeled Damarco's fashions as if she were cloaked in Gucci. Damarco was grateful to Gezebel for her outstanding performance and promised future projects. He understood that she was trying a make a comeback after damaging accusations ruined her image. Damarco took a liking to Gezebel, and promised to get her as much exposure as possible. He referred Gezebel to other 'up and coming' designers struggling to make their labels household names, and word spread among them like wildfire! They clamored for the services of this former top model. Gezebel modeled in nightclubs, auditoriums, at parties, and other social events. These modeling gigs kept her moving, despite the paltry compensation and amateurish productions. Gezebel had to claw her way back to the top and it was frustrating. But, some work in the business was better than no work at all. Her portfolio was becoming more impressive with each event, and she was convinced that there had to be light at the end of the tunnel. These unknown designers eventually became Gezebel's friends, and to them, she was a valuable asset.

Gezebel was focused on filing documents at an accounting firm in Manhattan, when the mobile phone attached to her trouser pocket vibrated against her hip. Gezebel answered the call in a hushed tone because her co-workers were within earshot.

"Yes!" Gezebel whispered into the handset.

"It's damarco." He sounded upbeat and in good spirits.

"Hey, what's up?" Gezebel whispered.

"i've got a gig that's going to blow your mind!" Damarco exclaimed.

"Really?" Gezebel asked.

Damarco was a colorful and creative soul. His speech and body language was just as outrageous as his fashion sense. He carried himself with an effeminate air that Gezebel found hilarious. Damarco wore makeup, donned tight clothes, and loved to play dress up. He kept his peers, models, and clients on their toes with his ever-changing hair, clothes and over the top fashion sense. Sometimes he presented himself in drag, or as a gay male. Other times he presented himself as a heterosexual man minus the feminine mannerisms. He possessed a dramatic flair, and invigorated his team with outlandish ideas, a buoyant spirit, and a mouthful of sarcastic remarks that kept those around him in hysterics. Gezebel considered him a girlfriend and treated him as such.

"You know that pop singer, Morrow?" Damarco asked breathlessly. Gezebel knew Damarco was fluttering his eyelashes even though she could not see him. She could tell from Damarco's tone that he thought this R&B singer was hot.

"Of course! He sings that hit song, "Got to have you." Gezebel replied.

"That's it girl! Well, one of my friends is directing a music video for that song! They need a girl to act as Morrow's love interest and guess what?" Damarco asked exuberantly.

"Go on, lay it on me!" Gezebel no longer whispered into the phone. Suspense was getting the best of her and her co-workers listened with interest.

"It's you babe! I got you that gig! Do you love me?" Damarco exclaimed. Gezebel squealed with delight into the phone, and her co-workers speculated that she won the lottery! They looked at her in hopes that she would share the good news.

"I can't believe this! Could this be the break i've been waiting for? Oh, damarco, I can't believe you hooked me up!" Gezebel exclaimed with delight.

"Girlfriend, when you get your groove back, and start making millions, don't forget us little people!" Damarco teased and Gezebel giggled.

Filming a music video was a new experience for Gezebel because she had to be up close and personal with the R&B star. She acted the role of his girlfriend, and that entailed laying in bed next to him and giving him a kiss. They danced with their bodies close, held hands, and pretended to be enamored with each other. At first, Gezebel was stiff and awkward. The crew had to do a couple of takes before she loosened up and got it right. The director announced "That's a wrap" and Gezebel breathed a sigh of relief.

Gezebel sat on her living room sofa, and viewed the music video as it played on the cable music video networks. She hoped this video would bring her a step closer to being a super model. After watching her performance, Gezebel decided to take a shower. She emerged refreshed and wrapped her body in the chenille robe that Lizette gave to her as a house warming gift. Lizette boasted that the robe was on sale at

Mayberry Dept Store where she worked, and when she added her employee discount, she paid only $20 for the designer robe. The doorbell buzzed. Gezebel peered into the peep-hole. It was Sylvester.

"Hey beautiful, I thought I would drop by with a bot-tle of champagne to celebrate your music video." Sylvester announced in a festive manner.

"Champagne? Sylvester, you shouldn't have!" Gezebel replied and moved aside to let him in. She disappeared into the kitchen and returned with two champagne glasses purchased from the $99 cent store.

"Anything for you, pretty lady!" Sylvester replied and licked his fudge colored lips. He popped the cork off the bottle and poured pink bubbly into a glass. He handed it to Gezebel and poured some for himself.

"Here's to the "come back kid!" Sylvester clowned and Gezebel couldn't help but giggle at his silliness.

"Here! Here!" She agreed and sipped the bubbly. To Gezebel, champagne was the perfect expression of celebration, con-tained in a bottle.

"Excuse me while I change out of this robe." Gezebel advised Sylvester.

"I think you look beautiful just the way you are. I would love to see what's underneath!" Sylvester remarked in a seductive voice. He didn't know if Gezebel would ask him to leave or indulge his fantasy.

Gezebel gulped the champagne and gazed at Sylvester. It was a long time since she made love and Sylvester was physically appealing. His dark skin, and rugged bad boy style of dress, was indicative of his neighborhood and culture. She stepped away from him and loosened the straps of her robe. The robe drifted from her body, and fell gently to the floor like a leaf falling from a tree in autumn. Gezebel was nude, and stood shamelessly in front of Sylvester. His eyes soaked up her toned body and flawless skin. Sylvester's eyes lingered on her breasts which reminded him of sun ripened raspberries, and his eyes drank in her tiny waist, and long shapely legs. Sylvester gazed into Gezebel's translucent gray eyes, and stepped closer. He took her in his arms, and flicked her nipples hungrily with his tongue. He groped her buttocks, and drew her close. They kissed ardently and savored the bittersweet champagne in each other's mouths. Gezebel unzipped his denim jeans, and fondled his rigid manhood. His manhood brushed against her pubic area and enticed her sensuously. Sylvester kneeled on the floor and aroused her sensitive vulva with his tongue. Gezebel knelt next to him, and his tongue invaded her mouth with such yearning that it almost took her breath away. She lay back on the floor and he positioned himself on top of her. His unyielding instrument of pleasure penetrated her warm caress and surpassed his wildest fantasies. Sylvester left Gezebel's apartment hours later, physically exhausted. He realized that fantasies really do come through.

Chapter Forty-One

Lizette was on her way to Gezebel's apartment with urgent news about Jack, and Gezebel was anxious. Was Lynn moving in with him? Did Jack propose to Lynn? Gezebel didn't know what to think. She opened the door for Lizette before the doorbell could ring twice.

"Hi honey, how are you?" Lizette asked and gave her a hug.

"I'm hanging in there." Gezebel replied anxiously.

"I loved the music video! I told the girls at work that we are best friends and they didn't believe me!" Lizette complained. She rolled her eyes and sucked her teeth. Gezebel snickered at the comical expression on Lizette's face when she pushed up her mouth.

"Gezebel, you look radiant! I mean you're glowing like a neon sign! You got yourself a man!" Lizette avowed and chuckled. She pointed her forefinger at Gezebel in an accusatory fashion. Gezebel ignored her, but the grin on her face substantiated Lizette's assumptions.

"You had some didn't you? I knew it! You can't fool me! So, who's the lucky stud?" Lizette asked eagerly.

"Oh, you busy body!" Gezebel complained.

"Uh huh, so, who is it?" Lizette brazenly pressed on, and Gezebel groaned good- naturedly.

"Is it Sylvester?" Lizette asked.

Gezebel giggled and shared information with Lizette about her sexual encounter with Sylvester. She gave her shadowy details of his sexual prowess but Lizette craved more. Gezebel entertained Lizette, and declared Sylvester an extremely well endowed buck! Lizette's eyes bulged and she squealed like a stuck pig! She lapsed into a song and dance in her native Spanish that caused Gezebel to laugh hysterically. Lizette's performance ended abruptly and Gezebel applauded. Lizette bowed in appreciation and plopped down on the couch. Then she focused on the reason for her visit.

"Mamie, look, I hate to deliver bad news now that things are looking up." Lizette advised Gezebel with a solemn expression. Gezebel held her breath and waited.

"Jack has prostate cancer." Lizette stated flatly.

"What?" Gezebel asked in an alarmed voice.

"He's been back and forth to the hospital taking all kinds of tests." Lizette stated.

"Man! This is not good! I should be there to help him through this! I'm going over there right now! Jack needs me!" Gezebel fought back tears.

"No! Don't!" Lizette warned Gezebel.

"Why not? Jack needs me!" Gezebel insisted.

"Because Lynn is there!" Lizette explained in a worried voice.

"I'm not scared of Lynn!" Gezebel stated with hardness to her voice.

"Honey, I know, but she's there 24/7. She may as well be living with the man!" Lizette quipped.

"I don't care!" Gezebel muttered between clenched teeth.

"Gezebel, be reasonable! You haven't spoken to Jack since you left, and the woman who accused you of a hit and run is practically living in his house! Do you really think you should go over there?" Lizette argued with Gezebel. Gezebel knew Lizette was right. Lynn would welcome the opportunity to nail her coffin shut! She decided not to argue with her friend.

"You're right! What was I thinking?" Gezebel stated meekly and sat next to Lizette.

"Now you're talking! Look, i've got to go. I'll call later. Love you." Lizette said with a sigh of relief and pecked Gezebel on the cheek before leaving the apartment.

Gezebel pondered the situation further and tears welled in her eyes. She wouldn't be able to forgive herself if Jack's condition took a turn for the worse and she wasn't there to comfort him. Gezebel grabbed her handbag and exited the apartment. She rode the train from Brooklyn to Manhattan. It was time to pay Jack a visit, even if it meant a confrontation with Lynn. Gezebel walked briskly from the subway to the stately home she once shared with Jack. Her heart pounded and she was numb with fear. She edged closer to his palatial townhouse, and stormy seas of trepidation raged in her soul. Gezebel was within a block of the home when she observed a red Mercedes exiting Jack's garage. It was Lynn with her oversized retail bosom leaving Jack's house. Gezebel waited until the vehicle pulled away from the building before she rang the doorbell. She wrung her hands frantically, and worried about how Jack may respond to seeing her after all this time. Gezebel closed her eyes. Brisk footsteps clamored closer to the door, and she half-hoped it was Inez.

"Gezebel!" Jack stated with surprise. Gezebel opened her eyes and threw her arms around his neck.

"Oh, Jack!" Gezebel cried and wiped tears from her eyes.

"Welcome back!" Jack stated happily and ushered Gezebel into the house. They rode the elevator to the third floor, and by the time they entered the penthouse, Gezebel was despondent.

"Hey, what's wrong? Did someone hurt you? Why didn't you call? I've been worried sick!" Jack asked, unable to veil the pain in his voice. He guided her to the leather sectional so they could sit and talk.

"Jack, I was miserable! You believed Lynn's lies instead of trusting me when I told you I did not hit her with the car! I felt confined. I had to leave in order to establish my own independence." Gezebel explained between sobs.

"I figured that was the reason you took off. I was just trying to protect you because Lynn was hell bent on ruining your career. As long as you were here with me, I was able to protect you, but, when you left, the situation was beyond my control. I never wanted to lose you." Jack remarked softly. He took Gezebel in his arms and kissed her passionately. "i've missed you so much." Jack whispered in a throaty voice.

"i've missed you too. I've been modeling for every unknown designer in New York, and I managed to land a lead role in a music video. But, that's not important. I heard you were sick." Gezebel remarked with concern.

"Sick?" Jack asked sheepishly.

"Jack, do you have prostate cancer?" Gezebel cried.

"Damn!" He yelled and slammed a fist on the center table! Jack knew the only person who could have told Gezebel was Inez's malicious sister, Lizette. He was well aware of the friendship between the two girls.

"Yes… I have prostate cancer." Jack admitted and furrowed his brow.

Gezebel cried. Jack took her in his arms and kissed her. He slipped his hands under her frilly knee length skirt and caressed her warm body. Gezebel lay back on the leather sectional and Jack pulled her skirt down her silky smooth legs. His tongue reacquainted itself with all those crevices he loved to ravish. Gezebel moaned as he soothed her tears away. Her body throbbed and quivered with pleasure.

Jack requested Inez prepare lunch for two, and when she arrived with the food, she was pleasantly surprised to see Gezebel. Jack and Gezebel lunched on salmon, salad, and jasmine rice, while Jack informed Gezebel about his medical situation. During a routine visit with his physician, a lump was detected and the doctor ordered a biopsy. The biopsy confirmed that the lump was a malignant stage one tumor. Lucky for him, the tumor was still localized, and doctors were able to pose a variety of treatment options to combat the disease. Jack's prognosis was positive, and he was upbeat. Gezebel thought he looked incredibly handsome, and she leaned over and kissed him, just like old times. After they lunched, Gezebel thought it was best to leave because she wanted to avoid Lynn at all costs. She didn't want anything to spoil her reunion with Jack.

"Jack, I have to go. Please take care of yourself." Gezebel whispered and embraced him.

"Gezebel, I know you have a life of your own but this is still your home. I need you here with me." Jack declared with love.

"What about Lynn?" Gezebel asked and folded her arms across her chest.

"I see Lizette has done a fine job keeping you informed!" Jack exclaimed and feigned disdain for Lizette. Gezebel smirked.

"You're the one I want!" Jack advised Gezebel with brute force.

"We'll see!" Gezebel replied firmly.

"Gezebel, marry me! I love you! I've always loved you! Can't you see that?" Jack implored her.

"Jack, getting married is the furthest thing from my mind! I'm working to regain my footing as a supermodel and I can't make such a commitment until it happens!" Gezebel touched his lips tenderly with her fingers and hurried out the door.

Jack wanted to own Gezebel's mind, body and spirit. But, her son, Baron deserved those things too. Gezebel felt a sense of relief when she arrived in the trendy Brooklyn neighborhood where she lived. She walked in and out of shops dotted intricately along Fulton Street and compulsively purchased items she didn't need. Her thoughts lingered on Baron. She missed him dearly. Was the sacrifice really worth it? Would her family allow her back into his life and pick up where she left off? She wiped tears from her eyes. It was imperative for her to get back on top. Only then she could face her family with a sense of accomplishment and claim her son.

Chapter Forty-Two

Gezebel fielded a multitude of calls from producers and other low profile designers after the music video aired. She accepted the most lucrative offers and worked tirelessly to reinvent her image. But still, the top fashion houses eluded her. Lynn's accusations had severely wrecked her reputation, and renowned designers were scared of bad publicity. Gezebel was determined to emerge victorious and refused to give up. She missed Jack but wanted to prove she could do this on her own. The responsibility to succeed or fail was all hers.

Damarco became Gezebel's unofficial agent and booked her for every feasible gig he was privy to. He arranged a photo shoot for a small ethnic magazine, which agreed to put her face on the cover. Her portfolio functioned like a sword to slice through some of the obstacles in her career path, but things were not happening fast enough. Fashion week in New York was only a few months away, and she had to get in on the action but hook or by crook! Photographers were wrapping up after the photo shoot for the magazine concluded when damarco paid her a surprise visit.

"Hey Gezebel!" He exclaimed happily.

"damarco! You look absolutely ravishing my dear!" Gezebel teased, and bat her eyelashes to mimic him.

"Don't I always?" Damarco asked, and did a 360 degree turn in hip hugging black jeans. His studded leather belt, powder blue long-sleeved shirt, and black patent leather shoes made him look as though he just stepped off the pages of a magazine. A few buttons on his shirt were left unbuttoned to show off toned Pecs. Silver chains of various lengths hung stylishly from his neck and his hair was slick with gel. He was clean-shaven, and smelled like a fragrant rose garden.

"Girl! Have I got news for you! A new fragrance is about to hit the market and the word is, the creator is being very selective about the model chosen to represent the product. Three top models were rejected because of over exposure. Gezebel, I think you should give it a try." Damarco advised her. He knew how hard Gezebel worked for the little people and he wanted her to be in the limelight again. If she spiraled her way back to the top, there's no telling what that could mean for him.

"Hum… a fragrance? What's the name of it?" Gezebel asked excitedly.

"Heck if I know! It's some top-secret mess!" Damarco replied sarcastically.

"Hey, why not? I'll give it a whirl!" Gezebel mused over auditioning for a job she knew little about.

"I knew you would! Let's grab a bite to eat and i'll tell you all I know. I'll also tell you about my finder's fee!" Damarco joked and they laughed. Gezebel linked her arm with dam-arcos' and the two of them left the studio chatting excitedly about the fragrance that was about to set the world on fire!

The audition was held in the fashion district near West 37th street in Manhattan, and it was a testy experience. Gezebel waited three hours before it was her turn to strut her stuff. The crew informed the models that the girl chosen to be the face of the fragrance would also model the designer's fashions during fashion week in New York, and other venues around the world. The audition required each girl walk on a runway, read lines from a teleprompter and change her facial expression when asked to do so. They were looking for a girl that was seductive and mysterious, yet innocent. The girl had to be youthful, yet mature enough to wear a sexy fragrance. It wasn't going to be easy!

Gezebel's turn had come, and she was ordered to change into six-inch stilettos, don a weighty white gown that dragged on the floor, and walk on a hastily built runway erected for this purpose. The producer bellowed at her, "SEDUCTIVE!" And Gezebel hunched her shoulders and softened her face. She sashayed her hips slightly when she walked, but the dress got tangled beneath the stilettos, and she prayed she wouldn't trip! Gezebel managed to discreetly kick the folds of the dress away from her ankles when she walked, and the producer bellowed, "INNOCENT!" Gezebel adopted an unassuming strut, opened her eyes wide, and masked her face with a clueless expression, but, before she could perfect the image, the producer bellowed, "AGGRESSIVE yet GENTLE!" And Gezebel struggled to conjure up this look. She placed a hand on a hip, walked with a proud gait, and plastered a smile on her face. Then she was ordered to face the teleprompter and read. Gezebel read the lines with as much enthusiasm as possible and it was over! The audition was over in five minutes, and Gezebel was informed that she would receive a call for a second auditiion if they were interested. There were no smiles, no handshakes, and not a single ray of hope offered by the crew. She was reduced to being one of the hundreds of girls vying for an incredible opportunity in New York.

"Thanks for the audition... i'll be leaving now!" Gezebel sputtered, and addressed the production crew. She hoped they would tell her to come back tomorrow, but they ignored her, and buried their heads in paper work. Life sucked!

The crew was oblivious to her departure, and Gezebel went into the dressing room and changed. She exited the studio, and walked into the chilly corridor. Gezebel took notice of a petite, harried looking, bespectacled young woman sitting in an office. She appeared to be of some importance to the production. The nameplate on the door read, "Sophie Berg – Production Coordinator." The young woman was so engrossed in her work that she didn't notice Gezebel. She got up from her desk and hustled into the hallway to call the next girl on the list. Gezebel eyed the open briefcase on the coordinator's desk, and wondered if the creator of the fragrance was noted on the papers. She wanted to sift through the briefcase, and inched closer to the office door. Gezebel heard footsteps coming toward the office so she hid behind a corner and waited. Out of the corner of her eye, she spied the coordinator walk into the office and lock the door! Gezebel was peeved! She exited the building and walked dejectedly past hundreds of models scheduled to audition. Gezebel wanted to scream! She had never felt so powerless! Winning this contract was a big deal. The model stood to earn millions, not to mention having her face plastered in top magazines all over the world! She had to be the face of this fragrance! Something big had to happen!

Finally, a long day of auditions had come to an end. Sophie, the coordinator, was glad to call it quits. Since 7:00am, she had been screening hundreds of girls to find that special one. Sophie removed a sample of the secret fragrance from her briefcase and sniffed. The soft scent made her feel like a princess. She placed the sample into her briefcase and locked it. This campaign was going to be big, and the perfume was going to be a top seller. She was impatient to find the right model for the job because the creator devised a stringent schedule for her to follow. Sophie looked over a few photos the team thought were top picks. She like Gezebel's the most. Her eyes were hauntingly beautiful and mysterious. They seemed to capture the essence of what the perfume conveyed. However, her image was tainted by scandal. But, that was a long time ago. Sophie didn't care about scandal, and she hoped the creator of the fragrance didn't either. Why should this model suffer because of rumor? Sophie sighed, and put Gezebel's photo on top of the other nine. She grabbed her briefcase, locked the door, and bade goodnight to the crew. Sophie rode the elevator to the lobby, and walked out into the twilight. It was almost 9:00pm, and a few people were out enjoying the mild weather. Sophie ventured across the street to purchase a cup of coffee from a nearby café, when the unthinkable happened. Something hard was pressed against the side of her head and there was a tug at the briefcase!

"Drop it!" A gruff voice demanded.

Sophie turned, and faced a figure dressed in black, wearing the mask of a cartoon character! She dropped the briefcase and sprinted down the block screaming at the top of her lungs! The masked figure picked up the briefcase and ran in the opposite direction! The goon turned the corner, dipped into an alley, and removed the mask and overalls, which were

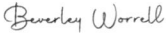

then stuffed into a bag. The goon slinked out of the alley and disappeared underground into the nearest subway station! The assailant arrived home and giggled devilishly when the image of the terrified coordinator entered her mind. It was so funny! Gezebel used the handle of her hairbrush as the stick up weapon! Her heart beat wildly in her chest. She had never done anything so daring! So fun! Gezebel sank to her knees because they felt like jelly and burst into nervous laughter. The coordinator didn't even put up a fight, but dropped the briefcase, and ran screaming for her life! It was so easy!

Gezebel sifted through the contents of the briefcase, and scanned the documents for information about the creator of the fragrance. If she knew who the creator was, perhaps she could find a way to convince that person to give her the job. Something rolled around at the bottom of the briefcase. Gezebel removed the papers and found an opaque perfume bottle. It had a round base and a cap designed like a trumpet flower petal. Inscribed in script on the front of the bottle, was "Lady of the Night by Sisi." Gezebel removed the cap and sniffed. This was Sisi's fragrance! This was it! Gezebel read the documents and learned that Sisi owned a Fashion House in London." Her label was already on the racks in European stores, and she was ready to make her debut in North America during fashion week in New York! Gezebel was thrilled! She couldn't sleep at all that night! It was time to give Uncle Jeffrey a call, first thing tomorrow morning!

The next morning, before she got out of bed, Gezebel dialed her uncle at his office in London. A woman with a thick British accent screened the call, and identified herself as his secretary. Jeffrey, over the years, had worked to become CFO of a chain of five star hotels. Gezebel informed the militant secretary that she was Jeffrey's niece, and was transferred to her uncle within seconds.

"Gezebel, is that you?" Jeffrey asked in shock.

"Yes, it's me, Uncle Jeff. How are you?" Gezebel asked.

"Couldn't be better! You vanished from the island without a trace and I haven't seen or heard from you since! What the hell is going on with you?" Jeffrey demanded impatiently.

"Uncle Jeff, I felt trapped! I had to leave in order to try something new!" Gezebel explained.

"That's it? I don't think you can justify your disregard for other people's lives by claiming you wanted to try something new! There could have been some other way!" Jeffrey punished her with his words.

"Perhaps! I intend to resume my responsibilities and pick up where I left off!" Gezebel promised in a prudish manner. Jeffrey chuckled at her foolhardy words.

"Gezebel, this can't be a social call. You suddenly remembered your uncle in London? Have you hit hard times? Are the stories in the tabloids true?" Jeffrey asked curiously.

"Uncle Jeff, those stories are totally false! That girl is crazy! She was jealous of my relationship with Jack Chagall!" Gezebel grumbled. Jeffrey remained silent.

"Uncle Jeff, I hope you believe me!" Gezebel stressed.

Jeffrey's thoughts languished over Ernest's dirty deeds years ago when he worked for The Network Foundation. That scandal was still in the news, and investigators uncovered new information every few years. Some low-level affiliates were imprisoned, along with others that had an indirect connection to the foundation. Perhaps the apple didn't fall far from the tree after all.

"Gezebel, I'm here for you if you need me." Jeffrey advised his niece.

"Uncle Jeff, my career has slowed down after a promising start, and i've been doing office work. I've been modeling for small time designers to earn money. I even had the lead role in a music video! And... I also auditioned to be the face of Sisi's fragrance!" Gezebel stated coyly.

"What? This was supposed to be top secret!" Jeffrey shouted angrily into the phone.

"Not anymore!" Gezebel sang wickedly and giggled.

"Gezzy, i've got Sisi buzzing me on the other line. Don't hang up!" Jeffrey pleaded with her.

"Sweetheart, I'm sorry to disturb you, but last night Sophie was robbed at gun point by someone wearing the mask of a cartoon character! The robber got away with the brief case filled with information about the fragrance!" Sisi informed her husband.

"Honey, I'm so sorry! Is Sophie alright?" Jeffrey asked.

"Yes, she wasn't harmed. She just dropped the briefcase and ran for her life! Poor girl! I think i'll arrange for car service to take her home from now on." Sisi replied.

"Darling, I think that would be best because we don't want anything to happen to her. Do you think Sophie was targeted by competitors in order to find out more about the fragrance?" Jeff asked.

"Who knows?" Sisi remarked.

"I have Gezebel on the other end." Jeffrey stated and changed the subject.

"Gezebel? Is she alright?" Sisi asked.

"Yes, she is. I have her on hold. Let's talk later. I love you." Jeffrey said.

"I love you too." Sisi replied and hung up.

"Gezebel, thanks for holding. Sisi just gave me some rather alarming news. Her coordinator, Sophie, was robbed of her briefcase in New York. All the information about the fragrance was inside that briefcase!" Jeffrey informed her.

"Ohmigosh! Uncle Jeffrey, that's terrible! Was she hurt?" Gezebel asked innocently.

"No, she wasn't." Jeffrey replied gruffly and Gezebel stifled a giggle.

"Gezebel, how did you find out about the fragrance? Perhaps you can assist the police with their investigation!" Jeffrey remarked icily.

"Uh, I don't think so. I overheard the production crew talking while I was in the changing room." Gezebel lied.

"I see." Jeffrey replied but he didn't believe her. His gut told him that Gezebel knew more about the robbery.

"Uncle Jeff, I want to be the face of Sisi's fragrance. Can you picture any other model acting as spokesperson? It would also help my struggling career. I've missed out on so much of Baron's life, and I can't go home a failure. Will you help me?" Gezebel pleaded with her uncle.

"Gezebel, you expect me to ask Sisi to do what? You disappeared out of our lives only to surface when you need a spring board? How insulting! You want to use her for your own personal gain! I don't know what type of jackass you take me for! Now, tell me, what do you know about the robbery?" Jeffrey shouted into the telephone receiver.

"Nothing! And, I'm not using Sisi! She should be honored to have me represent her! Uncle Jeffrey, please!" Gezebel shouted.

"You little liar! I don't know who you're protecting, but careful you don't find yourself knee deep in horseshit!" Jeffrey lashed out verbally.

"Uncle Jeffrey, please!" Gezebel burst into tears.

"Gezebel, I love you, but your decisions have had an adverse affect on our family, and I don't hear remorse for any of it! If you want to represent the fragrance, ask Sisi yourself! I won't attempt to sway her decision either way. She's disgusted with you for running away in the middle of the night, but I'm sure you'll work your way back into her good graces. Is there anything else?" Jeffrey asked icily.

Gezebel slammed the phone down and threw it at the wall! It cracked in half and fell to the floor. She booted her computer and booked a flight to London. Fashion week was only four months away. Sisi was going to see things her way!

Chapter Forty-Three

The month of May showered the city of London with mild spring weather and Gezebel hustled through the busy airport. She flagged down a taxi and handed the driver the address to Jeffrey's office. Jeffrey was bemused when his secretary informed him that his niece had just arrived from New York and was waiting to see him. He gritted his teeth at Gezebel's ruthlessness, but welcomed her with open arms.

"Gezebel! Good Lord Almighty! What a pleasant surprise!" Jeffrey remarked ecstatically. He got up from his desk to greet her.

"Uncle Jeff it's so good to see you. I had to come." Gezebel replied and hugged her uncle.

"If I knew you were coming, I would've picked you up from the airport. You look fantastic!" Jeffrey exclaimed.

"Thank you! Uncle Jeff, please convince Sisi to let me represent the fragrance! I feel as though it's already a part of me!" Gezebel replied mulishly. She refused to waste time with frivolous chatter. She was in London with a definite purpose in mind.

"Again, that decision is Sisi's!" Jeffrey responded in an aggravated tone.

"Uncle Jeff…" Gezebel whined tenaciously. Jeffrey ignored her and returned to his desk. He buzzed the secretary, and advised her to have car service drive Gezebel to his home.

"Gezebel, a car will be waiting outside in five minutes to drive you to the house. Sisi has transformed our basement into a design studio. It's where she spends most of her time. I'll let her know you're in town, and she'll take care of you until I get home." Jeffrey advised Gezebel and sent her on her way.

Gezebel was driven to an impressive estate in the district of Winnington, not far from London. Manicured lawns girdled the home and the shrubs were sculpted into traditional shapes. Gezebel stood anxiously outside the towering brick home and waited for the driver to remove her bags from the vehicle. He set the bags on the ground close to her feet and drove away. Gezebel contemplated her next move and rang the doorbell.

"Gezebel! What a surprise! It's so good to see you!" Sisi exclaimed in a heavy British accent. She embraced Gezebel and welcomed her into the house.

"Sisi, it's good to see you too!" Gezebel gushed.

"Why didn't you tell us you were coming? I could have planned things for us to do. Right now I'm up to my neck in work preparing for fashion week in New York." Sisi informed Gezebel apologetically.

"Sisi, don't worry about that. We can do those things some other time. " Gezebel reasoned. She observed that Sisi hadn't changed a bit. Her dark skin was flawless and seemed immune to wrinkles.

"Let me show you around." Sisi responded and Gezebel followed her lead.

Gezebel followed Sisi through the lovely home that reflected Sisi's keen eye for texture, color, and design. The home had eight bedrooms, seven baths, a pool, gym, and reception areas. Various degrees and awards lined the walls of the corridors, and boasted of the family's various accomplishments. Sisi advised Gezebel she could stay in the guestroom of her choice, and she selected one close to the where the boys slept. She unpacked quickly because the boys would soon be home from school, and she didn't want to be distracted from the task at hand. Gezebel joined Sisi in the kitchen after she unpacked, and found her preparing dinner.

"All done?" Sisi mused, and sliced onions on a wooden cutting board on top of the granite counter top. She was cooking beef stew. Gezebel smiled and nodded her head. She sensed that Sisi was suspicious of her visit and had to work fast to gain her trust.

"Gezebel, why did you leave your family? How could you leave your son? Sisi asked in an accusatory manner.

"Hell! Here we go again!" A miffed Gezebel thought to herself.

"I left because I needed to live my own life! I'm not proud of what I did but I can't change the past!" Gezebel replied in an exasperated tone. She wished the family would get over this.

"Baron and your family deserved better!" Sisi reprimanded her harshly.

Gezebel remained silent. Why should she lament about something that happened three years ago? Baron wasn't left on a stranger's doorstep! He wasn't left destitute and hungry! He was left in the care of her family so what was the big deal? This was old news and she didn't fly all the way to London to cry over spilled milk!" Gezebel thought peevishly to herself. Sisi sighed, and realized Gezebel was not about to delve into the matter. She raked the onions off the cutting board and into the pot. Then she started to peel potatoes.

"Sisi, I understand that Lady of the Night fragrance will debut in New York during fashion week!" Gezebel remarked slyly. Dropping this bombshell should take the focus off her and redirect it towards what she wanted. Sisi gasped.

"Gezebel, the coordinator hired to find the right girl to represent the fragrance was robbed! Her briefcase was stolen and it contained information about the fragrance! How did you find out?" Sisi asked bitterly and diced potatoes on the cutting board. She was on the verge of tears.

"Sisi, I auditioned for the job knowing nothing about your perfume line. After my audition, that irresponsible coordinator, what's her name again? Oh yeah, Sophie! She left documents in one of the changing rooms with details about the fragrance, and that's how I found out! Who knows how many other girls looked through those papers! While I was changing, I overheard Sophie complaining to the crew about being overworked and underpaid! She joked about leaking information to the press just to earn a few extra bucks! Sophie said you were ignorant about what was happening on the New York fashion scene! She said, and I quote, "a black woman could never create a fragrance with universal appeal!" And "this perfume wasn't good enough to freshen up the dead!" I couldn't bear to listen anymore and ran out the studio!" Gezebel lied in a voice cloaked with emotion. She sniffed back tears for dramatic effect. Sisi was dismayed by the information shared by Gezebel. She rinsed the potatoes off and placed them in the pot with chunks of cubed beef that simmered in onions, carrots, and other spices.

"Sisi, The robbery may have been planned! I flew to London to tell you in person because I know how hard you've worked to make this happen! I wasn't about to let Sophie trash your perfume line!" Gezebel lied with sincerity.

Sisi was acutely disturbed by Gezebel's revelations about Sophie. She hired an employment agency to scout for a talented person that was trustworthy. She traveled to New York to personally meet the candidates, and Sophie was chosen because of her strong background in project management and marketing. She was highly recommended by other designers that hired her on past projects. Communication with Sophie had always been positive, until the robbery. Where did she go wrong? Gezebel's message was loud and clear! She couldn't afford to fail because the greater part of her and Jeffrey's savings was invested into the perfume line. Sisi hoped it wasn't too late to safeguard their investment. She was grateful to Gezebel for confiding in her; otherwise she would be at the mercy of Sophie!

"Gezebel, I don't know how to thank you for flying all the way from New York to tell me this. I will relieve Sophie from her dowdy duties and find a suitable replacement! I don't have much time!" Sisi stated miserably.

Later that day, before the sun set on Gezebel's manipulative heart, a bewildered Sophie was fired, and the hunt was on for her replacement! Gezebel's plan worked better than she hoped for. Sisi was vulnerable, and Gezebel made her next move. She entered the spacious basement that Sisi transformed into a fashion design studio. This was where Sisi's creativity came alive. Here, her designs were birthed in yards of silks, satins, cottons and spandex. Fabric dyes were placed on shelves constructed against the walls, and velvety mannequins stood in various poses with their bodies draped in colorful fabrics. Sequins, measuring tapes, and trimmings littered the sturdy fabric cutting table where Sisi was in the process of putting her Midas touch on a piece. Gezebel leaned on the table and pretended to inspect the sequined gown Sisi was working on. Sisi was engrossed in a heated discussion on the phone.

"Yes, I understand that finding a replacement on such short notice is difficult, but it must be done! Look, if you can't deliver, then i'll find another agency that can! Uh huh... Uh huh... Sounds good! I'll be waiting for your call!" Sisi sighed and hung up.

Gezebel plopped her languid figure into the plush tangerine loveseat used by Sisi for short naps. She feigned a morose expression on her face and moved in for the kill!

"Sisi, i've been thinking." Gezebel remarked pensively.

"Gezebel, I don't want to talk about Sophie!" Sisi stated in a sharp voice. Introduction of her fragrances was in limbo because of Sophie and Sisi felt betrayed.

"Oh Sisi, if I didn't rat on that backstabbing witch you wouldn't be going through this! I feel responsible for this mess!" Gezebel stated meekly. She wanted Sisi to feel as though she owed her.

"Gezebel…please… this is not your fault!" Sisi assured her.

"Sisi, i'll represent the fragrance!" Gezebel suggested and held her breath. Sisi looked at Gezebel in wonder and her expression changed from one of misery to one of elation!

"What? Gezebel… that's a terrific idea! I was so caught up with worry that it hadn't dawned on me to hire you! Would you really do that for me? Wait, I have to warn you, the schedule is grueling!" Sisi advised Gezebel in an exuberant manner.

"I'm up for the challenge! It's what I do!" Gezebel stated victoriously.

"Gezebel, you're a perfect fit! This makes it so much easier! Now I can concentrate on the shows instead of finding a model!" Sisi exclaimed and hugged Gezebel.

Gezebel laughed and hugged her back. The trip was not in vain after all. The prize was firmly in her grasp. She switched on the radio and danced like a clown. Sisi laughed, and released all the tension that gripped her psyche.

"Sisi, you need to lighten girl! Especially after all you've been through!" Gezebel yelled and snapped her fingers to the music. Sisi joined Gezebel's silliness, and jumped around the room flailing her arms and kicking her legs.

"Mummy, we're home!" Yelled Adam. He was Jeffrey and Sisi's first son.

"Cousin Gezzy!" Exclaimed Winton. He was their youngest.

The boys had just got home from school and were elated to see Gezebel. She hugged them both in an ebullient fashion, and remarked how Adam was the splitting image of Jeffrey. Adam was blessed with a cinnamon complexion and hazel eyes. Winton resembled both parents with skin the color of whipped mocha. Gezebel roused their wavy hair, and marveled at how handsome and athletic the boys were.

"Guess what? Your auntie is going to represent the perfume line! Isn't that fantastic?" A delighted Sisi informed the boys. They hollered with joy, and joined the ladies clowning around the room.

"Now, that's what I call a slam dunk!" Gezebel thought to herself.

Gezebel spent two weeks in London with her Uncle and his family. Their attorneys hashed out the terms of her contract, and Gezebel was declared the official face of the fragrance. Gezebel hoped this marketing campaign would propel her career back into the spotlight. Jeffrey drove Gezebel to the airport on the day of her departure, but he remained mystified at how she managed to pull off this feat.

"Uncle Jeff, I had a wonderful time. Thanks for taking me to visit my mother's family." Gezebel uttered graciously as they stood in the waiting area for departing passengers.

"Gezebel, you're always welcome. I hope you visit the family in Barbados soon. Your son needs you." Jeffrey reminded her.

"I will. I miss him." Gezebel promised and averted her gaze.

"Gezebel, the family isn't against you. A sincere apology is all they really want. You don't have anything to prove." Jeffrey advised her. Tears welled in her eyes, and she looked down at the open toe sandals on her feet. She hated being emotional but couldn't help it when the subject involved her son.

"All I think about is my son! No one in New York knows I have a child! Not even Jack!" Gezebel wailed and sniffed back tears. Jeffrey smirked. He felt no pity for his fickle niece, and couldn't believe that she had been keeping her only child a secret!

"Gezebel, how did you convince Sisi to give you the contract?" Jeffrey asked. She dried her eyes and looked at her uncle with interest.

"Didn't she tell you?" Gezebel asked quizzically and furrowed her brow. If he wasn't aware of the sordid lies she told Sisi about Sophie, she wasn't about to enlighten him! Jeffrey would instinctively know that she lied, and Sophie was being investigated by police because of her. Sophie's impeccable reputation was now in question.

"I know that Sophie was fired because of a rumor that the robbery was staged, and you were going to be the face of the fragrance!" Jeffrey stated flatly.

"Uncle Jeff, I spoke to Sisi at length about my interest in the job and she hired me on the spot!" Gezebel retorted smartly. Her lips curved in a cocky grin. She raised an eyebrow and stared at her uncle with defiance.

"I don't know how you did it, but I'm 100% sure that you are responsible for Sophie's dismissal! I'm convinced you know more about the robbery than you're telling!" Jeffrey ranted and shook his forefinger in her face. Gezebel rolled her eyes and sucked her teeth. She turned to leave but he grabbed her arm and spun her around.

"Ouch! Uncle Jeffrey, let me go!" Gezebel muttered with spite. Jeffrey's hardened eyes flung daggers at her. He commanded her full attention and respect! Jeffrey refused to be toyed with!

"Don't turn away from me when I'm talking to you! Make sure you honor that contract, and work your diva fingers to the bone! You better not mess this up or disappoint my wife, otherwise you'll have many regrets!" Jeffrey's voice rumbled like thunder in the midst of a storm, and bystanders took notice.

"Damn it! Alright!" Gezebel countered angrily between clenched teeth. She tried to wriggle out of his grasp.

"And, one other thing! After this modeling piss off of yours is done, you better make time for your son!" Jeffrey added in an uncompromising tone. He released Gezebel's arm with a slight shove that sent her reeling into a crowd of people! Gezebel stumbled and landed on her backside! Onlookers hid their faces, and chuckled at the spectacle of the clumsy young woman sprawled on the ground! Gezebel scrambled to her feet, brushed the dust off her backside, and boarded the aircraft in a hurry!

Chapter Forty-Four

———⌇———

Gezebel returned to New York with a renewed spirit. Her battery was charged, and she continued to work temp assignments and model for low budget designers. She jogged in Prospect Park and sculpted her body at the gym. It was her desire to be in the best possible shape when fashion week commenced. She wanted to surprise those highly tiered echelons of couture that ignored her all this time. Gezebel thought about Jack's marriage proposal, and how advantageous it would be to wed him. Jack loved her, and wanted to make a commitment, but the relationship would have to be on her terms this time around. She visited him frequently at his posh Manhattan townhouse where they made love for hours with reckless abandon. The opportunity to bed Jack behind Lynn's back was too good to pass up! On one of these glorious days, Gezebel was in the company of Jack when Lynn barged into the bedroom unannounced! Jack was lying on his back with Gezebel on top of him!

"What the hell is going on here?" Lynn's shrill voice threatened the peace like a bomb. Jack and Gezebel were sexually intoxicated with each other. The anguish in her voice was like a splash of cold water on their backs. Gezebel hastily rolled off Jack and covered her nakedness with the sheet. Jack lay naked with an erect penis, and a bewildered expression on his face.

"Lynn, what are you doing in here?" Jack asked in an exasperated tone. He couldn't believe she had the valor to invade his privacy. Jack thought he set the alarm for the penthouse, but what he didn't know, was that Gezebel always disarmed it. She knew that Lynn would eventually show up unannounced.

"I thought this hag was out of your life!" Lynn shouted hysterically.

"Jack couldn't resist the scent of my crotch!" Gezebel quipped nastily.

Lynn glared at Gezebel with rancor. Gezebel sat up in bed with her dark hair falling wildly around her shoulders. Her eyes seemed devoid of color, and gave Lynn goose bumps. She was haunted by images of this she-devil that attempted to run her over with a sports car, but she refused to back down.

"Gezebel, what are you doing in this house? You couldn't make it on your own, so you ran back to Jack offering him used goods?" Lynn retorted hotly. Gezebel stared at her with frigid eyes; her face, a mask of hate.

"I'm here because you suck in every way! Jack is repulsed by that beat up tire you've been dragging around town! By the way, I hear it's waterlogged! I'm glad you stopped by though… this way, I can personally inform you, that your services are no longer required!" Gezebel spat the words out indignantly. She always managed to make Lynn feel like a worthless tramp.

"Lynn, I want you to leave, and never enter my home without permission!" Jack shouted in a frosty tone.

Lynn was agitated, and she felt betrayed. She stood in the bedroom wearing black leggings and a t-shirt that was so tight, her implants threatened to bust through! Lynn had finished working out at a nearby gym that afternoon when she decided to pay Jack a surprise visit. He had been distant lately, and calls she placed to his home phone, and cell phone, went unanswered. She placed her hands on her hips and showed off pink lacquered nails that reminded one of cotton candy. Lynn stood her ground.

"Jack, what about me? Don't I give you everything you could ever want?" Lynn challenged him. She was determined to run Gezebel off.

"I asked you to go!" Jack shouted with fury. He sat up on the bed with his manhood poking out in front of him.

"Oh Lynn, I almost forgot to add… Jack asked me to marry him! Your invitation will be personally hand-delivered by me!" Gezebel hissed. She twirled a strand of hair around her forefinger and smirked with satisfaction at Lynn's stunned expression.

"You're a liar! Jack, tell me this isn't true!" Lynn hollered with disbelief. She wanted Jack to denounce Gezebel and throw her out of the house! Her hopes of getting hitched to a multi-millionaire were dashed!

Jack's loud silence infuriated Lynn and spurned her into action! She couldn't accept the possibility that Jack wanted to marry someone else! Lynn lunged across the bed, grabbed

Gezebel's hair, and dragged her onto the floor! Gezebel hit the floor like a sack of potatoes! She lashed out at Lynn and clawed her cheek with her sharp nails! Lynn winced in pain and let go of Gezebel's hair! Gezebel, no longer concerned about her own nakedness, speedily got to her feet, and Lynn put her in a headlock! Gezebel's face was smothered against Lynn's silicone bosom, and she felt as though she was going to suffocate! She kicked Lynn in the knee with her bare footed heel! Lynn stumbled backward and fell to the floor! Jack threw on his underpants and stepped between the two alley cats! He put a swift end to the bedroom brawl!

"Lynn, get out of this house before I have you arrested!" Jack yelled in a decisive tone that indicated he was serious.

"Jack, please don't do this! I've always been there for you! She can't make it without you and that's why she came back! Can't you see?" Lynn bawled with ire. Her pimple-scarred face was bloodied with scratch marks delivered by Gezebel. She stubbornly stood her ground, begging and pleading with Jack.

Jack picked up the phone and proceeded to dial 911. Lynn realized he meant business and vowed vengeance against Gezebel! She vowed that a marriage between them would never happen because she would not allow it! Lynn ran out of the bedroom and slammed the door shut!

"Darling, are you alright?" Jack asked Gezebel tenderly. He smoothed her hair and kissed her angel face.

"Now, where were we?" Gezebel asked sexily and slipped her tongue between his lips. She returned to bed and got under the sheets. Jack crept playfully under the sheets and sucked

her toes. He inched his way up, and munched gently on her thighs. Gezebel moaned in ecstasy. This made the drama worthwhile!

Lynn mashed her ear against the bedroom door and listened to Gezebel moan with pleasure. Tears of wrath rolled down her face like molten lava. She wanted to be the object of Jack's affections instead of Gezebel! Jack was her ticket to power in the realm of adult entertainment. She should be the trinket on his arm! Jack was representative of the reasons why she abandoned a poverty stricken life in a small southern town to strike it rich in show business.

Chapter Forty-Five

G lamorous, hectic, fun, exciting, described fashion week in New York City. Weeks before the fashion shows, Gezebel was involved in photo shoots, rehearsals, and personal appearances for House of Sisi Design and Fragrance. Renowned photographers whose skill behind the lens made unknown models shoot to stardom waited patiently to photograph the elusive Gezebel. Gezebel quit her temporary job in the administrative field as the world of high fashion beckoned once again. She worked fourteen-hour days and was constantly on the move. Sisi joined Gezebel in New York a month before the inauguration of fashion week, to add her personal touch to all the work that had been put into the marketing campaigns. She too, was overworked, and anxiously agonized over microscopic details the hired help overlooked. Sisi chose to reside in a midtown hotel during her stay to be in close proximity of the fashion district. She wanted to be in walking distance of shops, restaurants and tourist attractions.

Sisi's agent in New York booked Gezebel for highly publicized fashion shows that were worthy of prime time news. Rehearsals for these shows were time consuming, and production crews gave life to the outlandish imaginations of the creative teams. Gezebel's first experience with fashion week three years ago was a joke compared to this. Jack wasn't there to order meals, limos, or to fend off the press. Even though he wasn't there to protect her, the experience she obtained hustling for nondescript designers gave her the resilience to deal with unforeseen obstacles. She and Sisi worked hard. Each woman had a stake in ensuring that Sisi's design label and fragrance was a reverberating success.

The marketing campaign for the fragrance was launched with a television advertisement. The set was designed to reflect a bleak snow-covered forest, where the only sign of life was a red butterfly. The butterfly fluttered its wings, and landed on the lone green shrub sprouting white trumpet flowers. The camera then focuses on Gezebel who appears to be lost. She runs through the forest dressed in a shimmering white gown. Her hair is loosely curled around her face. She seems afraid because its twilight, and soon, the forest will be dark. Gezebel observes the red butterfly perched on the green shrub and approaches it. She picks one of the trumpet shaped flowers and it's magically transformed into an opaque perfume bottle. Gezebel twists off the trumpet shaped cap and sniffs. She tilts her head, and touches the tip of the cap along her neck. In an instant, the sun rises, and the forest is transformed into an exquisite garden. Gezebel replaces the cap and smiles. She balances the fragrance in the palm of her hand and walks dreamily out of the garden, followed by the red butterfly. The television advertisement was slated to run on all networks at the start of fashion week. Posters of Gezebel with all three Lady of the Night fragrances lined the windows in upscale department stores. Her haunting eyes gazed seductively at shoppers, and they ventured in to make the purchase.

Fashion week started with a bang, and Gezebel fastidiously stomped the catwalks, determined to be a showstopper. She turned heads with a fierce signature stalk that was unstoppable! Gezebel's mesmerizing stare and sensual swagger left designers scurrying to find out who her agent was. They tried to steal her away from Sisi's campaign, and offered to double her pay, but Gezebel turned them down! Sisi's fashion line got superb reviews, and Gezebel modeled with grace and style. Gossip columnists and the paparazzi drove themselves into a reporting frenzy, and touted her as the hottest model on the fashion circuit. Her name was the butt of jokes on late night talk shows when comedians compared her to the biblical Jezebel, but she didn't care. She wanted the world to know that she was back! Bigger and badder than ever!

Chapter Forty-Six

Jeffrey and the boys joined Sisi in New York at the start of fashion week. He was proud of Sisi and imperiously pleased with Gezebel for her loyalty to Sisi's campaign. Jeffrey watched her model with confidence, and felt as though he was admiring someone he really didn't know. He asked the family to fly to New York and witness Gezebel in the prime of her life and they agreed. Daddy St. John's three sisters joined the rest of the family, in addition to Beulah, Dwight, and her best friend Joi.

They were impressed with the way in which she commanded the audiences' attention with every step. Gezebel was unaware of the fact that her family attended the shows, and basked in the glory of her amazing comeback. She captured everyone's imagination and breathed life into Sisi's fashions. Photographers couldn't get enough of the striking beauty, and other top models were in awe of her captivating presence. The family chose to wait until fashion week concluded before making their presence known.

Trouble for Gezebel brewed outside the shows in the form of protest. A porn superstar with an ax to grind strove to hinder Gezebel's rise to stardom. Lynn waved signs of protest at venues where Gezebel was scheduled to appear. The signs blatantly read, "GEZEBEL, GUILTY, HIT & RUN!" Lynn ranted belligerently at attendees, "Shame on you! Boycott Gezebel!" She enlisted the help of professional hecklers to hold up signs and chant the same words. Lynn's verbal slugfest drew the attention of the media, and she was granted airtime to publicly denounce Gezebel. She snatched every opportunity to be on national TV, and bellyached to the press about her shocking ordeal. Speculation and doubt about whether Gezebel committed this questionable act threatened to overshadow all that Sisi had worked for.

The family convened privately, and decided it was time for Gezebel to talk to the press. She couldn't afford to ignore Lynn any longer because Lynn was not going away! Gezebel succumbed to a brief interview with a well-respected journalist during a prime time program, and put the word out that Lynn was a woman scorned. She stressed that the police concluded Lynn's claims were without merit, and that's why the investigation was closed. Gezebel delivered her message with sincerity and tact. The tactic worked, and her analysis of Lynn's wild accusations was credible. The public viewed Lynn as a delusional porn star rejected as a supermodel, and rejected in love. Gezebel pushed forward with her career and put the subject of Lynn to rest.

Fashion week in New York came to a close, and Gezebel was invited to join her Uncle and his wife in their hotel suite for a celebration. Jack was Gezebel's escort. He was incensed by Lynn's publicity stunt and severed all business ties with the vengeful porn star. The suite was decorated with colorful balloons in anticipation of Gezebel's arrival. Family and friends were ready to forgive, but they would never forget. They understood that their controlling antics probably helped drive her away. Gezebel knocked rapidly on the door and Sisi

opened it. She ushered them in, and the group yelled out in unison, "Surprise!" Gezebel could not believe her eyes! She dropped to her knees, and cried uncontrollably. In this room, were all the people she missed and loved.

Corine hurried over to her daughter, and hugged her. Ernest assisted Gezebel to her knees and she hugged her dad. He gazed at his daughter with love and forgiveness in his eyes. His little girl was all grown up, and he realized that the two of them were cut from the same cloth. Gezebel gasped when she saw grandmother Estele standing regally in the room with a heart warming smile on her face. She was beautifully made up and her hair was elegantly coiffed. Gezebel ran over to her grandmother and cried like a baby on her bosom. Estele soothed her granddaughter with kind words and cried tears of joy. She had waited for this moment for so long, and was relieved that Gezebel made it through. Someone approached Gezebel from behind and tapped her on the shoulder. Gezebel turned around and put her hands to her mouth to stifle the squeals of joy that burst forth from her lips when she saw her best friend Joi! The two ladies hugged and laughed just the way they used to when they were teenagers. Beulah stood crying next to Ernest. She was so happy that this strenuous ordeal was finally over. The family was back together. Daddy St. John's three sisters walked over to Gezebel and embraced her warmly. They were elated that she was back into the family's protective fold. Gezebel stood in the middle of the room surrounded by family and cried. She wanted to tell them how much she loved them, but was too overcome for words.

"Gezzy?" A familiar voice called out.

Gezebel turned in the direction of the voice and there was her Aunt Bella, smiling at her with Baron in her arms.

Gezebel walked over on tottering legs and threw her arms around them. She gently took her son out of Bella's arms and hugged him. Baron looked at his mother curiously and whimpered. He reached for Bella because he did not know who Gezebel was. The realization that her son no longer knew her wounded Gezebel's heart, but she understood that he was just a baby when she left. She kissed him and ran her hands through his soft hair.

"Baron, that's mommy." Bella spoke soothingly to the toddler as he tried to wriggle out of Gezebel's arms.

Gezebel placed her son on his feet because she was overwhelmed! She almost forgot to introduce Jack who stood by the door quietly observing the family reunion. He felt responsible for the ultimate disassociation between Gezebel and her family when he encouraged her to move to New York. Gezebel walked over to Jack and held his hand. She had an announcement to make.

"I want you to meet Jack. He's the man who paved the way for me in this business. Jack is important to me and I hope you accept him as the man in my life." Gezebel stated in a voice cloaked with emotion.

Estele walked gingerly over to Jack and extended her hand. Jack reciprocated, and members of the family followed suit. They were desperate to learn more about the mysterious millionaire in Gezebel's life. The group settled down, and talked amicably over drinks, delicious food, and tasty desserts. Contemporary music wafted through the air from hidden speakers, and laughter filled the air. Gezebel and Joi busied themselves entertaining energetic Baron.

Jack held a glass of champagne in his hand, and charmed the ladies with tales about how he started his entertainment company as a young entrepreneur. Even though Jack was in his late forties, the ladies were able to discern why a young woman like Gezebel would find him attractive. He was wealthy, attractive, and charismatic, so why not? Jack was dressed fashionably in a dark blue dinner jacket, matching slacks, and a white designer shirt. His patent leather shoes added a touch of class to his smart outfit.

Ernest eyed Jack, and was unable to form an opinion about the man. He couldn't shake the creepy feeling that he crossed paths with this stranger at some juncture in his life. Ernest squired Jack away from the talkative ladies in order to learn more about the man his daughter loved. The men talked at length, and Ernest was enlightened about Jack's life as the son of a wealthy businessman in London. Jack dreamed about striking it rich in New York, and relocated to the Empire State after graduating at the top of his class from the University. In time, he worked his way to becoming a self-made millionaire. Ernest studied Jack's facial expressions and body language with interest. He realized that he was looking into the beady eyes of a man he knew extremely well! Images of their activities in London more than a decade ago came rushing back like a tsunami! Jack abruptly refrained from speaking, and a puzzled expression flooded his face. His beady eyes hardened, and he peered at Ernest with intense scrutiny. Gezebel sipped champagne from a red flute, and monitored the strained body language between her father and Jack. She disengaged her self from the company of Joi and Baron. Gezebel inched closer to the men and listened to their animated conversation. Jeffrey observed the hardened expression on Jack's face, and Ernest's pale complexion. He followed Gezebel's cue.

"Lerwick!" Ernest confirmed in astonishment! The man who supposedly perished in a fire along with millions of dollars was alive and kicking! His facial features were slightly altered thanks to cosmetic surgery, but those beady eyes were a dead giveaway!

"Ernest!" Lerwick barked, equally stunned! He recalled that Ernest pilfered close to a million pounds from TNF offshore operations and fled!

"Lerwick? It can't be!" Jeffrey exclaimed! He arrived just in the nick of time for the shock of his life.

"Why you calling Jack, Lerwick?" A perplexed Gezebel asked.

"Because that's who I am! By the way, thanks for telling me you had a kid!" Lerwick complained sarcastically.

"Oh Please, Jack! Lerwick! Or whatever the hell your name is! It's obvious I haven't been the only one keeping secrets!" Gezebel declared brazenly with a hand poised on her hip.

"i'll divulge my life story to you between the sheets! Here's to secrets, kid!" Lerwick smirked and raised his champagne flute toward Gezebel for a toast.

Gezebel touched her glass to his and winked.

As an Ursuline Convent student in Barbados, West Indies, I discovered that writing was my passion. I've always dreamed of writing books with interesting story lines and unforgettable characters.

The idea for this book took root during a creative writing class at the University of Maryland, where I graduated with a Bachelor of Arts in Communication Studies.

It gives me great pleasure to bring you my first work of fiction.